Oxford Pocket English Grammar

Oxford Pocket English Grammar

Oxford Pocket English Grammar

A. J. Thomson
A. V. Martinet

Oxford University Press

Oxford University Press
Walton Street, Oxford OX2 6DP

Oxford   New York   Toronto
Delhi   Bombay   Calcutta   Madras   Karachi
Petaling Jaya   Singapore   Hong Kong   Tokyo
Nairobi   Dar es Salaam   Cape Town
Melbourne   Auckland

and associated companies in
Berlin   Ibadan

Oxford, Oxford English and the *Oxford English* logo
are trade marks of Oxford University Press.

ISBN 0 19 431301 8

© Oxford University Press 1990

First published 1990
Fourth impression 1991

The phonetic alphabet on page vii is
reproduced from *A Basic English Grammar* by
John Eastwood and Ronald Mackin (Oxford
University Press, 1982). The drawings are by
Trevor Ridley.

Typeset by Pentacor Ltd in 9¼/10½ Meridien
and 8¾/9¾ (Exercises)

Printed in Hong Kong.

Contents

Introduction

The *Oxford Pocket English Grammar* is for the learner who has used or studied English for some time but wants to know more about its grammar. The book explains all the main structures in simple language and shows how they are used. It deals clearly with the more difficult points. There is a full index at the end, and a glossary of grammatical words on pages viii–x.

Exercises follow many of the sections. These are useful for checking that the section has been understood. They are easy and can be done quickly. The answers are on pages 275–298.

In the examples of spoken English and in the exercises, the sign '~' means that there is a change of speaker.

Phonetic alphabet

iː	see	ɒ	top	ɜː	third	aʊ	how
ɪ	big	ɔː	saw	ə	away	ɔɪ	boy
e	get	ʊ	good	eɪ	day	ɪə	near
æ	man	uː	soon	əʊ	go	eə	fair
ɑː	bath	ʌ	bus	aɪ	by	ʊə	sure
p	pen	tʃ	cheap	s	say	n	new
b	book	dʒ	job	z	zoo	ŋ	long
t	time	f	fine	ʃ	shop	l	last
d	dog	v	very	ʒ	measure	r	room
k	can	θ	think	h	help	j	yes
g	game	ð	that	m	mine	w	water

Glossary

abstract nouns are names of things which our physical senses cannot perceive: *anger, freedom, humour, justice* etc.

active and passive verbs A transitive verb can be put into the passive:
Active: *The policeman **arrested** the thief.*
Passive: *The thief **was arrested** (by the policeman).*

adjectives tell us about nouns or pronouns: ***brown** eggs; He is **happy**.*

adverbs tell us about verbs: *Bill lived **here**. Tom walks **slowly**.*

affirmative *Bill lived here* and *Tom walks slowly* are affirmative sentences. *lived* and *walks* here are affirmative verbs. Compare **negative**.

agent The subject of an active verb becomes the agent if that verb is put into the passive. But the agent is often omitted: *The crew were rescued (by **helicopter**).*

auxiliary verbs/auxiliaries Principal auxiliaries are *be, have, do*. For other auxiliaries, see **modal auxiliaries**.

clauses are groups of words containing subject and verb. See also **main clauses** and **subordinate clauses**.

cleft sentences are sentences such as: *It was **Tom** who told me. It's **food** that we need.* The form gives extra emphasis to the word following the verb *be*.

collective nouns are names of groups: *crew, family, team*.

colloquial, or informal English, is the style normally used in ordinary conversations and personal letters.

compound adjectives/adverbs/nouns/tenses consist of two or more parts: *a **ten-ton** truck; a **hall door**.*

conjunctions are words like *and, but* and *or* which join words or phrases/clauses; also words like *after, since, till* when they begin clauses: *I'll wait **till** Ann comes.*

consonants See **vowels**.

contractions are shortened forms of auxiliary verbs: *he's; he isn't.*

countable nouns are nouns which can have a plural form: *man, men; car, cars.*

direct objects In *He gave me a job, a job* is the direct object, *me* is the indirect object.

direct speech See **reported speech**.

emphasizing pronouns have the same form as reflexive pronouns: *He built the house **himself**.*

gerunds are *-ing* forms of verbs used as nouns: *He is fond of **gardening**.*

imperatives are used for giving orders: *Come by bus. Don't delay.*

indirect objects See **direct objects**.

indirect speech See **reported speech**.

infinitives are the basic verb forms. The full infinitive is *to* + verb: *I want to **help**.* The bare infinitive has no *to*: *Let me **help**.*

interrogative verbs and forms are used in asking questions: *Who is he? What does he want? Where have you been?*

intransitive verbs are verbs like *lie, rise, sleep* which cannot have an object. Compare with **transitive verbs**.

link verbs usually connect a noun/pronoun subject with an adjective. *be, become* and *seem* are examples of link verbs.

main clauses When a sentence has more than one clause it has at least one main clause: *If you haven't a pen, I can lend you one. We'll go when you're ready.* The clauses *If you haven't a pen* and *when you're ready* are **subordinate clauses**.

modal auxiliaries/modals These are *can/could, may/ might, must, ought, shall/should, will/would*. Semi-modals are *dare, need* and *used*.

negative *Bill didn't live here* and *Tom can't walk* are negative sentences. *didn't* and *can't* here are negative verbs. Compare **affirmative**.

nouns are usually the names of people, animals or things: *Ann, boy, dog, pen*.

objects In *I bought **a pen*** and *He saw **Ann**, a pen* and *Ann* are the objects of the verbs. See also **direct objects**.

participles We form the present participle with infinitive + *ing: love, **loving**; want, **wanting**;* and the past participle of regular verbs with the infinitive + *d* or *ed: love, **loved**; want, **wanted**.*

phrasal verbs are verb + preposition/adverb combinations: *look for, look out, go on, pick up*.

phrases are groups of words which do the work of an adjective, adverb or noun. *in time* is an adverb phrase. Phrases can contain a participle or infinitive: *Fans waiting to get in became angry.*

possessive adjectives are *my, your, his, her, its, our, your, their.*

prefix In *disobey* and *unjust, dis* and *un* are prefixes.

prepositions are words like *at, into, with,* normally placed before nouns or pronouns: *Go with Ann. Look at this.*

pronouns are words like *I, me, you, she, her, mine, yours, hers,* used instead of repeating a noun or noun phrase.

reflexive pronouns are words like *myself, herself, ourselves.*

reported speech *She said, 'I'm going'* is direct speech. *She said (that) she was going* is reported or indirect speech.

stress is extra emphasis given in speech to certain words or syllables: *He ad'mitted that he had 'made a mis'take.*

subject In the sentences *Bill went; The boys will help; They are here* the words *Bill, The boys* and *They* are the subjects of the verbs.

subjunctive is a verb form used to indicate doubt or unreality: *If Tom were here I'd ask him.* (But Tom is not here.)

subordinate clauses do the work of an adjective, adverb or noun. In *This is the tape that he made, that he made* is a subordinate clause. See also **main clauses** and **that-clauses.**

suffix In *actor* and *hopeful, or* and *ful* are suffixes.

syllable The word *boy* has one syllable; the word *sis·ter* has two syllables; the word *fa·mi·ly* has three syllables.

that-clauses are noun clauses introduced by *that.* But in colloquial speech the *that* is often omitted: *I'm glad (that) you came.*

transitive verbs are verbs which can have a direct object, such as *eat, drink, read, say, write: She ate a pear. Tom drinks beer.* Compare with **intransitive verbs.**

uncountable nouns have no plural form and are always treated as singular: *grief, knowledge, luggage, weather.*

verbs are words which usually express an action, such as *come* and *go,* or a state, such as *be, have, know.*

vowels are a, e, i, o, u; all other letters are **consonants.**

wh- words are *what, when, where, who, whose, why.*

1   a/an, one, the, this, that

1   *a/an* [the indefinite article]

A We use *a* before a consonant sound:
a baby   a dog   a university   a European

We use *an* before a vowel sound:
an apple   an old man   an hour   an MP

a/an is the same for all genders:
a boy   a girl   a table

B We use *a/an* with a singular countable noun

when we mention it for the first time and it doesn't
mean any particular one (compare with 3 B):
They live in a flat.   The sun was hot, so he bought an ice-cream.

when it is one example of a class:
A dog needs exercise. (All dogs need exercise.)

when we say what somebody or something is:
Bill is an actor.   That was a bomb.

in exclamations:
What a hot day!   Such a long queue!

in certain phrases of price, speed etc.:
They cost 25p a kilo.   It's cheap at £1 a metre.
He drives at sixty kilometres an hour.
We eat three times a day.

C We also use *a/an* in certain phrases of quantity:
a few, a lot, a great deal, a great many, a couple

and before some numbers:
a hundred, a thousand, a million (261 C)
a fifth, a quarter, a third, a half (262 F)

D We do not use *a/an*

before plural nouns, so the plural of *a dog* is *dogs*:
I'd like a pet but my mother doesn't like dogs or cats.

before uncountable nouns (14)

before names of meals unless these follow an adjective
or they are special meals:
> *We have **breakfast** at eight o'clock* BUT
> *He gave us **a good breakfast**.*
> *I was invited to **a dinner** given to welcome the new ambassador.*

Exercise 1

▶ Put in *a* or *an*:

□ *a* man	3 ____ useful tool	6 ____ onion
1 ____ atlas	4 ____ X-ray	7 ____ hour
2 ____ uncle	5 ____ one-way street	8 ____ hospita

▶ Put in *a* or *an* if necessary:

□ Bill is *an* author.
9　He writes ____ travel books.
10　He makes ____ lot of money.
11　We had ____ lunch with him yesterday.
12　It was ____ excellent lunch.
13　The meal cost him ____ hundred and ____ fifty pounds.
14　What ____ expensive restaurant!
15　He gave the waiter ____ twenty pounds.
16　That was ____ good tip.

2　*a/an* and *one*

A When counting or measuring time, distance, weight
etc. we can use either *a/an* or *one* for the singular (261 C):
> £1 = *a/one pound*　£1,000,000 = *a/one million pounds*
> *You can take **an/one** hour for lunch.*

However, *a/an* and *one* do not normally mean the same:
> *A box is no good.* (A box is the wrong sort of thing.)
> *One box is no good.* (We need two or three boxes.)

B We use *one*

with *another/(the) others*:
> *One day he came early, another day he came late.*
> *One (boy) read a book, (the) others watched TV.* (57)

before *day/week/month/year/summer* etc. or before the
name of the day/month/season to show when
something happened:
> *One day a telegram arrived.*　*One winter the snow fell early.*

before *day* to mean 'at some future date':
> *One day you'll be sorry you treated him so badly.*
> (*Some day* would also be possible here.)

C *one* is the pronoun equivalent of *a/an* + noun:
> *Did you get a ticket? ~ Yes, I managed to get one.*

The plural of *one* used in this way is *some*:
> *Did you get tickets? ~ Yes, I managed to get some.*

Exercise 2

▶ Put in *a* or *one*:
Peter, the only son of (□) *a* millionaire, lives (1) _____ and
(2) _____ half miles from his school. (3) _____ day, when he was
walking to school, (4) _____ car with three men in it stopped
beside him. (5) _____ of the men opened the door, leant out,
and tried to pull Peter into the car. Luckily, just then
(6) _____ policeman rode up on (7) _____ bicycle, and the men
drove off. 'I know that gang,' said the policeman, 'and
(8) _____ day we'll catch them!'

3 *the* (the definite article)

A We use *the* with singular and plural nouns and for all
genders:
> *the boy, the boys   the girl, the girls   the day, the days*

B We use *the*

before a noun which can refer to only one particular
thing or group of things:
> *Ann is in the garden.* (the garden of this house)
> *The beds are comfortable.* (the beds in this hotel)
> *the earth, the sky, the moon, the stars*

before a noun which is mentioned for a second time:
> *His car hit a tree. You can still see the mark on the tree.*

before a noun which is defined by a phrase or clause:
> *the mark on the tree   the man we met yesterday*
> *the girl in blue   the place where we met*

before a singular noun to mean a class of people or things:
> *The small shopkeeper is having a difficult time.*
> *The helicopter has made travel easier for the businessman.*

before an adjective only, to mean a class of people:
the old = old people in general (27)

before superlatives, *first/second/third* etc. and *only*:
the best (day)   the first (week)   the only way

and in a *the* + comparative . . . *the* + comparative
construction (24 E).

Exercise 3

▶ Choose *a* or *the*:
One day we set out to climb (□) **a/the** highest hill in the area.
The campers in (1) **a/the** next tent lent us their map. They told
us to follow one of (2) **a/the** routes marked on (3) **a/the** map.
But Tom said that he was sure that there was (4) **a/the** better
way. (5) **A/The** way that he chose was so steep that we had to
stop for (6) **a/the** long rest on the way up. But we got to
(7) **a/the** top in (8) **a/the** end.

4   *the* with proper names

A We use *the* before certain types of geographical name:

seas	*the Atlantic*	mountain ranges	*the Alps*
rivers	*the Thames*	groups of islands	*the Azores*
deserts	*the Sahara*	regions	*the Crimea*

the Bay of Biscay   *the Black Forest*
the Republic of Ireland   *the United States*

When *east/west* etc. are nouns, we use *the*:
the north of Spain   the Middle East   the West

When *east/west* etc. are adjectives, we use *the* in a few
names:
the West Indies   the North Pole   the South Pacific

but we normally don't use *the* with names of countries:
South Africa   North America   West Germany

B We use *the* before some other proper names:

galleries, museums	*the National Gallery,*
	the British Museum
theatres, cinemas	*the Royal Shakespeare (Theatre),*
	the ABC (Cinema)

hotels	*the Savoy (Hotel)*
orchestras, pop groups	*the Hallé Orchestra, the Beatles*
newspapers	*the Telegraph, the Guardian*
ships	*the QE2, the Titanic*
names with *of*	*the Tower of London*
	the Houses of Parliament
plural family names	*the Smiths* = Mr and Mrs Smith

Exercise 4

▶ Put in *the* if necessary:
We walked past (□) *the* Tate Gallery and (1) _the_ Houses of
Parliament to (2) _the_ Westminster Bridge, and down
(3) _the_ steps beside (4) _the_ bridge to (5) _the_ Westminster
Pier. Here we bought tickets for a trip down (6) _the_ Thames.
A river boat was waiting at (7) _the_ pier. We were just in time
for (8) _the_ 2 o'clock trip.

We passed under several famous bridges and finally under
(9) _the_ Tower Bridge, which is (10) _the_ most famous of all.
We hoped to see (11) _the_ Thames Flood Barrier, which was
built to protect (12) _the_ city from floods, but we didn't see it
because (13) _the_ boat didn't go any further than
(14) _____ Greenwich.

5   Omission of *the*

We do not use *the*

before proper names, except as shown in 4 above

before abstract nouns, used in a general sense:
    Men fear death. BUT
    The death of the Prime Minister left his party without a leader.

after a noun in the possessive case, or before a
possessive adjective:
    the boy's uncle (the uncle of the boy)
    It is my book. (The book is mine.)

before names of games:
    He plays golf and tennis.

before parts of the body and articles of clothing, as we
normally use possessive adjectives:
    He injured his back.   *She put on her coat.*

before names of meals used in a general sense:
The Scots have porridge for breakfast.

before plural nouns, used to refer to a class of things:
I hate cars.   I like bicycles.

Exercise 5

▶ Put in *the* if necessary:
We have (□) — soup for (1) ___ supper. After (2) *the* meal
Tom and I play (3) ___ chess. Bill prefers (4) ___ cards.
(5) *the* game he likes best is bridge. He says that (6) *the*
chess requires (7) *the* patience and he is not patient. He also
says that (8) ___ life is too short to waste in this way.

▶ Put in *the* or *his* or *your*:
The boy took off (□) *his* coat and dropped it on (9) *the* floor.
'Pick (10) *your* coat up', said his mother, coming into
(11) *the* hall. 'And look at (12) *the* mud on (13) *his*
boots! Why don't you leave them outside (14) *the* door?
(15) ___ father always leaves (16) *his* boots there.'

6 Omission of *the* before *home, work, bed* etc.

A *home*

When we use *home* on its own, we omit *the*:
He is at home.   They went home.

When *home* is preceded or followed by a word or
descriptive phrase, we use *the*:
*We arrived at **the** bride's home.*
*The orphanage was **the** only home we had ever known.*

B *work/office*

work (= place of work) is used without *the*:
He's on his way to work/way back from work.   He is at work.
but *office* (= place of work) needs *the*:
*He is at/in **the** office before eight o'clock every morning.*

C *bed, church, court, hospital, prison, school/college* etc.

We do not use *the* before these words when the places
are visited or used for their main purposes. We go:

to bed to sleep or rest   *to hospital* as patients

to church to worship   *to prison* as prisoners
to court as witnesses etc.   *to school/college/university* to study

For similar reasons we can be *in bed/church/court/
hospital/prison*, and *at church/school/college/university*. Later
we can *be/get back* (or *be/get home*) *from school* etc., *leave
hospital/school* etc., and *be released from prison*.

When we visit or use these places for other purposes,
we use *the*:
     *He goes to **the** prison sometimes to give lectures*.

Exercise 6

▶ Put in *the* if necessary:
'You'll have to go into (□) ——— hospital,' said (□) *the* doctor.
'Can't I stay at (1) ——— home?' asked the old man. 'I hate
(2) ——— hospitals. I was in (3) ——— hospital for six weeks
when I was a boy and it was like being in (4) ——— prison.'
'(5) ——— hospitals are more cheerful now,' the doctor assured
him, 'and (6) ——— food at the County Hospital is excellent.
(7) ——— beds are comfortable too and you'll like
(8) ——— nurses.' 'Shall I have to stay in (9) ——— bed all the
time?' 'Oh no!' 'And can (10) ——— people come to
(11) ——— hospital to see me?' 'Of course.'

7   *this/these, that/those* [demonstratives]

A   As adjectives

this and *that* are the only English adjectives which have
a plural form (*these/those*) for plural nouns:
     ***This** beach was quite empty last year*.
     ***These** people are staying in **that** hotel over there*.
     *Look at **those** birds at the top of **that** tree*.

B   As pronouns

     ***This** is my umbrella. **That's** yours*.
     ***These** are the new classrooms. **Those** are the old ones*.
     *Hello, Tom. **This** is my brother Hugh, and **this** is my sister*.

this/that can refer to a previously mentioned noun,
phrase or clause:
     *They're digging up my road. They do **this** every summer*.
     *He said I wasn't a good wife. Wasn't **that** horrible?*

those can be followed by a defining relative clause:
Those who couldn't walk were carried on stretchers.

C With *one/ones*

When there is some idea of comparison or selection, the pronoun *one/ones* is often used after *this/these, that/those:*
This chair is too low. I'll sit in that one.
I like this one best.   I like that blue one/those blue ones.

Exercise 7

▶ Put in *this, that, these* or *those:*
Bill: All the books on (□) *these* shelves (the ones near us) are non-fiction. The fiction is on (□) *those* shelves (the shelves on the opposite wall).
Tom: I see. So (1) _____ are biographies etc. and (2) _____ are novels and plays.
Bill: (3) _____'s right. Do you want to borrow a book?
Tom (taking out a biography of Jane Austen): Can I borrow (4) _____ ?
Bill: Yes, of course; and you'll find her novels on (5) _____ shelves over there.

2 Nouns

8 Kinds and function

A There are four kinds of noun in English.

Common nouns: *dog, man, table*
Proper nouns: *France, Madrid, Mrs Smith, Tom*
Abstract nouns: *beauty, love, courage, fear, joy*
Collective nouns: *crowd, flock, group, swarm, team*

B A noun can function as

The subject of a verb: *Tom arrived.*
The complement of a link verb (*be, become, seem* etc.):
Tom is an actor.

The direct object of a verb: *I saw Tom.*
The indirect object of a verb: *I gave Tom the book.*
The object of a preposition: *I spoke to Tom.*

A noun can also be in the possessive case: *Tom's books.*

9 Gender

A Men, boys and male animals are masculine.

Women, girls and female animals are feminine.

Things, plants, animals whose sex we don't know, and sometimes babies whose sex we don't know, are neuter (pronoun: *it/they*). Exceptions: countries, ships, and sometimes cars and other vehicles, are feminine.

B Most nouns referring to people have the same form whether they are male or female:

   baby   child   cook   doctor   driver   parent   teenager

but a few have different forms. Here are some examples:

boy, girl	*brother, sister*	*uncle, aunt*
bridegroom, bride	*father, mother*	*actor, actress*
husband, wife	*nephew, niece*	*king, queen*
widower, widow	*son, daughter*	*waiter, waitress*

C Many domestic animals and some large wild animals have different forms for the male and female:

   bull, cow   cock, hen   dog, bitch   lion, lioness   tiger, tigress

Exercise 9

► Find the nouns which have different feminine forms and write the feminine form:

□ actor   *actress*

1	driver	9	waiter	17	host
2	elephant	10	camel	18	snake
3	guide	11	manager	19	player
4	son	12	uncle	20	brother-in-law
5	bull	13	lion	21	bridegroom
6	nephew	14	bachelor	22	doctor
7	cousin	15	widower	23	secretary
8	dog	16	assistant	24	teacher

10   Regular plural forms

A   We form the plural of most nouns by adding *s* to the singular:

    cat, cats   day, days   dog, dogs   change, changes

s is pronounced /s/ after an *f, k, p* or *t* sound, but /z/ after other sounds. When *s* is placed after *ce, ge, se* or *ze*, the final *es* is pronounced /ɪz/:

    change /tʃeɪndʒ/ becomes *changes* /tʃeɪndʒɪz/

B   We form the plural of nouns ending in *ch, o, sh, s* or *x* by adding *es*:

    church, churches   brush, brushes   box, boxes
    tomato, tomatoes   bus, buses

es after *ch, sh, s* or *x* is pronounced /ɪz/: *buses* /bʌsɪz/.

Exercise 10

▶   Write the plural form of these nouns:

□ watch	*watches*						
1	box	4	case	7	day	10	tax
2	bus	5	cliff	8	match	11	tomato
3	bush	6	clock	9	potato	12	kiss

11   Irregular plural forms

A   Nouns ending in a consonant + *y* change the *y* to *ies*:

    baby, babies   country, countries   fly, flies   lady, ladies

B   Some nouns ending in *o* add *s*:

    kilo, kilos   photo, photos   piano, pianos   radio, radios

C   Some nouns ending in *f* or *fe* change the *f* or *fe* to *ves*:

    half, halves   life, lives   shelf, shelves   wife, wives

    Others are *calf, knife, leaf, loaf, thief, wolf.*

D   A few nouns form their plurals by a vowel change:

    foot, feet   man, men   tooth, teeth   woman, women

E   The plural of *child* is *children*.

F Some nouns do not change at all in the plural:
    aircraft deer series sheep

fish does not usually change, but *fishes* is possible.

(For numbers and measurements which do not change, see 261 D, 264.)

Exercise 11

▶ Write the plural forms of these nouns:

□	knife		*knives*				
1	baby	6	key	11	man	16	storey
2	child	7	kilo	12	photo	17	story
3	country	8	woman	13	piano	18	thief
4	aircraft	9	leaf	14	sheep	19	tooth
5	foot	10	loaf	15	shelf	20	wife

12 Plurals of compound nouns

A In compound nouns only the last word is normally made plural:
    boy-friends break-ins travel agents lady doctors

But where *man* or *woman* is the first word both are made plural:
    men *drivers* **women** *teachers*

The first word is made plural in noun + preposition + noun compounds:
    sisters-in-law ladies-in-waiting
and in:
    hangers-on lookers-on runners-up

B Initials can be made plural by adding *s* at the end:
    MPs (Members of Parliament)
    VIPs (very important persons)

Exercise 12

▶ Write the plural form of these nouns:

□	girl-friend		*girl-friends*		
1	brother-in-law	4	lady doctor	7	time bomb
2	house agent	5	MP	8	woman driver
3	juke-box	6	runner-up		

13 Plural or singular?

A Some nouns are always plural and take a plural verb:

arms (= weapons)	*greens*	*savings*
clothes	*police*	*stairs*
earnings	*premises/quarters*	*surroundings*
goods	*riches*	*thanks*

Also some clothes, instruments etc. which have two parts:

glasses	*pants*	*scales*	*tights*
jeans	*pyjamas*	*scissors*	*trousers*

B Some nouns are always plural in form but take either a plural or a singular verb:

works (= factory)	*headquarters*	*politics*
means	*mathematics*	*athletics*

C *news* and the names of some games and diseases are always plural in form but always take a singular verb:
*The **news** is on television at nine o'clock.*
***Measles** is not usually a fatal disease.*

D Singular collective nouns (*government, crew, family, team* etc.) can take a singular or a plural verb:
*Our **team** is the best.* (The team is a single group or unit.)
*Our **team** are wearing new jerseys.* (The team is a number of individuals.)

E Uncountable nouns are singular and take a singular verb (see 14).

Exercise 13

▶ Choose the correct verb form, singular or plural:
  ☐ The police **is**/*are* are watching the house.
  1 His trousers **is/are** too long.
  2 Rabies **is/are** a very dangerous disease.
  3 The news **was/were** better today.
  4 The stairs **leads/lead** to the cellar.

14 Uncountable nouns

A The names of things which cannot be counted as separate objects are called uncountable nouns. They include:

Names of substances
  bread   coffee   gold   paper   cloth   glass   oil   stone   wood

Abstract nouns
  advice   death   help   information   news   beauty
  experience   horror   knowledge   work (= occupation)

Some other nouns
  baggage   damage   luggage   shopping   parking   weather

B Uncountable nouns are always singular and take a singular verb:
  *This coffee **is** cold.   The weather **was** dreadful.*

They are not used with *a/an*, but are often used with *some, any, no, a little* etc.:
  *I don't want **any** advice or help. I want **some** information.*

or with nouns such as *bit, piece, slice* etc. + *of*:
  *a **bit of** news   a **piece of** glass   a **slice of** bread*

work (= occupation) is uncountable, and so always singular, but *job* is countable:
  *He's looking for **work*** BUT *He's looking for **a job**.*
  *There'll be **work** for everyone* OR *There'll be **jobs** for everyone.*

C Many uncountable nouns can be used in another sense which is countable. With a countable meaning they can take *a/an* in the singular and can be used in the plural.

UNCOUNTABLE	COUNTABLE
Her **hair** is black.	She found **a hair** in the milk.
I prefer **tea** to coffee.	I'll have **two teas** and **a coffee**.
Their house was made of **wood**.	We picnicked in the **woods**.

NOTE
work (= occupation) is uncountable.
works (plural only) can mean 'factory' or 'moving parts of a machine'.
works (usually plural) can mean literary or musical compositions: *Shakespeare's complete **works**.*

D Some abstract uncountable nouns can be used in a special sense with *a/an*:

> *A good map would be **a help**.   It was **a relief** to sit down.*
> *He had **a dislike/dread/hatred/horror/love** of violence.*
> *It would be **a pity** to cut down these trees.*
> *It's **a shame** you couldn't come to the party.*

Exercise 14

▶ Put in *a* or *an* if necessary:

- ☐ These toys are made of ____ wood, not ____ plastic.
- ☐ We picnicked in *a* wood.
1 Someone threw ____ stone at the speaker.
2 The garden wall was made of ____ stone, not ____ concrete.
3 Paper is made from ____ wood.
4 I bought ____ paper to see who had won the match.
5 All you need now is ____ experience. Then you'll be able to get ____ work.
6 But how can I get ____ experience if I can't get ____ job?
7 We need ____ help. Could you give us ____ hand?
8 A good torch would be ____ help.
9 We had ____ fine day for our trip. ~ You were lucky. We had ____ terrible weather.

15 The possessive case: forms

A We add *'s* to singular nouns and plural nouns not ending in *s*:

> *a child's voice   Russia's exports   the people's choice*
> *the horse's mouth   the government's decision   men's clothes*

B We use the apostrophe alone (') with plural nouns ending in *s*:

> *a girls' school   the eagles' nest   the Smiths' car*

C Names ending in *s* take *'s* or the apostrophe alone:

> *Mr Jones's/Mr Jones' house   Yeats's/Yeats' poems*

D In compounds and titles the last word takes the *'s*:

> *my brother-in-law's guitar   Henry the Eighth's wives*

We can use *'s* after initials:

> *the PM's secretary   the MP's speech*

Exercise 15

▶ Rewrite these phrases:
   □ the luggage belonging to the travellers
      the travellers' luggage
   1 the room belonging to the child
   2 the clothes belonging to the children
   3 the car belonging to Mr Smith
   4 the luggage belonging to the VIP
   5 the flat belonging to her son-in-law
   6 the canteen used by the workers

16 The possessive case: use

A We use the possessive chiefly with people, animals and
   countries. But we can also use it

   in time expressions:
      a week's holiday   today's paper   tomorrow's weather
      in ten years' time   ten minutes' break   two hours' delay

   in expressions of money + *worth*:
      a pound's worth of stamps   ten dollars' worth of ice-cream

   in some other expressions:
      for heaven's sake   a summer's day   the water's edge
      the ship's mast   the plane's wings   the train's departure

B We can use some nouns in the possessive without a
   following noun when it is clear what we mean, usually
   when we are referring to a shop, office or house:
      You can buy it at the chemist's (shop).
      I bought my ticket at a travel agent's (office).
      We had lunch at Bill's (house) yesterday.

Exercise 16

▶ Complete these phrases:
   □ A *day's work* is work taking a day to complete.
   1 A ＿＿ is a holiday lasting a week.
   2 ＿＿ is a newspaper dated today.
   3 A ＿＿ is a wait lasting ten minutes.
   4 ＿＿ are the fashions of last year.
   5 A ＿＿ are the wages for a month.
   6 ＿＿ is the news about yesterday.

17 *of* + noun for possession

A We use *of* + noun chiefly with things (but see B):
the walls of the town   the roof of the church   the keys of the car

But instead we often make a compound noun and say:
the town walls   the church roof   the car keys

The first noun is like an adjective and is not made
plural: *the roofs of the churches* becomes *the church roofs*.

of + noun cannot always be replaced in this way, so
when in doubt use *of*.

B We use *of* + noun with people and animals when these
are followed by a phrase or a clause:
I took the advice of a couple I met on the train and hired a car.
I stroked the nose of a horse looking out of his stable.

18 Compound nouns

A There are three main types of compound nouns.
Noun + noun: *kitchen table, Oxford Street, petrol tank*
Noun + gerund: *fruit picking, lorry driving, coal mining*
Gerund + noun: *waiting list, dining room, swimming pool*

B In these compounds the first word gives information
about the second word. It is like an adjective. It can say
the following things about the second word:

What it is for	*coffee cup, reading lamp, tin opener*
What it is about	*detective story, telephone bill*
What it is a part of	*shop window, college library, garden gate* (but we say *a piece of cake, a slice of bread* etc.)
Where it is	*city street, country lane, corner shop*
When it is	*summer holiday, Sunday paper*
What it is made of	*steel door, stone wall, rope ladder* (but *wood* and *wool* have adjective forms: *wooden, woollen*)
What it produces	*fish farm, oil rig, car factory*
What power/fuel it uses	*gas fire, petrol engine, oil stove*
What work is done there	*inspection pit, assembly plant*

C We often use these compounds to refer to occupations, hobbies, sports and competitions and to the people who take part in them:

sheep farming	*pop singer*	*water-skiing*	*football match*
sheep farmer	*disc jockey*	*water-skier*	*beauty contest*

D There is no rule for the use of hyphens in compounds. In case of doubt it is usually safe to write the words separately without a hyphen, but where possible the student should look the word up in a good dictionary.

We often use hyphens with noun + gerund combinations:

bird-watching   ice-skating

and can use them with gerund + noun combinations:

diving-board   swimming-bath

Some noun + noun combinations can also be written with a hyphen:

space-suit   hand-luggage

Some very common compounds can be written either with a hyphen or as one word:

ice-cream, icecream   day-light, daylight

and some can be written in three ways:

tooth-brush, toothbrush, tooth brush

Hyphens are used in some compounds showing family relationships:

son-in-law   brother-in-law

When noun compounds are used as adjectives they are usually written with a hyphen:

a bird-watching expedition   a dining-room table

Exercise 18

▶ Combine the words in CAPITALS to make a compound noun:

   □   a DRIVER of a LORRY   *a lorry driver*
   1   the SHOP at the CORNER
   2   the ROOM for WAITING
   3   the KEYS of the CAR
   4   an ICE-CREAM flavoured with COFFEE
   5   a LAMP for READING by
   6   a DRESS made of SILK
   7   a MINE where GOLD is produced

3 | Adjectives

19 Introduction

A We use adjectives to describe nouns and pronouns:
a clever woman   most people   It was hot.

B There are several kinds of adjectives.
Demonstrative: *this, that, these, those* (7)
Adjectives of quality: *dry, good, happy, small* etc. (20–21)
Distributive: *each, every* (53–54), *either, neither* (52)
Quantitative: *some, any, no* (55), *many, much* (32),
little, few (31), *one, two* etc. (261)
Interrogative: *which? what? whose?* (58–59)
Possessive: *my, your, his, her, its, our, their* (61–62)

This chapter is mainly about adjectives of quality.

20 Adjectives of quality: form and use

A In English, adjectives of quality have the same form in
the singular and plural, and for all genders:
a good boy, good boys   a good girl, good girls
a good film, good films

B When two or more adjectives follow a verb, we put *and*
before the last one:
The day was cold, wet and windy.

We can put *but* if there is a contrast of ideas:
The case was small but heavy.

When two or more adjectives of colour precede a noun,
we put *and* before the final one, but we don't need *and*
when there is only one adjective of colour:
a green and brown carpet BUT a *big green carpet*

C We can use present participles (*-ing*) and past participles
(*-ed*) as adjectives. Note the difference in meaning:
The play was boring. The audience was bored.
The noise was terrifying. Everyone was terrified.

D We can use many adjectives followed by
   1 an infinitive: *I'm surprised to see you here.* (28)
   2 a *that*-clause: *I'm afraid (that) I can't help you.* (29)
   3 a preposition + noun/pronoun or gerund: *He's good at games. He's fond of dancing.* (90 A)

Exercise 20

▶ Put in *and* if necessary before the final adjective:
   □ The case was large   heavy   *The case was large and heavy.*
   1 a yellow   green flag
   2 a big   red car
   3 He was tall   thin
   4 He was a tall   thin man
   5 a cold   wet day

▶ Put in the present (-ing) and past (-ed) participles of the verbs in brackets:
   □ The match was *exciting*. The spectators were *excited*.   (excite)
   6 The listeners were ____. The radio programme was ____.
     (interest)
   7 The delays were ____. The travellers were ____.   (annoy)
   8 The play was ____. The audience were ____.   (amuse)
   9 We were all ____. The work was very ____.   (tire)

21 Adjectives of quality: position

A Most adjectives of quality can go either before a noun:
   a rich man   a happy cat   a cold day
   or after a link verb:
   He was rich.   The cat looks happy.   The day turned cold.

   The link verbs are *be, become* and *seem. appear/look*
   (= seem), *feel, get/grow* (= become), *keep, make, smell,
   sound, taste, turn* can also be used as link verbs.

B A few adjectives like *chief, main* and *poor*
   (= unfortunate) can go only before a noun:
   *This is the **main road**.   The **poor child** had no home.*

C Some can go only after a link verb:
   He's asleep.   I'm awake.   She seems upset.

   Also: *afraid, alike, alive, alone, annoyed, ill/well, sorry.*

D The meaning of some adjectives depends on their position.
*the **late** train* means 'the train scheduled to run late in
the day'. *The train is **late*** means that it is later than its
proper time. Similarly with *the **early** train* and *The train
is **early***.

Exercise 21

▶ Put in adjectives from the list. Use each adjective once.
dark, good, late, little, poor, ready, sorry, sure, upset

The (□) *poor* mother was very (1) ____. Her (2) ____ boy, Tom,
hadn't come home yet and it was nearly (3) ____. 'I'm (4) ____
that Tom is in trouble', she said. But just then Tom rushed in.
'I'm (5) ____ I'm (6) ____, Mum,' he said. 'Is supper (7) ____?
It smells (8) ____.'

▶ Put in the adjectives from the list: *horrible, ill, interesting, sour.*

9   The milk smells ____. Let's throw it away.
10 He looks ____. Should we ring the doctor?
11 What did you put in the soup? It tastes ____.
12 Your idea sounds ____. Let's try it.

22 Order of adjectives before a noun

When we use two or more adjectives together before a
noun, we must put them in a certain order.

Several variations are possible, but a fairly usual order is:
1 possessive adjectives (*my* etc.) and *this, that, these, those*
2 size (*big, small*)
3 general description (*dirty, smart*)
4 age (*old, young*) and the adjective *little*
5 shape (*round, square*)
6 colour (*blue, green*)
7 material (*steel, wooden*)
8 origin (*Austrian, French*)
9 purpose (*dining, reading*)

> *a **green plastic** bucket   my **smart new velvet** curtains
> an **elegant little French** clock   a **small round dining** table*

nice, fine and *lovely* can go before adjectives of size, shape
etc. when used to express approval. *a **nice big** room*

shows that we like big rooms. *The room is nice and big* has the same meaning. Similarly *a fine sandy beach*.

Exercise 22

► Put the adjectives into the correct order:
   □ big/black/this box   *this big black box*
   1 a heavy/leather/old case
   2 blue/her/new dress
   3 handmade/expensive shoes
   4 a nice/carving/sharp knife
   5 a little/noisy/English car
   6 a sunny/lovely day

23 Comparative and superlative forms

A The three degrees of comparison

ADJECTIVE	COMPARATIVE	SUPERLATIVE
dark	*darker*	*darkest*
difficult	*more difficult*	*most difficult*

We form comparatives and superlatives as follows.

B Adjectives of one syllable

We add *er/est*, or *r/st* if they end in *e*:
   short   *shorter*   *shortest*
   brave   *braver*   *bravest*

But note: *hot, hotter, hottest; sad, sadder, saddest*. (265 A)

C Adjectives of two syllables

We normally put *more/most* before the adjective:
   foolish   **more** *foolish*   **most** *foolish*
but if they end in *er* or *y*, we usually add *er, est*:
   clever   *cleverer*   *cleverest*
   pretty   *prettier*   *prettiest*

Note that the *y* becomes *i*.

D Adjectives of three or more syllables

We use *more/most*:
   interested   **more** *interested*   **most** *interested*

E Irregular forms

bad	worse	worst	
far	farther	farthest	(30)
	further	furthest	(30)
good	better	best	
little	less	least	
many/much	more	most	(32)
old	elder	eldest	(33)
	older	oldest	(33)

Exercise 23

▶ Write the comparative and superlative forms of these adjectives:

☐ happy *happier, happiest*

1 brave   5 fat   9   difficult
2 busy   6 many   10 exciting
3 clever   7 bad   11 far
4 dry   8 beautiful 12 good

24 Making comparisons

A To compare two people or things, we can use

as + adjective + *as* in the affirmative:
*A boy of sixteen is often **as tall as** his father.*

not as/so + adjective + *as* in the negative:
*Your coffee is **not as/so good as** my mother's.*

B We can also use a comparative adjective + *than*:
*The new tower blocks are **higher than** the old buildings.*
*He makes **fewer mistakes than** you (do).*

In colloquial English we often omit *than* and use a superlative instead of a comparative:
*This is the **best way**. (This is better than the other way.)*

C To compare three or more people/things, we use *the* + superlative adjective + *in/of*:
*This is **the oldest** theatre **in** London.*
or *the* + superlative + relative clause:
*He is **the kindest** man (that) I have ever met.*

ever is used in these relative clauses, not *never*. We can express the same idea with *never* + comparative:
  *I have **never** met a **kinder** man.*

most + adjective, without *the*, means 'very':
  *This is **most important*** means 'This is very important'.

most meaning *very* is used mainly with adjectives of two or more syllables: *annoying, exciting, helpful, important* etc.

D To talk about gradual increase or decrease, we use comparative, *the* + comparative:
  *The weather is getting **colder and colder**.*

E To talk about parallel increase, we use *the* + comparative, . . . *the* + comparative:
  You want a big house? ~ *Yes, **the bigger, the better**.*

Exercise 24

▶ Put in the comparative or superlative form of the adjective in brackets (+ *than* if necessary):
  The 8 o'clock train is much (□ *fast*) *faster than* the 7.30 one. Of course it is (1 *crowded*) _____ the 7.30 train and the tickets are (2 *expensive*) _____. You get (3 *cheap*) _____ fares before 8 o'clock. Still, it's the (4 *quick*) _____ way of getting to Bath, unless you want to fly, and getting to the airport is much (5 *difficult*) _____ getting to the station.

▶ Put in *as, the* or *than*:
  □ What about this one? It's better *than* the one we saw in Harrods.
  6 It's bigger _____ the one in our local shop.
  7 But it's more expensive _____ the others.
  8 Do we want one _____ big _____ that?
  9 Yes, _____ bigger, _____ better.
  10 Let's buy it. It's _____ best we've seen so far.

25 Comparisons with *than/as* and auxiliaries

A When the same verb is required before and after *than/as*, we normally use an auxiliary instead of the second verb:
  *I earn less than he **does**.* (I earn less than he earns.)

We need not use the same tense for each verb:
  *He **knows** more than I **did** at his age.*

B When *than/as* is followed by *I/we/you* + verb, and there is no change of tense, we often omit the verb:
> *He has more time **than I/we** (have).* (formal)
> *He has more time **than me/us**.* (informal)

C When *than/as* is followed by *he/she/it/they* + verb, we normally keep the verb:
> *You are stronger **than he/she is** OR **than they are**.*

But we sometimes omit the verb after *he/she/they* and use *him/her/them*:
> *You are stronger **than him/her/them**.*
> *You are stronger **than he/she/they** is possible, but formal.*

Exercise 25

▶ Put in *I/she/we* + *be/have/do*. An object pronoun (*me/her/us*) without a verb is also possible.
   □ My brother is younger than *I am*/than *me*.
   1 Tom and I work for the same company but he started later than ____.
   2 So I have been in the company for longer than ____.
   3 And I earn more than ____.
   4 We are both a bit jealous of our sister, Ann. She earns more than ____.
   5 And she's younger than ____.
   6 But she had a better training than ____.
   7 And she can learn new techniques faster than ____.

26 Adjective + *one/ones*

A If we want to refer to a noun that has just been mentioned, we can use most adjectives followed by *one/ones*:
> *I lost my old camera. This is a **new one**.*
> *Don't buy expensive apples. Get **cheap ones**.*

Similarly with a number + adjective:
> *We haven't got a large loaf. Will **two small ones** do?*

B We can use *first/second* etc. with or without *one/ones*:
> *Which train did you come on? ~ Oh, I caught the **first** (one).*

We use *the* + superlative in the same way:
    They've got four children. **The eldest (one)** *is only ten.*

the + comparative is possible but rather formal.
Informally we use a superlative instead:
    Which (of the two) is **the strongest (one)?**

Exercise 26

▶ Omit the nouns in CAPITALS and replace them by *one* or *ones* if
  necessary:
  ☐ Which coat do you like? ~ I like the blue COAT.
     I like the blue one.
  1 I don't want big bananas. I want small BANANAS.
  2 These are Tom's boys. Bill is the eldest BOY.
  3 Which train shall I catch? ~ Get an early TRAIN. The 8.30
     is the best TRAIN.
  4 A hard mattress is better than a soft MATTRESS.

27 *the* + adjective with a plural meaning

A We use *the* before some adjectives without a noun to
  mean a class of people:
    The poor *get poorer:* **the rich** *get richer.*

  These expressions have a plural meaning. They take a
  plural verb and the pronoun is *they*.

  Adjectives that can be used in this way are those which
  describe the human character or condition, for example:
  blind, deaf, disabled, healthy/sick, living/dead, rich/poor.

B We use *the* similarly with national adjectives ending in
  ch, sh, se and *ss*:
    the Dutch   the Spanish   the Welsh
    the Burmese   the Chinese   the Japanese   the Swiss

C *the* + adjective without a noun refers to a group of
  people considered in a general sense only. When we
  speak of a particular group, we add a noun:
    Those seats are for **the disabled**. BUT
    The disabled members *of our party were let in free.*
    The French *like to eat well.* BUT
    The French tourists *complained about the food.*

Exercise 27

► Replace the phrases in CAPITALS by *the* + adjective:

☐ PEOPLE WITH MONEY get richer. PEOPLE WITHOUT MONEY
get poorer. *The rich get richer. The poor get poorer.*

1 PEOPLE WHO ARE UNEMPLOYED draw unemployment
benefit.

2 These parking places are for PEOPLE WITH A PHYSICAL
DISABILITY.

3 There are special TV programmes for PEOPLE WHO
CANNOT HEAR.

4 PEOPLE WHO COME FROM WALES speak their own language.

28 Adjectives + infinitives

Here are some adjectives which we can use with
infinitives. They are divided into groups according to
their meaning. In most of these groups the construction
begins with *it*. For example: *It was good of you to call.*

A Character or sense

brave	foolish	good/nice	idiotic	silly
clever	generous	kind	sensible	stupid

of + object is usual here:
*It was **kind of you** to wait.* (You waited. This was kind.)
*It was **stupid of him** to leave his car unlocked.*

B Ease or safety

dangerous/safe	hard (= difficult)
easy/difficult	possible/impossible

for + object is optional:
*Is it **safe (for children)** to drink this water?*

With all except *possible* we can use constructions of the type:
*This cake is **easy** to make.   Is the iron **safe** to use?*

C Feelings and reactions

1	amusing	dreadful	marvellous
	annoying	exciting	nice
	awful	interesting	terrible
	disappointing	lovely	wonderful

*It was **interesting** to watch the team training.*
*It's **nice** (for the children) to have a garden to play in.*

2

amazed	disappointed	pleased
annoyed	glad	relieved
astonished	happy	sad
delighted	interested	sorry

Note that here we begin the sentence with the person who has the feelings or reactions, and not with *it*:
*He was **disappointed** to find nobody at home.*

With most of the adjectives in C we can also use a *that*-clause:
*I'm **delighted** that you can come.* (257)

D Willingness

anxious	ready	unwilling
prepared	reluctant	willing

*He's not **prepared** to lend you any money.*
*I'm **anxious** to help him.* (I want to help him.)

(*anxious* used alone, or *anxious about*, means 'worried'.)

E Necessity

advisable better, best important necessary

*It's **best** to buy tickets in advance.*
*It's not **necessary** for us to tell the police.*

Exercise 28

► Combine the sentence and the adjective in brackets:

☐ He offered to pay. (generous)
   It was generous of him to offer to pay.
1 He forgot the key. (stupid)
2 She arrived late. (foolish)
3 You offered to help. (kind)

☐ She saves money. (hard)
   It is hard to save money.
4 She hitchhikes alone. (dangerous)
5 He parks in the high street. (difficult)
6 They leave (their) cars unlocked. (not safe)

□   I was back home again.   (nice)
    It was nice to be back home again.
7   We felt the house shaking.   (terrible)
8   We saw the cars burning.   (dreadful)
9   We canoed down a fast river.   (exciting)

□   He found that there were no seats left.   (annoy)
    He was annoyed to find that there were no seats left.
10   I heard that he had got the job.   (glad)
11   He saw nobody he knew at the party.   (disappointed)
12   She saw him again.   (delighted)

29   Adjectives with infinitives or *that*-clauses

A   *afraid* + infinitive or *that*-clause
    *I was **afraid** to speak.*
    (I didn't speak because of my fear.)
    *I am **afraid** (that) I can't help you.*
    (I'm sorry to say that I can't help you.)

B   *bound, certain, sure, likely* + infinitive
    *Tom is **bound/certain/sure/likely** to win the race.*

This sentence expresses the speaker's opinion.

C   *certain* and *sure* with *that*-clauses
    *Tom is **certain/sure** that he will win.*

The above sentence expresses Tom's opinion.
We cannot use *bound* or *likely* here.

D   *it is* + *probable/likely/possible* + *that*-clause

We can say *It's **probable** that George will come last.*

But more often we use the adverb *probably* or *be* + *likely*
+ infinitive:
    *George will **probably** come last.*
    *George is **likely** to come last.*

We can say *It is **possible** that Bill will come second.*

But more often we use *perhaps* or *may/might/could*:
    ***Perhaps** Bill will come second.*
    *Bill **may/might/could** come second.*

But we often use *It's possible/probable* in short answers or comments. We can also use *It's likely/quite likely/very likely, not very likely* etc.:

> *Do you think taxes will go up?* ~
> *It's **quite possible/probable/likely*** OR
> *It's **not very likely/probable**.*

▷ For adjectives + *that*-clauses, see also 256.

30 *far* and *near*

A We can use the comparative and superlative forms of *far* and *near* in the same way as those of other adjectives:

> *Paris is **farther/further** than Lyon.*
> *Bath is our **nearest** town. It's **nearer** than Wells.*

We can also use *further* to mean 'additional':

> **further** *delays/demands/information/instructions/supplies* etc.
> *We are awaiting **further** instructions.*

B *the **near** bank/end* etc. means 'the bank/end nearest to us'.
*the **far** bank/end* etc. means the other one:

> *Most of the players were at **the far end** of the field.*

C We don't use *far* or *near* before a noun except as shown in B above. Instead of *far* we can sometimes say *distant* or *remote*; and instead of *near* we can say *nearby* or *neighbouring*:

> *a **distant** country   the **neighbouring** town*

D We can use *far* with an interrogative or negative link verb:

> *How **far** is (it to) Lyon?* ~ *It isn't **far**.*

With the affirmative we must say *a long way (away)*:

> *Paris is **a long way away**.   It's **a long way** to Paris.*

But we can use *as/so/too* + *far* and *far enough*:

> *Paris is **too far**. Lyon is **far enough**.*

E We can use *near* after a link verb if we modify it with *quite, so, too* or *enough*:

> *the airport is **quite near**.*
> *We can walk to the station. It's **near enough**.*

Exercise 30

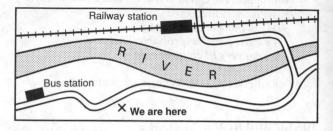

Railway station

R I V E R

Bus station

✕ We are here

▶ Put in *far* or *farther* or *a long way*:

☐ The railway station is much *farther* than the bus station.
1 It isn't ____ from here.
2 But it's ____ by road.
3 It's on the ____ side of the river.
4 How ____ is the bridge? ~ Two miles. ~ That's not too ____ to walk.

▶ Put in *nearer, nearest, quite near* or *neighbouring*:

☐ We do our shopping in one of the *neighbouring* towns.
5 Is Bath your ____ town?
6 Yes. It's ____ than Bristol.
7 We shop in the supermarket because there's a car park ____.
8 If we lived any ____ to Bath we'd pay more rent.

31 *little* and *few*

A We use *little* and *a little* before uncountable nouns:
   little salt   a little salt
and *few* and *a few* before plural nouns:
   few trees   a few trees

B We can also use them as pronouns:
   *How much of this do you understand? ~ Very **little**.*
   *Do you go to the lectures? ~ I go to **a few** (of them).*

C *a little* is a small amount. *a few* is a small number. We can add *only* to emphasize the smallness of the amount or quantity:
   *I have **only a little** time.   **Only a few** people know this.*

D But *little* and *few* without *a* have an almost negative meaning. We use them chiefly in formal English:

> *The minister has done **little** to help us.*
> ***Few** people realize the danger.*

In conversation we normally replace *little/few* by *hardly any/anyone/anything*:

> ***Hardly anyone** realizes the danger.*
> *He has done **hardly anything** to help us.*

But we can use *little* and *few* after *so, too, very* etc.:

> *We have **too little** free time.*
> *You see **very few** butterflies nowadays.*

Exercise 31

▶ Put in *a little* or *a few*:

    □ *a little* milk

1	____ litres of milk	4	____ rolls
2	____ oil	5	____ bread
3	____ drops of oil		

▶ Replace the phrases in CAPITALS by *very little* or *very few*:

    □ He eats HARDLY ANY meat.   *He eats very little meat.*

6 We've had HARDLY ANY tourists this year.
7 He worked hard but he made HARDLY ANY money.
8 We had HARDLY ANY rain that summer.

32 *many, much* and *a lot (of)*

A We use *many* with countable nouns and *much* with uncountable nouns (14):

> *He didn't make **many mistakes**.*
> *We haven't got **much coffee**.*

We can use *a lot of/lots of* with countable and uncountable nouns.
many and *much* have the same comparative and superlative, *more* and *most*:

> ***more** mistakes **more** coffee **most** men **most** fruit*

B We can also use *many, much, more, most* and *a lot/lots* without a noun, as pronouns:

> *Letters? She gets **a lot** but I don't get **many**.*
> *Money? You have **lots** but I haven't **much**.*

C We can use *much*, *many* and *a lot of* in negative and interrogative sentences:

>*We didn't eat **much** meat/**a lot of** meat.*
>*Did you see **many** films/**a lot of** films?*

But we use *much/many* after *how?*:

>*How **much** meat?   How **many** films?*

D In affirmative sentences we normally use *a lot of* or *lots of* instead of *many* and *much*:

>*A lot of/Lots of people came to the meeting.*
>*There was a lot of noise.*

We sometimes use *many* as part of the subject:

>*Many people came to the meeting.*

But we don't often use *much* except in formal English:

>*Much will depend on what the Minister says tonight.*

We don't normally use *many* or *much* as objects of a verb, so we say:

>*I saw a lot of birds.* (not *many birds*)
>*He eats a lot of meat.* (not *much meat*)

But we use *as/so/too/how* + *many* and *much*, also *a great many*, *more* and *most* as subjects and objects:

>*Most people eat too much meat.*
>*I know how much you earn.*

E With uncountable nouns we can use *a great/good deal of* instead of *a lot of*.

Exercise 32

▶ Put in *many, much, more, most, a lot of,* or *a great many*. Sometimes there are two possibilities.

George applied for (□) *a great many/a lot of* jobs and spent (1) _____ time travelling to interviews, but without success. The interviewers always said, 'How (2) _____ experience have you had?' Then they said, 'We need someone with (3) _____ experience than that.' Finally he had an interview in an office near his home. The interviewer was friendly. She asked (4) _____ questions and then said, 'For (5) _____ of our vacancies we need people with (6) _____ experience, but for this one we just need someone who can learn quickly. How (7) _____ did

you earn at your last job?' George told her. 'We can offer you
(8) _____ than that,' she said.

33 *elder* and *older*

We use *elder/eldest* mainly in comparisons within a
family:
    my **elder** brother   her **eldest** boy/girl

But we do not use *elder* with *than*; we use *older than*:
    My brother is **older than** I am.

We often use *eldest/oldest* (and *youngest*) when there are
only two sisters/boys etc.:
    His **eldest** boy's left home. The other's still at school.

---

4   Adverbs

34 What are adverbs?

A Adverbs are words used to show how, where, when,
how often or to what extent an action takes place. In the
sentence *I am going **home tomorrow**,* the word *home*
shows where I am going and *tomorrow* shows when I
am going. Both these words are adverbs. They give
information about, or modify, the action of the verb *am
going*.

B Adverbs can also modify

an adjective:
    I am **dreadfully** tired.

another adverb:
    Don't speak **so** quickly.

or a whole sentence:
    Perhaps we'll see you again next week.

C There are also adverbial phrases:
   at home   in bed   every Monday morning

Exercise 34

▶ Find the 15 adverbs and one adverb phrase in this story:
Once she came home rather late. She opened the front door
quietly and then remembered that she needn't have been so
quiet because her parents had gone away that morning,
leaving the house empty. But suddenly she realized that the
house wasn't empty; someone was moving about upstairs.
She stood quite still, her heart beginning to beat very fast.

35 Kinds of adverb

Manner (how?)
bravely, fast, happily, hard, quickly, well (41)

Place (where?)
home, down, here, near, there, up (42)

Time (when?)
now, soon, still, then, this morning (43)

Frequency (how often?)
always, every day, never, often, twice (45)

Degree (to what extent?)
almost, fairly, rather, quite, very, so (46–50)

Sentence
certainly, definitely, luckily (51)

Interrogative
how? when? where? why? (60)

Relative
when, where, why (69 E)

Exercise 35

▶ What kind of adverb is each of the following?

   □ now   *time adverb*
   1 politely   4 very   7 hard
   2 sometimes   5 angrily   8 quite
   3 everywhere   6 home   9 late

▶ Put in an adverb or adverb phrase from this list. Use each
once.

That Easter	before	Soon
in a hotel	completely	immediately
much less	then	slowly
On our second day	halfway up a mountain	there

(□) *That Easter* we camped in the Lake District. We had been
(10) ____ (11) ____ but (12) ____ had stayed (13) ____.
Camping was (14) ____ comfortable. (15) ____ we had a
violent thunderstorm. We were (16) ____ when it started. We
turned back (17) ____, but had to go (18) ____ because the
rocks were slippery. (19) ____ we were (20) ____ soaked.

36 Adverbs ending in *-ly*

A We form most adverbs by adding *-ly* to adjectives:
brave, bravely   slow, slowly

B Sometimes there is a spelling change.
1 A final *y* changes to *i*: *happy, happily*
2 Adjectives ending in a consonant + *le* drop the *e* and
add *y*:
gentle, gently   sensible, sensibly   simple, simply
3 *true, due* and *whole* become *truly, duly* and *wholly*

C We cannot form adverbs from adjectives which
themselves end in *-ly*. Instead we use another adverb or
an adverb phrase:

ADJECTIVE		ADVERB
likely	→	probably
friendly	→	in a friendly way

Exercise 36

▶ Write the adverb form of these adjectives:

□	complete		*completely*		
1	gentle	5	sensible	9	legible
2	angry	6	true	10	simple
3	sincere	7	happy	11	easy
4	beautiful	8	immediate	12	careful

D Some adverbs have a narrower meaning than their adjectives, or a different meaning. *coolly, coldly, hotly* and *warmly* are used mainly of feelings:

> *We were old friends. He greeted me **warmly**.*

▷ For *barely, scarcely*, see 49; for *surely*, see 51 C.

37 Adverbs with the same form as adjectives

A

back	*far*	*left*	*low*	*still*
early	*fast*	*little*	*much*	*straight*
enough	*ill*	*long*	*more*	*well*

The following have *ly* forms also, usually with other meanings (see a good dictionary):

deep	*hard*	*last*	*near*	*round*
direct	*high*	*late*	*pretty*	*short*
first	*just*	*most*	*right*	*wrong*

B The forms in A above can have similar meanings:

ADVERB	ADJECTIVE
*The train went too **fast**.*	*This is the **fast** train.*
*She went **straight** home.*	*Draw a **straight** line.*
*You can dial Rome **direct**.*	*The **direct** route is best.*

or different meanings:

*Come **back** soon.*	*She came in by the **back** door.*
*They trained us **well**.*	*He looks **well**.* (= healthy)
*Turn **right** here.*	*You are quite **right**.* (= correct)

Exercise 37

▶ Write adverbs corresponding to these adjectives. In some cases there is no change.

	□	quick	*quickly*		
1	quiet		7	slow
2	straight		8	good
3	real		9	still
4	early		10	careful
5	fast		11	long
6	back		12	enough

▶ Put in a suitable adverb formed from one of the following adjectives. Sometimes no change is needed.

direct, good, high, late, long, loud, low, slow, straight, truthful, warm

☐ We didn't climb very *high*.

13 He answered ____.
14 The old man walked ____.
15 He speaks Dutch ____.
16 They welcomed us ____.
17 The fans cheered ____.
18 He arrived ____ and missed his plane.
19 You mustn't fly ____ over the town.
20 I didn't wait ____.
21 You can dial Paris ____ .
22 He didn't stop anywhere. He drove ____ home.

38 Comparative and superlative forms

	ADVERB	COMPARATIVE	SUPERLATIVE
Regular			
One syllable	*hard*	*harder*	*hardest*
Two or more syllables	*quickly*	*more quickly*	*most quickly*
Exception	*early*	*earlier*	*earliest*
Irregular	*badly*	*worse*	*worst*
	far	*farther*	*farthest*
		further	*furthest*
	little	*less*	*least*
	much	*more*	*most*
	well	*better*	*best*

39 Adverbs in comparisons

A With the base form of adverbs we use affirmative verb + *as* + adverb + *as* . . . :

He worked as fast as he could.

or negative verb + *as/so* + adverb + *as*

It didn't take as/so long as he expected.

B With comparative adverbs we use adverb + *than*:
   *He arrived **earlier than** the others.*
   or *the* + adverb . . . *the* + adverb:
   ***The earlier** you start **the sooner** you'll finish.*

C With superlatives we do not need any special phrase:
   *He likes tennis **best**.* (better than other games)

D We can use adverb + *than/as* + auxiliary:
   *She ran **faster than** he did.* (than he ran)
   *I don't speak Greek **as well as** she does.*

E We use *like* with noun/pronoun:
   *We eat with chopsticks **like** the Chinese.*
   or *as* or *like* with a clause:
   *We eat with chopsticks **as** they do in China.* (formal)
   *We eat with chopsticks **like** the Chinese do.* (informal)

Exercise 39

▶ Put in the correct form of the adverb in brackets:
   □ Do men drive *better* than women?   (well)
   1 You can buy fruit ____ in the market than in the
      greengrocer's.   (cheaply)
   2 Bill came ____ than Tom.   (early)
   3 Try to come in ____ than you did last night.   (quietly)
   4 Her boys behave ____ at school and behave even ____ at
      home.   (badly)
   5 I'll come as ____ as I can.   (soon)
   6 Mary works ____ than you.   (hard)
   7 The ____ we start, the ____ we'll be finished.   (soon)
   8 We can't go any ____; the bridge has collapsed.   (far)

40 Position of adverbs in a sentence

A We put adverbs in various positions in sentences.
   Sections 41–3 below deal mainly with the positions we
   use for different kinds of adverb. In these sections the
   following terms are used:
      front position   end position   mid-position

B Front position means 'at the beginning of a sentence or
   clause':
   ***Yesterday** the bus drivers went on strike.*

C Mid-position means

after the simple tenses of *be*:
  *She is **always** busy.*

before the simple tenses of other verbs:
  *She **never** watches television.*

after the auxiliary in compound tenses:
  *They're **now** living in Bath.*
  *He has **never** been abroad.*

after the auxiliary in other auxiliary + verb combinations:
  *It was very foggy. I could **hardly** see the road.*

before or after an auxiliary used alone:
  *Do you work late? ~ Yes, we do **sometimes**/we **sometimes** do.*
  *Did he pay you? ~ Yes, he **usually** did.*

D End position means 'at the end of a sentence or clause':
  *I had to walk to work **yesterday**.*

E Adverbs can also come between a verb and a
preposition + noun/pronoun:
  *He listened **patiently** to everyone's complaints.*

41 Adverbs of manner

A We often put these in end position. So we have:

Verb + adverb or verb + object + adverb
  *He ran **fast**.   She speaks **well**.   She speaks Greek **well**.*
Do not put an adverb between verb and object.

Verb + preposition + object + adverb
  *He spoke to everyone **politely**.*

B We can also put these adverbs between a verb and a
preposition:
  *He spoke **politely** to everyone.*

This order is usual with *badly* and *well*:
  *He worked **well** for his last boss.*
  *The team played **badly** in their first match.*
and with longer objects:
  *He shouted **angrily** at a group of latecomers.*

Exercise 41

▶ Put the adverb in brackets into the sentence. Sometimes there are two possibilities.

  □ He repaired the car.   (quickly)   *He repaired the car quickly.*

1 He pays his staff.   (badly)
2 He spoke to me.   (politely)
3 He speaks to all his regular customers.   (politely)
4 He doesn't get on with some of his staff.   (well)

42   Adverbs of place and direction

A

abroad	here	along	in London
away	there	behind	in front
back	anywhere	in/out	out of the house
home	everywhere	on/off	off the bus
outside	somewhere	through	through the wood
upstairs	nowhere	up/down	down the ladder

B We usually put these adverbs and adverb phrases in end position. So we have:

Verb + adverb
  *This herb grows **everywhere**.   You can park **anywhere**.*
  *Are you going **anywhere**?   I can't find my keys **anywhere**.*
  *He ran **off**.   We flew **above the clouds**.*

Verb + object + adverb
  *I sent him **away**.*
  *Let's have lunch **somewhere by the river**.*
  *He left his car **outside**.   I met Bill **in London**.*

C In sentences with verb + preposition + object, adverbs and adverb phrases of place follow the object; so we have:

Verb + preposition + object + adverb
  *I'll talk to him **here**.   Wait for me **by the back door**.*

Adverbs or adverb phrases of *direction* follow the verb; so we have:

Verb + adverb + preposition etc.
  *Come **home** with me.   They went **to Rome** for a holiday.*

D Notes on certain adverbs of place and direction

1 *along, back, in/out, on/off, through, up/down* etc. and *home* come before other adverbs or adverb phrases:
> He ran **off** down the street.   Come **back** here!

2 *here/there* + *be* + noun subject is also possible:
> **Here** are the tickets.   **There's** Jack!

but pronoun subjects come before *be*:
> **Here** they are.   **There** he is!

3 We can use *anywhere* (meaning 'it doesn't matter where') and *nowhere* in short answers:
> Where shall we go? ~ **Anywhere** OR **Anywhere** you like.
> Where are you going? ~ **Nowhere**.

Exercise 42

▶ Put the adverb in brackets into the sentence:
   □ We went with plenty of money.   (out)   *We went out with plenty of money.*
   1 We came without a penny.   (home)
   2 She buys her clothes.   (abroad)
   3 He went with his wife.   (there)
   4 She sent the children.   (upstairs)
   5 They ran from me.   (away)
   6 He has gone to Rome.   (back)

▶ Put in *somewhere, anywhere, nowhere* or *everywhere*:
   7 I've left my watch ____ and now I can't find it.
   8 Have you seen my watch ____?
   9 You can camp ____. There are no restrictions.
   10 He lives ____ in Kent now.
   11 You can see these advertisements ____.
   12 Where shall we have lunch? ~ ____ you like. I leave the choice to you.
   13 I couldn't find a parking place ____.
   14 Where are you going this summer? ~ ____. I'm not going ____.

43 Adverbs of time

A

afterwards	*first/last*	*today*	*at 5.30*
before	*immediately*	*tonight*	*on Monday*
early/late	*now/then*	*yesterday*	*in June*
lately	*soon*	*last night*	*for ages*

We usually put adverbs of time in end position or front position:

> *He gave a lecture on Monday* OR *On Monday he gave a lecture.*

But we use end position, not front position,
with very short sentences: *He came yesterday.*
with phrases with *till*: *I'll stay till six.*
with imperatives: *Write soon.*
with *before, early, last* and *late*:

> *I've been here before.   He left early.   Tom came last.*

now, soon and *then* can also be in mid-position:

> *He's now living in Rome.   She soon found work.*

B We use *just* after the auxiliary in compound tenses:

> *He has just left the house.   He is just getting into the taxi.*
> but *just now* and *just then* come in front or end position.

(For *just* as an adverb of degree, see 46 C, G.)

C *yet* and *still* mean 'up to the time of speaking'.

We normally use *yet* with a negative or interrogative perfect tense. It is usually in end position:

> *He hasn't come yet.   He hasn't paid me yet.*

We use *still* mainly with affirmative or interrogative verbs. It usually comes in mid-position:

> *He is still in bed.   Are you still waiting for him?*
> *I've still got your camera.   Do you still work for Tom?*

▷ For *since*, see 81 B; for *long*, see 50 D; for the adverbs *afterwards/then* and the preposition *after*, see 80 C.

Exercise 43

▶ Decide if the adverb or adverb phrase in CAPITALS is in the right or wrong position in these sentences. If it is wrong rewrite the sentence.

　　□ Have you BEFORE been here?   WRONG – *Have you been here before?*
　1 LATE Bill arrived.
　2 She is NOW working in a bank.
　3 FOR TWO YEARS he waited for her answer.
　4 We stop ON SATURDAY work early.

5   The fog will lift SOON.
6   TODAY stay in bed.
7   There have been some terrible fires RECENTLY.

▶ Put the words in brackets into the sentence:

□   I'm getting up.   (just)   *I'm just getting up.*
8   We're not taking on any more staff.   (just now)
9   We have finished lunch.   (just)
10   There was a knock on the door.   (just then)

▶ Put in *yet* or *still*:

□   You can't borrow the book. I'm *still* reading it.
11   Tom's not ready ____. He's ____ in the bath.
12   They're ____ standing there! What are they waiting for?
13   It isn't time to start ____.
14   Hasn't it stopped raining ____? No, it's ____ raining.
15   Is he ____ in London or has he moved?

44   Order of adverbs of manner, direction, place and time

A   Manner and direction

Adverbs of manner usually follow adverbs of direction:
   *He walked away **sadly**.   She came in **quietly**.*
   *She ran off **happily**.   We climbed down **carefully**.*
but they can come before or after adverb phrases of
direction:
   *I climbed up the rope **slowly*** OR *I climbed **slowly** up the rope.*

B   Manner and place

Adverbs of manner usually come before adverbs and
adverb phrases of place:
   *They were playing **noisily** outside (the house).*
   *You can buy fruit **more cheaply** here.*

C   Manner, place and time

Time expressions sometimes come last:
   *A burglar climbed up the fire escape **during the night**.*
but front position is neater when there are other adverbs:
   ***During the night** a burglar climbed quietly up the fire
   escape.*

Exercise 44

► Put these words/phrases into a correct order. Sometimes more than one order is possible.

□ slowly/he walked/home   *He walked home slowly.*

1 some tennis players play/on hard courts/ best
2 to school/by bus/the children go
3 he waited/outside the telephone box/impatiently
4 beautifully/she sang/at the Festival Hall
5 he/spends the weekend/quietly/often/at home
6 I don't drive/on motorways/fast/ in foggy weather
7 on a hard bed/well/he says he/ sleeps/ always

45 Adverbs of frequency

A *always, frequently, occasionally, often, sometimes, usually*

These can be in mid-, front or end position.
*Is it **always** his fault?   He is **sometimes** late.*
*We **often** camped here.   I **usually** get up at six.*
*Sometimes I go by bus.   I go by bus **sometimes**.*

But note that *always* is never in front position except with imperatives:
Always lock this door when you go out.
and that if we put *often* in end position after affirmative verbs we must modify it by *quite/so/too/very* or *enough*:
*We camp here quite **often**.   He took risks so **often** that . . .*
*We don't go out **often** enough.*

B *again, once, twice, three times, once/twice a week*

These usually come in end position, and always do so with imperatives:
*It happened **again**.   I've seen the play **twice**.*
*Do it **three times**.*
but they can be followed by a time expression:
*It happened **again** last night.   I've seen it **twice** since then.*

once can also be in front position:
*She's very careless. **Once** she lost £100.*

C   *ever* (= 'at any time')

We use *ever* chiefly in the interrogative and in mid-position:
> *Is she **ever** on time?   Do you **ever** drive to work?*
> *Has he **ever** passed an exam?*

We can use *ever* + negative verb, usually in a perfect tense:
> *I haven't **ever** driven a Rolls Royce.*
but *never* + affirmative verb is much more usual:
> *I have **never** driven a Rolls Royce.*

We can use *ever* + affirmative verb in comparisons and after *if*:
> *That was the best holiday I have **ever** had.* (24 C)
> *If I **ever** go to Australia . . .*

D   *never, hardly ever, rarely* and *seldom*

We use these with affirmative verbs, not with negatives.
They usually come in mid-position:
> *She is **never** late.   He **hardly ever** eats meat.*
> *I can **rarely** hear what he says.   She **seldom** reads novels.*

Exercise 45

▶ Put the adverb in brackets into the sentence. Sometimes
   several positions are equally good.
   □ I walk to work. (sometimes)   *I sometimes walk to work.*
   1   Ann goes by bus. (always)
   2   The buses are very crowded. (usually)
   3   She has to stand all the way. (often)
   4   But she is late for work. (never)
   5   You've been late this week. (three times)
   6   He fell asleep at the controls. (once = on one occasion)
   7   Take these pills for the first week. (twice a day)
   8   He woke us up last night. (again)

▶ Put in *ever, never* or *hardly ever*:
   □ I wonder if he *ever* writes to his wife.
   9   I have ____ drunk better beer. This is the best beer I have
       ____ drunk.
   10 Doesn't your boss ____ say 'Thank you'? ~ No, he ____
       does.
   11 She says that he ____ makes mistakes. ~ That's not true.
       But he ____ makes one.

46 Adverbs of degree

A

almost	*extremely*	*much*	*really*
badly	*fairly* (47)	*nearly*	*scarcely* (49)
barely (49)	*far* (50)	*only*	*so*
completely	*hardly* (49)	*pretty* (= *very*)	*too*
enough	*just*	*quite* (48)	*very*
even	*a little*	*rather* (47)	*well*

B Most adverbs of degree, except *badly* and *well*, modify adjectives or other adverbs.

They normally precede the adjective or adverb:
  *My bag's **very** heavy.   Don't speak **too** fast.*
but *enough* follows its adjective or adverb:
  *This room isn't big **enough**.*

C Some adverbs of degree can also modify verbs.

almost, hardly, just, nearly, quite, rather, really precede the main verb:
  *He **almost** succeeded.   I can **hardly** see anything.*
  *I **nearly** missed my train. I only **just** caught it.*
  *Ann **quite/rather** enjoys driving at night.*

enough, much and *a little* come after verb or verb + object:
  *I don't practise (the piano) **enough**.*
  *It rained **a little** during the night.*

D *badly* and *well* usually modify past participles:
  *He was **badly** injured.* (seriously injured)
  *The hostages were **well** treated.* (opposite: **badly** treated)
or combine with a past participle to form adjectives:
  *a **badly-lit** street   **well-trained** dogs   **well-known** faces*

E *even* can modify a comparative adjective or adverb:
  *The second hill was **even** steeper than the first.*

We can also use it with nouns, pronouns and verbs:
  *Everything was expensive, **even** bread.*
  *He didn't **even** smile.*

F *far* and *much* require *too* + adjective or a comparative:
  *You are **far** too fat to wear those trousers.*
  *He is **much** taller than you.*

G *just* precedes the verb it modifies:
   *I **just** caught the train.*
and usually precedes other words and expressions:
   *I had **just** enough money.   He arrived **just** in time.*

H *a little* can come after a verb or verb + object:
   *I play (the oboe) **a little**.*

It can also come before adjectives and adverbs such as
anxious, anxiously, disappointed, sad, sadly:
   *a **little** sad   a **little** anxiously*
and before comparative adjectives and adverbs:
   *He's **a little** older than you are.*
   *Try to talk **a little** more quietly.*

I *only* can modify adjectives, adverbs, nouns, pronouns
and verbs. In formal English it comes next to the word
it modifies:
   *I need **only** one.* (not more than one)
but we usually put *only* before the verb and stress the
important word: *I only need 'one.*

Exercise 46

▶ Put the adverb in brackets into the sentence:
   □ The first house was big.   (too)
      The first house was too big.
   1 The second house wasn't big.   (enough)
   2 The third house was expensive.   (rather)
   3 Prices are high in this area.   (extremely)
   4 The house we bought was over 100 years old.   (nearly)
   5 We could have got it cheaply.   (fairly)
   6 But it was in a bad state of repair.   (very)

   7 They were stronger than we were.   (much)
   8 One of our team was injured.   (badly)
   9 The referee lost his temper once.   (nearly)
  10 We won.   (almost)
  11 But I'm afraid we don't train.   (enough)
  12 If we trained we'd win more often.   (more)

▶ Now put these adverbs into the sentence in a mid-position.
  (In one of these sentences you need to insert a hyphen; which
  one?)
  13 Were the children fed?   (well)
  14 The church was damaged by fire.   (badly)
  15 The workers were paid.   (badly)

16 But the offices were full of paid officials.   (well)
17 It will take a minute.   (only)
18 I had enough money for my fare.   (just)
19 He didn't give it to me. He lent it to me.   (only)
20 We will have time for a meal.   (just)
21 He didn't say anything. He didn't say 'Goodbye'.   (even)

47 Degree: *fairly* and *rather*

A Both *fairly* and *rather* can mean 'moderately', but we use *fairly* chiefly with 'favourable' adjectives and adverbs (*good, well, quietly* etc.), and we use *rather* chiefly with 'unfavourable' adjectives and adverbs (*bad, noisily* etc.):
   *This street used to be **fairly** quiet but now it's **rather** noisy.*

   a/an, if used, comes before *fairly* but can come before or after *rather*:
   *a **fairly** easy test*
   *a **rather** difficult test* OR ***rather** a difficult test*

B With 'neutral' adjectives and adverbs (*thin, thick, quickly, slowly* etc.) the speaker can express approval with *fairly* and disapproval with *rather*:
   *The ice was **fairly** thick. We were able to walk on it.*
   *He spoke **rather** quickly. I couldn't understand him.*

C We can also use *rather* before certain 'favourable' adjectives (*good, clever, interesting* etc.) but its meaning then changes: it becomes almost equal to *very* and expresses approval:
   *She said it was **rather** a good programme. I'm sorry I missed it.*
   rather here is much more complimentary than *fairly*.

   We can also use *rather* before *like* and *enjoy* to strengthen the verb or express a liking which might surprise people:
   *I **rather** like Tom.   Ann **rather** enjoys queueing.*

   Exercise 47

▶ Put in *rather* or *fairly*:
   You can get from Heathrow to Paris (□) *fairly* quickly. But it sometimes takes (1) ____ a long time to get to Heathrow. We got there (2) ____ easily last time as it was only 6 a.m. But then we had (3) ____ a long wait at the airport. We were (4) ____

worried because we had to make a connection in Paris. But in
the end we had a (5) ____ comfortable journey and arrived in
time.

48 Degree: *quite*

A *quite* with certain adjectives, e.g. *certain (sure), empty/full,
finished, ready, right/wrong, sure, well* (= healthy), and the
phrase *all right,* usually means 'completely':
  *You're **quite** right.* (completely right)

B With most other adjectives and with adverbs the
meaning of *quite* varies with the stress.

When *quite* is stressed it means 'moderately'; so it
weakens the adjective. *'quite good,* with stress on *'quite,*
is like *fairly good.*

When *quite* is unstressed it strengthens the adjective.
quite here is similar to *rather* (47 C) but not so strong.

C We can use *quite* similarly with the verbs *like, enjoy* and
understand (the reason for something).

49 Degree: *hardly, scarcely* and *barely*

A These adverbs are almost negative in meaning. We
therefore use them with affirmative verbs.

B We use *hardly* chiefly with *any, ever*:
  *He has **hardly** any friends.*
  *He **hardly** ever leaves the house.*
or with *can* + infinitive and other verbs:
  *I can **hardly** see anything. The fog is so thick.*
  *He **hardly** reads at all.*

Be careful not to confuse *hardly* with *hard*:
  *He **hardly** looked at it* means 'He gave it only a brief glance'.
  *He looked **hard** at it* means 'He stared at it'.

C *scarcely* usually means 'not quite':
  ***scarcely** forty men* (probably fewer than forty)

D   *barely* means 'not more than/only just':
    *The mother was **barely** fifteen.* (She was only just fifteen.)

> **Exercise 49**

▶ Finish these sentences, in the way shown. Use *hardly* each time.
    □ Tom has lots of friends but I *have hardly any (friends)*.
    1 Tom has plenty of money, but I ____.
    2 Tom will have plenty of spare time, but I ____.
    3 Tom has lots of records, but I ____.

    □ I usually drink coffee, but Tom *hardly ever drinks coffee*.
    4 I watch TV, but Tom ____.
    5 I read the newspapers, but Tom ____.
    6 I eat fruit, but Tom ____.

▶ Now use the words in brackets:
    □ This plate is very hot; I *can hardly hold it.*   (hold)
    7 This case is terribly heavy; I ____.   (lift)
    8 The handwriting is very bad; I ____.   (read)
    9 His voice was very faint; I ____.   (hear)

50   *far, near, long* and *much*

A   We use these adverbs chiefly in the negative and interrogative. With affirmative verbs we normally use a phrase as shown below. But we can use *far, near, long* and *much* in the affirmative if modified by *as, so, too, enough* or *how*.

B   *far*

    *How **far** did you go?* ~ *We didn't go **far*** OR *Not **far***.

    With affirmative verbs we use *a long way/a long way away*:
    *We went **a long way**.*   *I live **a long way away**.*
    *I went **far enough**.*   *You went **too far**.*

C   *near*

    *Don't come **near**.*   *How **near** can I come?*

    With affirmative verbs we can use *quite near* or *near* (preposition) in an adverb phrase:
    *He lives **quite near** the river.*   *I can park **near** here.*
    *You're **near enough** now.*   *Don't come **too near**.*

D *long*

> How **long** did it take? ~ It didn't take **long** OR Not **long**.

With affirmative verbs we use: *(for) a long time, for ages*:
> I waited (for) **a long time**.   I waited **for ages**.
> I waited **long enough**.   I waited **too long**.

E *much*

> Do you ride **much**? ~ No, not **much**.

With affirmative verbs we use *a lot/a great deal/a good deal*:
> But I used to ride **a lot**.
> He shouted **so much** that . . .   We all talk **too much**.

We can use *very much* after *enjoy/like/thank* + object:
> She enjoyed the party **very much**.

F **Comparatives and superlatives**

We can use the comparative and superlative forms of
far, near, long and *much* quite freely:
> You went **further** than I did.
> The storm lasted **longer** than we expected.

▷ For *far* and *near* as adjectives, see 30.
   For *much* as adjective, see 32.

Exercise 50

▶ Put in the words from the list. Use each word once.
   far, farther, farthest, too far, a long way
   1 How _____ do you want to go?
   2 This is the _____ you can go by car.
   3 The _____ you go, the worse the road gets.
   4 Bill's house is _____ from here.
   5 I couldn't walk home. It's _____. It's 20 km.

▶ Put in the words from the list:
   near (×2), nearer, nearest, quite near, too near
   6 Mary: I can park _____ the office.
   7 Ann: I live _____ so I can go home for lunch.
   8 Mary: You're lucky to live _____ enough to do that.
   9 Ann: Bill lives even _____ the office than I do.
   10 Mary: And Tom lives _____ of all. He has the flat above the
       office.
   11 Ann: Oh, I think that's _____!

▶ Put in the words from the list:
long (×2), *longer, too long, a long time*
12   It's a hired car. The _____ I keep it, the more I have to pay.
13   How _____ do these batteries last? ~ Ten hours.
14   I haven't lived here _____.
15   But Tom's been here _____.
16   I think you've kept this cheese _____. It smells horrible.

▶ Put in *much* (×3), *more, very much,* or *a lot* (×2):
17   Thank you _____ for the lift.
18   Your car is _____ more comfortable than mine.
19   I used to drive _____ but I don't drive _____ now.
20   The roads are _____ too crowded.
21   I walk _____ than I used to.
22   But my wife drives _____.

51 Sentence adverbs

These modify a whole sentence or clause, and usually
express the speaker's or narrator's opinion.

A   *actually* (= in fact), *certainly, definitely, obviously, probably*
can be in front position, mid-position or end position:
*Where did you go? ~ **Actually**, we didn't go anywhere.*
*The key's **probably** here* OR *The key's here, **probably**.*

B   *perhaps* is usually in front position:
Perhaps he doesn't know our number.

C   *surely?* is usually in front or end position:
*Surely we've met before?   We've met before, **surely?***

D   *(un)fortunately, honestly* (= truthfully), *(un)luckily,*
naturally are usually in front position, but end position
is possible. Note the commas:
*Honestly, it wasn't my fault.   It wasn't my fault, **honestly**.*
Naturally, he wanted to see her.

5   *neither, all, each, some* etc.

52   *neither, either*

A   *neither* means 'not one and not the other'. When used as subject, it takes a singular affirmative verb. We can use it alone or with a singular noun:

> *Two buses came.* ***Neither*** *was the one I wanted.*
> *It was a disappointing match;* ***neither team*** *played well.*

or with *of* + *the* + plural noun or *of* + *us/you/them/these/those/mine/yours* etc.

> ***Neither of the boys*** *went* OR ***Neither of them*** *went.*

B   *either* means 'any one of two'. When used as subject, it takes a singular verb. We can use it alone or with a singular noun or with *of*:

> *Take* ***either (bus)*** OR
> *Take* ***either of these buses/either of them***.

either can be the subject or object of an affirmative or interrogative verb:

> ***Either (bus)*** *will take us.*   *Do you want* ***either of these?***

either can also be the object of a negative verb. Negative verb + *either* means the same as affirmative verb + *neither*:

> *I* ***haven't read either*** *of them = I've read* ***neither*** *of them.*

Negative + *either* is more usual than affirmative + *either* in object position. But we cannot use *either* as the subject of a negative verb. *Neither boy knew* is not replaceable by *either* + negative verb.

▷   For *either . . . or, neither . . . nor,* see 244 B. For use of *they/them/their* with *neither,* see 63 D.

Exercise 52

▶   Rewrite the sentences. Use *neither of* with *us/you/them* and an affirmative verb.

   □   I don't like him. You don't like him.   *Neither of us likes him.*
   1   I can't swim. You can't swim.
   2   He wouldn't wait. She wouldn't wait.

3   He didn't know the area. You didn't know it.
4   He didn't see the programme. She didn't see it.

▶ Finish the sentences, using *either of* with *us, them* or *you*:
   □ He didn't like Tom or Bill. He didn't like ____.
      He didn't like *either of them*.
5   I didn't see him or her. I didn't see ____.
6   He didn't invite me or you. He didn't invite ____.
7   He hasn't paid you, Tom or you, Bill. He hasn't paid ____.
8   Do you want this one or that one? Do you want ____?
9   Does he teach you? Or you? Does he teach ____?

53 *all, each, every, everyone, everybody, everything*

When we have a number of people or things we can use
all + plural noun, but we often use *each* (54) for small
numbers and *every* for larger numbers:
   All the children in the crowd waved their flags.
   Each child in the class was given a flag.
   Every child in the crowd had a flag to wave.

Instead of 'all the people' we often use *everyone/everybody*,
and instead of 'all the things' we often use *everything*:
   Everyone does it is more usual than *All the people do it*.
   You can buy everything here is more usual than *You can
   buy all the things here*.

Note also the adverb *everywhere* (= in/at/to all places):
   He goes everywhere on foot.

Exercise 53

▶ Replace the phrases in CAPITALS by *everyone, everything* or
  everywhere:
   □ Did you see ALL THE GUESTS?   *Did you see everyone?*
1   He goes ALL OVER THE PLACE on his bicycle.
2   He has seen ALL THE THINGS.
3   ALL THE WORLD admires him.
4   You see tourists IN ALL AREAS.

54 *each, both, all*

A We can use *each* for two or more people or things. It is
   similar to *every* and often we can use either. But we do

not use *every* for very small numbers:
> *There are two volumes.* **Each (volume)** *costs £15.*

We can use *each* alone or with a singular noun or with *of*:
> **Each of the witnesses/Each of them** *told a different story.*

we each can replace *each of us* (subject). *us each* can replace *each of us* (indirect object). Similarly with *they/them each* and *you each*:
> *I'll give* **each of you/you each** *£10.*

each of us/you/them takes a singular verb but *we/you/they each* takes a plural verb:
> **Each of us** *has a map.* **We each** *have maps.*

B *both* means 'one and the other'. We use it of people or things. It takes a plural verb. We can use it alone or with a plural noun:
> *There are two doors.* **Both** *are open/***Both doors** *are open.*

or with *of* + *us/you/them* or (*of* +) *these/those/mine/yours* etc.:
> **Both of them** *are open* OR **Both (of) these doors** *are open.*

C We can use *all* with plural nouns and a plural verb:
> **All men are** *ambitious.* **All the men are** *on strike.*

or with uncountable nouns and a singular verb:
> **All the luggage was** *in the car.*

We can use *all* alone or with its noun or with *of* + *it/us/you/them* or with (*of* +) *this/these/that/those/mine/yours* etc.:
> **All of it** *was lost.* *Do you want* **all (of) these?**

D *we both/all* can replace *both/all of us* (subject).
us both/all can replace *both/all of us* (object).
Similarly with *you, they/them* and *it*.

SUBJECT OR OBJECT	SUBJECT	OBJECT
both of us	*we both*	*us both*
both of you	*you both*	*you both*
both of them	*they both*	*them both*
all of us	*we all*	*us all*
all of you	*you all*	*you all*
all of them	*they all*	*them all*
all of it	*it all*	*it all*

> **We both** *work.* *He saw* **us both.**

E When we use *we all, you both, they each* etc. as subjects of *be* or a compound tense, the *each/both/all* comes after *be* or after the auxiliary:

> *We all caught the* BUS *We are all here.*
> *You both know him* BUT *You have both seen him.*

except in the interrogative and in short answers:

> *Have you all paid?* ~ *Yes, we all have.*

Exercise 54

▶ Finish the sentences, using *them/us* and *both*:

☐ Did you see Tom or Bill? ~ *I saw them both* OR *I saw both of them.*

1 Does he want Jim or me? ~ He wants _____.
2 Will he pay you or me? ~ He'll pay _____.
3 Did she see Ann or Tom? ~ She saw _____.
4 Does he use this room or that? ~ He uses _____.
5 Does he write to Bill or to you? ~ He writes to _____.

▶ Answer the questions using *they/you/we* and *both*:

☐ Who goes to the class, you or Tom? ~ *We both go.*

6 Who helps you, Ann or Tom?
7 Who went, you or Bill?
8 Which of us pays, Tom or me?
9 Which of you was there?
10 Which of you has seen the programme?

55 *some, any, no, none*

A *some/any* with plural nouns means 'a certain number'. *some/any* with uncountable nouns means 'a certain amount':

> *Have we* **any** *lemons?* ~ *Yes, we have* **some**.
> *We haven't* **any** *coffee. Have* **some** *tea.*

We use *some* and *any* alone or with nouns or with *of*:

> *Did* **any** *of you buy milk?*   **Some** *of it is sour.*

B We use *some*
1 with affirmative verbs as shown above
2 in questions when we expect the answer 'Yes':
> *Were some of you late? I expect you were.*
3 in offers and requests:
> *Will you have* **some** *tea?*
> *Could you give me* **some** *information?*

C We use *any*

1 with negative verbs:
   *I haven't **any** money.*
2 with *hardly* (which is almost a negative):
   *He speaks **hardly any** French.*
3 in questions except those in B2 above:
   *Do **any** of these buses go to Victoria?*
4 after *if* and in expressions of doubt:
   *If **any** of you see Tom at the party tomorrow, tell him to
   phone me.* ~ *I don't think **any** of us will be at the party.*

D We use *no* and *none* with affirmative verbs:
   *He gets lots of letters. I get **no** letters/I get **none**.*

   no + noun and *none of* can be subjects of a sentence:
   ***No** rain fell that year and **none of** our crops ripened.*

E We can also use *some* and *any* with singular countable
   nouns. *some* here means 'unknown':
   ***Some** kind person sent me these flowers.* (I don't know who.)

   any here means 'every', 'no particular one':
   ***Any** bus from here will take you to the station.*

Exercise 55

▶ Put in *some* or *any* or *no* or *none*:
   □ Bill: Are *any* of you going to John's party?
   1 Tom: ____ of us would like to go but we haven't ____ way
      of getting there.
   2 Jim: ____ of us has a car.
   3 Bill: I thought ____ of you had bicycles.
   4 Tom: No, I don't think ____ of us have.
   5 Bill: Then what about trains?
      Tom: There's ____ station in his village.
   6 Jim: And hardly ____ buses go along his road.

56 *somebody, anybody, nobody, everybody* **etc.**

A Compounds of *some, any* and *no* follow the rules about
   some, any and *no* (55):
   ***Someone** has taken my map. Does **anyone** know the way?*

   Note also the adverbs: *somewhere, anywhere, nowhere.*

B We can add *else* to these forms and also to *everybody* etc.
(42) and *everywhere*:

somebody else = some other person
something else = some other thing
everybody else = every other person
anybody else = any other person
nothing else = no other thing
somewhere else = some other place

C Compounds with *-body* and *-one* can be possessive:
It is **everybody's/everyone's** duty to help the disabled.

D With compounds with *-body* and *-one* we normally use
plural pronouns and plural possessive adjectives (63 D):
Somebody will come soon, won't **they**? (not *won't he?*)
Has everyone got **their** books? (not *his books*)

Exercise 56

▶ Put in a word from the list. Use each word once.
anything, everyone, no one, someone, something, somewhere
   □ George, we must decide where we are going for our
      holidays this year. *Everyone* else has made plans already.
      Now what about Florida?
   1 I met _____ yesterday who goes there every year and loves it.
   2 I don't know _____ about the hotels but I could find out.
   3 Everyone we know is going _____ exciting this year.
   4 _____ is staying at home.
   5 Say _____, George. Don't just sit there looking gloomy.

▶ Replace the phrases in CAPITALS by *anyone/anywhere/no one/
someone/somewhere* + *else*:
   □ If the conductor doesn't know, ask ANOTHER PERSON.
      If the conductor doesn't know, ask someone else.
   6 But sometimes there isn't ANOTHER PERSON on the bus.
   7 Last night I was the only passenger. There was NO OTHER
      PERSON on the bus.
   8 That shop is too expensive. Let's go TO ANOTHER PLACE.
   9 There isn't ANOTHER PLACE open on Sundays.

57 *another, other, the other, (the) others*

A *another* is a singular adjective and pronoun:
Take this map. I have **another** (one).

other is an adjective used with plural nouns:
    *I have **other** maps/**other** ones.*

B   *the other* is an adjective and singular pronoun:
    the other book   **the other** books
    *One twin was dark; **the other** was fair.*

the others/others are plural pronouns. *the others* means 'all the others'; *others* can mean 'some of the others' or 'all the others':
    *One boy read a book. **The others** played.* (The other boys played.)
    *Some of the guests danced; **others** watched.*

Note the use of *one* and *some* with *other/others*.

Exercise 57

▶ Put in *another, one, others, the other* or *some*:
When we got on to the car ferry (☐) *some* of us went up on deck. (1) _____ hurried into the bars. There was one bar on C deck and (2) _____ on B deck. (3) _____ of the passengers were tourists, (4) _____ were fans on their way to a match. There were two groups of fans. (5) _____ group was fairly quiet, (6) _____ was noisy and aggressive.

6   Interrogatives: *wh-* words and *how*

58   *who, whom, whose, what, which*

A   We use these as follows.

	FOR QUESTIONS ABOUT:
who (pronoun)	people
whose (adjective/pronoun)	people
what (adjective/pronoun)	things
which (adjective/pronoun)	people or things when there are only a few to choose from.

We use the above forms as subjects or objects. In formal English we can use *whom* instead of *who* as object.

B We use *who, whose, what, which* as subjects of a verb:

> *Who found the stolen money?*   *What has happened?*
> *Whose horse won the race?*   *What answer shall I give?*
> *Whose are those old shoes?*   *Which key opens this door?*

In the sentences above we use an affirmative verb (95 C), but with *who/whose/what/which* + *be* + noun or pronoun we normally use an interrogative:

> *Who are you?*   *Whose is this?*   *What is his name?*

C We use *who, whose, what* and *which* as objects of a verb:

> *Who do you want to see?* ~ *The editor.* ~
> *We have two editors.* **Which** *of them do you want?*
> *Whose umbrella did you borrow?*
> *What did he say?*
> *Which would you like? Tea or coffee?*

Here we use an interrogative verb, as shown.

D We use *who, whose, what* and *which* as objects of a preposition. We normally put the preposition after the verb or verb + object:

> *Who was she talking to?*   *What are they looking at?*

In formal English we sometimes put the preposition before the *wh*- word:

> *From which account do you wish to draw this money?*

For people we then use the object pronoun *whom*:

> *To whom was she talking?*

Exercise 58

On Monday Ann and Bill went back to York. Tom borrowed his father's car and drove them to the station. There was a lot of traffic and they missed the 3.30 train. They caught the 4 o'clock train, but Ann was in such a hurry that she left her umbrella in Tom's car. She rang Tom that night to ask about it.

▶ Make questions to fit the following answers. Ask about the words in CAPITALS. Use *who, what* or *which* with an affirmative verb.

> □   *Who went back to York?* ~ ANN AND BILL went back to York.
> 1   _____? ~ TOM drove them to the station.
> 2   _____? ~ THE TRAFFIC delayed them.
> 3   _____? ~ ANN rang Tom.
> 4   _____? ~ ANN left an umbrella in the car. (Use *of them*.)

▶ Make questions with *who, what, which* or *whose* for these answers. Use interrogative verbs. Ask about the words in CAPITALS.

    ☐ *Whose car did he borrow?* ~ He borrowed HIS FATHER's car.
    5 ____? ~ They missed THE 3.30 TRAIN.
    6 ____? ~ They caught THE 4 O'CLOCK TRAIN.
    7 ____? ~ She left HER UMBRELLA in the car.
    8 ____? ~ She rang TOM.

▶ Put in *who* or *what* with a suitable preposition:

    ☐ *What* were they delayed *by?* ~ The traffic.
    9 ____ was Ann travelling ____? ~ With Bill.
    10 ____ did she speak ____ on the phone? ~ To Tom.
    11 ____ did she ask ____? ~ She asked about her umbrella.

59 Uses of *what*

A *what* is an interrogative pronoun and adjective:
    What did she want?   *What car do you drive?*

B *what + be + subject + for* can mean 'What is its purpose?':
    What is the red button for?

    what + action + for can mean 'Why?' It can also express disapproval of the action: *What did you do that for?* can mean 'It was a stupid thing to do'.

C *what + be + subject (a thing) + like* is a request for a description or comment:
    What was the beach like? ~ *It was nice but crowded.*

    what + be + he/she like is usually a query about character:
    What's your new boss like? ~ *He seems quite friendly.*

D *what + subject + look like* asks about appearance only:
    What does he look like? ~ *He's tall and thin with grey hair.*

E *what + be + he/she* means 'What is his/her profession?'
    What is she? ~ *She is a violinist.*

F Compare *what* and *how*. We use *what* in questions about date, time, weather, size and weight (105 B):
    What's the time?/What time is it?
    What size shoes do you take?   *What do you weigh?*

We can use *what* similarly with *age/depth/height/length*:
What is your height?/What height are you?

But in speech *how* + *old/deep/high/tall/long* is more usual:
How old are you?   How tall are you?

G   *what about* + noun/pronoun can be a request for information about a person or thing:
What about your wife? Will she agree?

what/how about + noun/pronoun or gerund is a useful suggestion form:
Where shall we go? ~ What about Rome?

Exercise 59

▶   Make questions to fit the following answers. Use *what?*, *what . . . for? what . . . like?* or *what . . . look like?*
□   *What is he? ~ He's an architect.*
1   _____? ~ It (the TV programme) was very interesting.
2   _____? ~ She's small and slim with blue eyes.
3   _____? ~ He's very cheerful and talkative.
4   _____? ~ It's for opening tins.
5   _____? ~ It (the restaurant) is good but expensive.

▶   Make questions to fit these answers using *how* + adjective:
□   *How old are you? ~ I'm 36 years old.*
6   _____? ~ He is 6 feet tall.
7   _____? ~ It (the river) is 10 feet deep.
8   _____? ~ It (the swimming pool) is 100 metres long.

60 Interrogative adverbs: *how, when, where, why*

A   We can use *how*

with adjectives:
How heavy is your case?   How tall are you? (59)

with adverbs:
How far did he go?   How fast can you run?

with *much* and *many* (pronouns/adjectives):
How much is it?/How much does it cost?
How many do you want?

how can also mean 'in what way?':
How did you get in? ~ I had Tom's key.

B *when* means 'at what time?' or 'in what period?':
    When did he leave? ~ He left last night.

C *where* means 'in/at what place?':
    Where shall we meet? ~ Let's meet at the station.

D *why* means 'for what reason?':
    Why did you follow him?

Exercise 60

▶ See Exercise 58 and make more questions about Ann and Bill's journey back to York. Put in *how, when, where* or *why*. The questions must match the answers.

  ☐ *How* did they get to the station? ~ Tom drove them.
  1 _____ did they arrive at the station? ~ Just before 4 o'clock.
  2 _____ were they going? ~ They were going to York.
  3 _____ did they travel to York? ~ They travelled by train.
  4 _____ did Ann ring Tom? ~ She wanted her umbrella.
  5 _____ did she ring from? ~ She rang from York.

7   Possessives, and personal and reflexive pronouns

61   Possessives and personal pronouns: forms

POSSESSIVE ADJECTIVES	POSSESSIVE PRONOUNS	SUBJECT PRONOUNS	OBJECT PRONOUNS
my	*mine*	*I*	*me*
your	*yours*	*you*	*you*
his/her/its	*his/hers*	*he/she/it*	*him/her/it*
our	*ours*	*we*	*us*
their	*theirs*	*they*	*them*

its (without an apostrophe) is the possessive adjective.
Note that *it's = it is*.

62 Possessives: use

A Possessive adjectives refer to the possessor only:
> *In this photo Ann is standing next to **her** father and Tom is standing behind **his** father.*

We can also use *his/her* of animals whose sex we know:
> *The hen is sitting on **her** eggs.*

We use *its* of animals whose sex we don't know and of things:
> *The crocodile lay on the bank with **its** mouth open.*
> *Does this tree drop **its** leaves in autumn?*

We use *their* for people, animals or things:
> *The children are with **their** father.*
> *Birds build **their** nests in spring.*
> *Trees drop **their** leaves in autumn.*

We use possessive adjectives with clothes and parts of the body:
> *He put on **his** shoes.   She broke **her** right arm.*

B Possessive pronouns = possessive adjectives + nouns:
> *This is **my** key. ~ No, it isn't. It's **mine**. (my key)*

a + noun + *of mine/his* etc. means 'one of my/his . . .'
> *a friend of **mine** = one of my friends*

Exercise 62

▶ Using the family tree, describe the relationships between Mary, Bill, Tom and Ann. Use possessive adjectives (e.g. *her*).

```
    Tom              Ann
  (father)    |    (mother)
       |_____|_____|
       |             |
     Bill           Mary
     (son)        (daughter)
```

☐   Bill → Mary   *Bill is her brother.*
1   Mary → Bill   *Mary is ____ .*
2   Mary → Ann
3   Mary → Tom and Ann
4   Bill → Tom and Ann
5   Tom → Ann

▶ Answer these questions. Use possessive pronouns (e.g. *his*).

Are you sure that:

☐ this tape recorder belongs to Tom? ~ *Yes, I'm sure it's his.*
6 these tapes belong to Ann?
7 this record-player belongs to me?
8 the dictionary belongs to you and me?
9 the photocopier belongs to you?
10 the radio belongs to the twins?

63 Personal pronouns

A Use of the subject pronouns *I/you/he/she/it/we/they*

These are subjects of a verb:
  I live here.   *He works hard.*   *She does nothing.*

B Use of the object pronouns *me/you/him/her/it/us/them*

These can be the direct object of a verb:
  I helped her.   *Tom saw them.*
or the indirect object:
  I gave him £5.   *He found her a job.*
or the object of a preposition:
  Bill wrote to them.   *Tom came with us.*
or the complement of *to be*:
  Who's there? ~ *It's me, Tom.*

C Position of object pronoun (see also 77, 259–260)

Instead of *I made a cake for her*, we can say *I made her a cake*. In this position *her* is the indirect object, while *a cake* is the direct object. The indirect object must precede the direct object. Similarly we can say *I sent the books to her* or *I sent her the books*.

But if the direct object is *it* or *them*, we normally use the *for/to* construction:
  I made it for her.   *I sent them to him.*

D With compounds of *one* and *body* and with *either/neither* and *none* we use *they/them/their* instead of *he/him/his* and *she/her*:
  Everyone passed the exam, didn't they? (56)

But with compounds of *thing* (*everything, anything, something, nothing*) we use *it*:

> *Everything was ready, wasn't it?*

Exercise 63

▶ Rewrite these sentences. Replace the words in CAPITALS by *it* or *them*. Use the preposition in brackets.

☐ John gave her THE BOOKS. (to) *John gave them to her.*
1 Joan bought her father A TIE. (for) *Joan bought it ____.*
2 I showed my mother THE PHOTOS. (to) *I showed ____.*
3 She read her children THE STORY. (to)
4 We got Ann A WORK PERMIT. (for)
5 I made you THIS CAKE. (for)
6 Tom sent me THESE FLOWERS. (to)

64 Uses of *it*

A We use *it* (subject and object) of a thing, of an animal whose sex we don't know, and sometimes of a baby:

> *This book isn't mine; it's yours.*
> *She found a kitten in her garden and gave it some milk.*
> *There's a new baby next door. It cried all last night.*

B We use *it* of people in sentences such as:

> *Phone for you, Ann! ~ Oh, who is it? ~ I think it's Tom.*
> *Is that Jack over there? ~ No, it's Bill.*

C We use *it* in expressions of distance, temperature, weather, time etc. (see also 105 B):

> *How far is it to the station? ~ Oh, it's only a short walk.*
> *It's cold/hot.   It's raining/snowing/freezing.   It was foggy.*
> *It's early/late.   It's 5 a.m.   It was Friday the 13th.*

D We use introductory *it*

with infinitives (*it* here represents the real subject, which is underlined):

> *It was foolish to leave your car there.* (191 A).
> *It would be a pity to cut down that tree.* (191 B)

with *that*-clauses (*it* represents the real subject):

> *It's luck that you brought your passport.* (256 A)
> *It's a pity that you can't come with us.* (256 B)

in cleft sentences (see Exercise 67):
> *It's Tom who signs the letters.* (not Bill)

We use *it* here even if the noun is plural:
> *It's more nurses that we need, not more doctors.*

E   We can say *it appears/occurs to me/seems* + infinitive or
that-clause and *it strikes me that, it turns out that* (257 A):
> *She told Tom to hire a car. Then **it turned out that**/she
> learnt that he didn't have a driving licence.*

F   *it* is also the subject of *say, believe, think* etc. in the
passive construction:
> *It is said that* . . . (People say that . . .)

G   *it* can represent a previously mentioned gerund,
infinitive, phrase or clause:
> *I suggested hiring a car but Tom was against **it**.*
> *You can't take photos here; **it's** not allowed.*

Exercise 64

▶ It's 6 a.m. on Saturday 2 January. Rain is falling. Our caravan
is six miles from the village. That's a two-hour walk. Use this
information to answer these questions:
  □ What's the date? ~ *It's 2 January.*
  1 What's the weather like?
  2 How far is it to the village?
  3 How long will it take to walk there?

▶ Combine two sentences into one sentence with the same
meaning. Begin each with *it*.
  □ You found your passport. That is lucky.
     It's lucky that you found your passport.
  4 You couldn't find a less expensive hotel. That's a pity.
  5 You have plenty of money. That's a good thing.
  6 Ann can't come with you after all. That's a shame.

▶ Now combine these sentences:
  □ Her sisters offered to pay her fare. That was generous of
     them.
     It was generous of them to offer to pay her fare.
  7 She booked before she knew her holiday date. That was
     foolish of her.
  8 You offered to postpone your own holiday. That was good
     of you.
  9 Her brother invited her to stay. That was kind of him.

65 The indefinite pronouns *you, one* and *they*

A   We can use *you* and *one* (possessive adjectives: *your* and *one's*) as subjects of a verb:
>   *You* have to show *your* passport.
>   *One* has to show *one's* passport.

but *one* is more impersonal than *you* and less common.

We normally use *you*, not *one*, as the object of a verb:
>   *They always want you to pay cash.*

B   *they* is used as subject only.

they can mean 'people in general':
>   *They say that elephants never forget.* (People say that . . .)

they can also mean 'the authorities concerned':
>   *They are rebuilding the underground station.*

66 Reflexive and emphasizing pronouns

These are *myself, yourself* (singular), *himself, herself, itself, ourselves, yourselves* (plural), *themselves*, also *oneself*.

A   We use reflexive pronouns when the subject and object are the same:
>   *He cut himself when he was shaving.*
>   *The record player switched itself off.*
>   *Ann and Tom blamed themselves for the accident.*

Note the difference if we use *each other* here instead of *themselves*:
>   *Ann and Tom blamed each other* means that Ann blamed Tom and Tom blamed Ann.

We use reflexive pronouns similarly after prepositions:
>   *We'll pay for ourselves.   He lives by himself.* (alone)
>   *They look very pleased with themselves.*

but if the preposition indicates place, we use ordinary pronouns:
>   *Did you take your children with you?*
>   *I haven't any money on me.*

B   We can also use *myself* etc. as emphasizing pronouns. They usually emphasize the subject, but can emphasize

other words. Note possible positions:
> *Tom went to York **himself** OR Tom **himself** went to York.*
> *Ann opened the door **herself** OR Ann **herself** opened the door.*

When one of these pronouns emphasizes another noun (and not the subject), it follows it directly:
> *I didn't meet the queen **herself**.*

Compare:
> *I did it **myself**. (It was I who did it.)* AND
> *I did it **by myself**. (I did it alone, without help.)*

Exercise 66

▶ Put in *myself, yourself, himself, herself* etc.:
  □ Hostess to friend: Help *yourself* to a drink.
  1 Hostess to friends: Help ____ to drinks.
  2 It was a buffet supper. The guests helped ____.
  3 She looked at ____ in the mirror. 'My hair is awful,' she said.
  4 He always goes on holiday by ____. (= alone)
  5 A dog came out of the water and shook ____.
  6 Does Tom have a secretary? ~ No, he types his letters ____.
  7 Does the garage wash your car for you? ~ No, we wash it ____.
  8 Do you send your sheets to the laundry? ~ No, I wash them ____.

8 | Relative pronouns and clauses

There are three kinds of relative clauses: defining (67–70), non-defining (71–73) and connective (74).

67 Defining relative clauses

A These clauses follow a noun and make clear who or what we are talking about:
> *People **who drink and drive** are a danger to everyone.*
> *This is the horse **that won last year's race**.*

They can also follow *all, none, one(s), those* and compounds
with *-body, -one* and *-thing* (*everybody, somebody* etc.):
*We need someone **who can speak French**.*

These clauses usually come immediately after their
noun/pronoun.

B Clauses after *a/an* + noun are also possible:
*The book is about a boy **who runs away from home**.*

This type of clause can also follow compounds of *-body*,
-one and *-thing*:
*There is someone here **who wants to speak to you**.*

C We use the same type of clause in cleft sentences (64 D):
*It's Tom **who makes mistakes**, not me.*

D We don't put commas between the noun/pronoun and
a defining clause:
*People **who drink and drive** . . .*

We don't put commas at the end of the clause either,
except in cleft sentences (C above). (See also 75.)

Exercise 67

▶ After a party, one of the guests doesn't remember it very
clearly.

   □ Ann did the decorations. ~ (Mary)
      No, it was Mary who did the decorations.

Reply to these sentences in the same way:

1   George sent out the invitations, didn't he? ~ (John)
2   Jack bought the wine. ~ (Tom)
3   Joan prepared all the food. ~ (Jill)
4   Bill got drunk, didn't he? ~ (Tom)
5   George sang for us, didn't he? ~ (Alan)
6   Alan drove us home. ~ (George)

68 Defining relative clauses about people

A *who* or *that* as subject of the clause

*The man **who hijacked the plane** wanted to get to Cuba.*
*The couple **who live next door** have the radio on all night.*

that is more usual than *who* after collective nouns and
everybody, somebody, nothing etc.:
> *The team **that won the championship** got a great
> reception.*

B *who/whom* or *that* as object of the clause

We normally use *that* or omit the pronoun altogether:
> *The people **that he met** warned him* OR
> *The people **he met** warned him.*

who is possible but less usual. *whom* is very formal.

C *who/whom* or *that* as object of a preposition

The formal construction is preposition + *whom*:
> *The man **from whom I bought it** told me . . .*

but it is more usual to move the preposition to the end
of the clause and use *that/who* or omit the pronoun:
> *The man **that/who I bought it from** . . .* OR
> *The man **I bought it from** . . .*

D *whose* (possessive pronoun)
> *A member **whose car breaks down** can ring this number.*

Exercise 68

▶ Combine these pairs of sentences into one sentence:
   □ Some people live above me. They are rather noisy.
     The people who live above me are rather noisy.
   1 A family have just bought the flat below me. They seem
     noisy too.
   2 A man sweeps the stairs. He doesn't sweep out the lift.
   3 Some men wash the windows. They haven't been for six
     months.
   4 Some men are repairing the roof. They want hot water for
     tea.

▶ Now combine these following pairs of sentences:
   □ We met a young man in the lift. He is Tom's assistant.
     The young man we met in the lift is Tom's assistant.
   5 We saw a girl sitting at the desk. She is Tom's secretary.
   6 We heard a man telephoning in the next room. He is
     Tom's partner.
   7 We passed a woman in the corridor. She is Tom's
     accountant.

69 Defining relative clauses about things

A *which* or *that* as subject of the clause

> *This is the programme **which/that won the prize**.*
> *We'll plant new trees to replace those **which/that fell**.*

which is more formal than *that* and less common.
We use *that* after superlatives, after *all, much, little, none, only* and compounds with *-thing*:

> *This is the best thing **that ever happened to him**.*

B *which* or *that* as object of the clause

We use *which* or *that* or omit the pronoun altogether:

> *The map **which/that he lent me** wasn't much use* OR
> *The map **he lent me** . . .*

But we use *that*, not *which*, after superlatives, *all, much* etc. (see A above):

> *Everything **(that) you need** now costs more.*

C *which* or *that* as object of preposition

The formal construction is preposition + *which*:

> *The safe **in which he kept his papers** was not locked.*

but it is much more usual to move the preposition to the end of the clause and use *that* or omit the pronoun altogether

> *The safe **(that) he kept his papers in** . . .*

D *whose* (possessive pronoun)

whose of things is possible but not common. We usually prefer a phrase with *with*. Instead of:

> *Cars **whose tyres are worn** are likely to skid.*

we usually say:

> *Cars **with worn tyres** are likely to skid.*

E *when, where, why* (relative adverbs)

when can mean *in/on which*, used of time, or *during which*:

> *a year **when no rain fell**   the night **when the roof fell in***

where can replace *at/in which*, used of place:

> *the town **where he lives**   the place **where this happened***

why can replace *for which*:

> *The reason **why he didn't answer** . . .*

F *what* (relative pronoun)

what can stand for 'the thing that/the things that':
> *Tell me **what he said**.   I showed him **what I had done**.*

Exercise 69

▶ Ann recently moved into a new flat. Her mother gave her a table. Her brother lent her some chairs. She brought a carpet from her old flat. She has just made some curtains. She bought a bookcase on Monday. The last tenant left a picture behind. Imagine that Ann is speaking. Complete the sentences.

☐ This is the table ____.
   This is the table *my mother gave me*.
1 These are the chairs ____.
2 This is the carpet ____.
3 These are the curtains ____.
4 This is the bookcase ____.
5 This is the horrible picture ____.

70 Infinitives and participles instead of relative clauses

A We can use an infinitive

1 After *the first/second* etc., *the last/only* and sometimes after superlatives. An infinitive is more usual than a clause:
> *The first guest to **arrive** . . .* (the first guest who arrives or who arrived)

Here the infinitive replaces a subject pronoun + verb.

2 After nouns or pronouns when there is an idea of purpose or permission or possibility. An infinitive is more usual than a clause here:
> *I have letters to **write**.* (letters that I must write)
> *The children loved the camp. There were ponies to **ride** . . .* (ponies that they were allowed to ride)
> *cushions to **sit on*** (cushions that we could sit on)

Here the infinitive replaces an object pronoun + verb.

B We can use a present participle when the verb in the clause expresses a continuous or repeated action:
> *Fans **watching** the match . . .* (fans who watched/were watching)

People living in the area . . .
(people who live/lived in the area)
A notice warning people . . .
(a notice that warns/warned)

Similarly with verbs such as *expect, hope, want, wish* (but not *like*):
Students wishing to come on this trip . . .
(students who wish)

Exercise 70

▶ Replace the clauses in CAPITALS by an infinitive or an infinitive + preposition:

   □   The only thing THAT WE COULD DO was to wait two hours for the next train.
      The only thing to do was to wait two hours for the next train.

1   The bookstall was closed so we couldn't buy anything THAT WE COULD READ.
2   The restaurant was closed so we couldn't get anything THAT WE COULD EAT.
3   There weren't even any other passengers TO WHOM WE COULD TALK.

Now replace the clauses in CAPITALS by present participles:

▶ Usually at a station there are people (4) WHO ARE WAITING for trains, or passengers (5) WHO ARRIVE or (6) LEAVE. There is usually a loudspeaker (7) WHICH ANNOUNCES arrivals and departures and there are people (8) WHO SELL papers and station staff (9) WHO COLLECT tickets. But here there was nothing.

71 Non-defining relative clauses

A   These follow a noun which does not need defining or explaining. They give some extra information about this person or thing, but the information is not essential and we can omit it without causing confusion.

     We cannot omit relative pronouns used with non-defining clauses.

B   Clauses placed immediately after the subject of the main verb are found chiefly in written English:
     Bill, who won the race last year, hopes to win again.

In conversation we would probably say:
Bill won last year and hopes to win again.

But clauses placed later in the sentence are quite common:
*He introduced me to his trainer, **who is fairly confident**.*

C Commas are used. We put a comma between the noun and its clause and at the end of the clause if the sentence continues:
*Bill, **who won last year**, hopes to win again.*

(For commas in relative clauses, see also 75.)

72 Non-defining relative clauses about people

A *who* as subject of the clause
*Peter, **who spoke French well**, offered to interpret.*

But in conversation we would probably say:
Peter spoke French well, so he offered to interpret.

B *who/whom* as object of the clause
*Bill, **who everybody liked**, was the team captain.*

But in conversation we would probably say:
Bill was the team captain. Everybody liked him.

whom is formal:
*Bill, **whom everybody liked**, was the team captain.*

C *who/whom* as object of a preposition

The formal structure is preposition + *whom*:
*Peter, **with whom we were travelling**, spoke French well.*

who with the preposition at the end is possible in conversation:
*Peter, **who we were travelling with**, spoke French well.*
but it would be more usual to say:
*We were travelling with Peter, **who spoke French well**.*

D *whose* (possessive pronoun)
*Ann, **whose pain was now worse**, called a doctor.*

But in conversation we would probably say:
Ann's pain was now worse so she called a doctor.

Exercise 72

▶ In my office Ann types the letters, Peter does the filing, Mary keeps the accounts. Joan manages the switchboard. John makes the tea and does the photocopying. Mrs Jones handles the foreign correspondence. Tom works the lift. Introduce these people to a new member of staff. Use relative clauses. Don't forget the commas.

☐ *This is Ann, who types the letters.*

Continue with (1) Peter (2) Mary (3) Joan (4) John (5) Mrs Jones (6) Tom.

▶ Replace the sentences in brackets by relative clauses. Put each after its noun, which is in CAPITALS. Use commas.

☐ Ann had hoped that TOM would offer to drive her to the party. (She liked Tom.)
Ann had hoped that Tom, who she liked, would offer to drive her to the party.

7 But BILL asked her so she had to go with him. (She didn't much like Bill.)

8 She enjoyed the party but was sorry to see Tom dancing with MARY. (Mary had apparently come with him.)

9 She knew that MARY'S FATHER wanted them to get married. (He was Tom's employer.)

10 And BILL said that Tom had recently bought an engagement ring. (Bill worked in a jeweller's.)

73 Non-defining relative clauses about things

A *which* as subject of the clause

> Harrods' sale, **which closed yesterday**, attracted huge crowds.

B *which* as object of the clause

> This cheque, **which he posted a fortnight ago**, has only just arrived.

C *which* as object of a preposition

The formal construction is preposition + *which*:
> His new car, **for which he paid £10,000**, has broken down.

But in conversation we could say:
> His new car, **which he paid £10,000 for**, has broken down.

D   *whose* (possessive pronoun)

> *Her car, **whose tyres were worn**, skidded on the wet road.*

In conversation we would probably say:
> *Her tyres were worn and she skidded . . .*

Exercise 73

▶ Put in *whose* or *which*:
Richard, (□) *whose* brother George has disappeared, receives a
message from Paul. Paul says that George is a prisoner in a
certain house. This house, (1) _____ is in a lonely part of
Essex, belongs to a mysterious organization (2) _____ activities
are puzzling the local residents. The leader of this group has
asked for George's briefcase. This briefcase, (3) _____ apparently
contains secret documents, is in George's safe, (4) _____
combination only George and Richard know.

74 Connective relative clauses

A   These clauses are similar in form to non-defining
relative clauses. Like them, they use *who, whose* and
which, and need commas.

But instead of describing their nouns like non-defining
clauses, they continue the story:
> *I asked Tom, **who said he didn't know**.*
> (I asked Tom but he said he didn't know.)
> *I met Bill, **whose dog growled at me as usual**.*
> (I met Bill and his dog growled at me as usual.)

B   Examples with *which*:
> *He ate chips, **which made him fat**.*
> (He ate chips and they made him fat.)

which can also stand for a whole clause:
> *They played the drums all night, **which annoyed us all**.*
> *He said that he was a refugee, **which was not true**.*

C   Be careful not to confuse the use of *which* here with the
relative pronoun *what* (69 F):
> *I didn't buy anything because I didn't see **what I wanted**.*
> (I didn't see the thing that/the things that I wanted.)
> ***What he needs** is a steady job.*

Exercise 74

▶ Join these pairs of sentences. Use the connective relatives *who* or *which*.

☐ Richard rang George's wife. She asked if he had any news.
  Richard rang George's wife, who asked if he had any news.

1 He told her what he knew. This didn't comfort her much.
2 He then drove round and knocked at the door. It opened at once.
3 In the safe he found only a small folder. He took it out.
4 The folder contained some papers. These didn't seem secret or important.
5 He rang Paul. Paul said, 'The briefcase must be somewhere; go on looking.'

▶ Put in *which* or *what*:

I've heard that the London sales are marvellous. ∼ Yes, that's (☐) *what* you hear. But people who come to London for the sales don't usually get (6) ___ they want, (7) ___ must be very disappointing. But they buy something, of course, and this is (8) ___ the shops want. I blame the advertisers. They say that there are hundreds of bargains, (9) ___ is not true. But people keep going to the sales, (10) ___ shows that there must be some bargains.

75 The importance of commas in relative clauses

Remember that a defining clause has no commas:
  *The passengers **who had visas** had no trouble at the frontier.*

who had visas is a defining relative clause, which defines or limits its noun *passengers*. The sentence implies that some passengers had visas, but that some hadn't. Those without visas presumably did have trouble at the frontier.

Note how the meaning changes if we add commas:
  *The passengers, **who had visas**, had no trouble at the frontier.*
This means that all the passengers had visas and therefore none of them had trouble. *, who had visas,* is a non-defining relative clause, which merely adds some information to the preceding noun.

9   Prepositions

76 Position

A We normally put prepositions before nouns, pronouns or gerunds:
> *The parcel **on the table** is for you.*   *He is terrified **of flying**.*

B But in questions with *wh-* words we usually put the preposition at the end of the sentence:
> ***Who** were you talking **to**?*

> ***To whom** were you talking?* is possible but very formal.

C Similarly in relative clauses we usually put the preposition at the end of the clause and omit the relative pronoun (68 C):
> *The people **I was travelling with** spoke French.*

> In formal speech and writing we can say:
> *The people **with whom I was travelling** spoke French.*

D In phrasal verbs the preposition (or adverb) must come after the verb (259–260). So we say:
> *Which bridge did they **blow up**?*

77 Prepositions with indirect objects: *to* and *for*

A Instead of saying *I gave the book to Tom*, we can say *I gave Tom the book*. (Note change of order.) We can do this after such verbs as *bring, give, lend, offer, pass* (= give by hand), *sell, send, show, sing, take*.

B Similarly, instead of *I'll find a job for Mary*, we can say *I'll find Mary a job*. We can do this after such verbs as *build, buy, cook, fetch, find, get, keep, leave, make, order*.

C We can normally use either construction. But:

1 We prefer the construction without *to* or *for* when the direct object is a phrase or clause:
> *Tell her the whole story.*   *Buy me anything you like.*

2 We prefer to use *to* or *for* when the indirect object is a phrase or clause:
   I had to show my pass to the man at the gate.
   We kept seats for everyone who had paid.

3 We must use *to* or *for* when the direct object is a personal pronoun:
   We sent it to George.   She bought them for Bill.

   This does not apply to other types of pronoun. We can say:
   We sent one to George OR *We sent George one.*
   She bought something for Bill OR *She bought Bill something.*

D After some verbs we can use indirect objects only, without direct objects. Examples:
   Read to me.   Play to/for us.   Show him.

Exercise 77

▶ Complete these sentences:
   □ I lent George (some) money. ~ Did you *lend money to anyone else?*
   1 I gave Bill a cheque. ~ Did you ____?
   2 I offered Ann a job. ~ Did you ____?
   3 I showed Tom these photos. ~ Did you ____?

   □ She says she made cakes for everyone. ~
   But she *didn't make me a cake.*
   4 She says she got tickets for everyone. ~ But she ____.
   5 She says she bought books for everyone. ~ But she ____.
   6 She says she found jobs for everyone. ~ But she ____.

▶ Replace the words in CAPITALS by the pronouns in brackets and make alterations in the sentence if necessary:
   □ I'll give Bill THIS BOOK.   (it)   *I'll give it to Bill.*
   7 I gave him A BOOK last year.   (one)
   8 I'm sending Ann THESE FLOWERS.   (them)
   9 I'd better send Mary FLOWERS too.   (some)

78 Verbs of communication with or without *to*

A Verbs of command, request, advice and invitation

   advise, ask, invite, order, remind, tell, warn (see also 239A) can be followed directly by the person spoken to:
   He advised us to go.   She invited him.   I warned them.

B Other verbs of communication

complain, describe, explain, say, speak, talk etc. need *to* before the person addressed:

He explained the problem to me. She spoke to them in English.
They didn't say anything to us.

Exercise 78

▶ Put in *to* if necessary:
The director spoke (□) *to* us and advised (□) ⎯ us not to go on strike. He warned (1) ⎯ us that strikes damaged the company. We told (2) ⎯ him that we didn't want to strike, but asked (3) ⎯ him to take our complaints seriously. He promised to talk (4) ⎯ the other directors. We reminded (5) ⎯ him that we had had promises before but no action.

79 Time: *at, on, in*

A *at*

We use *at* with a point in time or someone's age:
at 4.30   at dawn   at midnight   at (the age of) six
She was married at sixteen.

Exceptions: *at Christmas, at Easter, at night*

B *on*

We use *on* with a day or a date:
on Monday   on Christmas day   on 4 June
and with the morning/afternoon etc. of a day or a date:
on the morning of 6 December   on Friday evening

on time means 'at the time arranged' – not before, not after:
The 8.15 train started on time. (It started at 8.15.)

on arriving/leaving/hearing he . . . means 'when he arrives/arrived, he . . .' 'when he leaves/left, he . . .' etc.

C *in*

We use *in* with periods of time:
in five minutes   in 1934   in the 19th century
in the morning/afternoon/evening (but *at night*)

(For *during*, see 81 D.)

in time (for) means 'not late (for)':
*Make sure you're there **in time** for the train.*

Exercise 79

► Put in *at, in* or *on*:
He likes travelling (□) **at** night and usually starts his journey
very late (1) ___ the evening or very early (2) ___ the
morning. Last year he set out (3) ___ Christmas Eve and
arrived (4) ___ the morning of Christmas Day. The station
master said, 'If your train had been (5) ___ time (= if it had
arrived (6) ___ the correct time) you would have caught the
bus. But there'll be another one (7) ___ about an hour.'

80 Time: *by, before, after*

A *by*

by with a point in time or a date means 'at or earlier than':
*Be at the station **by** 6. Your train leaves at 6.15.*
*She wants the job finished **by** the end of May/**by** 31 May.*

B *before*

before means 'earlier than':
*If you get home **before** me, you can make the supper.*

We can use *before* instead of *by* in the sentences in A
above. But if we say *Come back **before** Friday*, we mean
'Come back on Thursday or earlier'.

We also use *before* with gerunds:
*Always check your bill **before** paying.*

Note other uses of *before*:
*I've seen her somewhere **before**.* (adverb)
*Read the contract carefully **before** you sign it.* (conjunction)

C *after*

We use *after* to mean 'following':
*Don't go swimming immediately **after** a meal/**after** eating.*

Instead of *after that* we often use the adverbs *afterwards*
or *then*:
*We had a meal and **afterwards/then** went to the cinema.*
We do not use *after* in place of *afterwards* or *then*.

We can use *after* as a conjunction:
  After he had tuned the guitar it sounded quite different.

Exercise 80

▶ Put in *after, before* or *by*:
'If you bring it back (□) *after* this date you'll have to pay a
fine,' said the librarian. 'You must bring the book back (1)
_____ this date.' 'Can I bring it back before this date?' I asked.
'Sometimes (2) _____ reading the first chapter I decide that I
don't like the book.' 'Bring it back the next day if you like,'
said the librarian. 'By the way, (3) _____ you hand your book
in, check that you haven't left anything in it. Yesterday
(4) _____ a reader had gone we found a £5 note in his book!'

▶ Put in *after* or *then*:
  Ann: Let's go for a walk.
  5 Tom: Not till _____ lunch. I'm hungry.
  6 Ann: All right. We'll have lunch and _____ go for a walk.
     Tom: What's for lunch?
  7 Ann: Well, there's soup. What would you like _____ that?
  8 Tom: I'd like a steak and _____ a pudding and some bread
     and cheese.
  9 Ann: You plan to eat all that and _____ walk ten miles?
  10 Tom: No. My plan is to have lunch, _____ a rest and _____ a
     five-mile walk.

81 Time: *from, till/until, to, since, for, during*

A *from, till/until, to*

We use *from* with the beginning of a period of time:
  I'll be at home from ten o'clock tomorrow.
and *till/until* or *to* with the end of the period:
  I'll be at home from ten till/until/to twelve.

If we do not say *from . . .*, we use *till/until*, not *to*:
  I'll be at home till/until twelve.

till/until with a negative verb emphasizes lateness:
  We didn't get back till/until 2 a.m.

We often use *till/until* as a conjunction of time:
  We'll stay here till/until it stops raining.

Note that we can use *to* for time or place but that we use
till/until for time only.

B *since*

since means 'from a point in time up to the time of speaking' (see also 155 B). We can use it as preposition, adverb or conjunction:

> *He has been here **since** Monday.* (from Monday till now; preposition)
> *She left in 1983. I haven't seen her **since**.* (adverb)
> *He has worked for us (ever) **since** he left school.* (conjunction)

C *for*

We use *for* with a period of time. The action lasts from the beginning to the end of the period (see also 155 A):

> *Cook it **for** two hours.   He has worked here **for** a year.*
> *I hired a car **for** the holidays.*

D *during*

We use *during* to talk about a particular period of time. It means 'in the course of'. The action can last for the whole period or occur at some time within the period:

> ***During** the summer his health improved a lot.*
> *It rained all day but stopped **during** the night.*

during and *in* are similar and often we can use either:

> *Strikes were common **during/in** this period.*

but *during* is more usual when we wish to emphasize that the action lasted for the whole period:

> *In 1989 prices went up.* (probably at one point in 1989)
> ***During** 1989 prices went up.* (There may have been a continual rise in prices.)

Exercise 81

▶ Put in *till*, *for*, *at* or *to*:

In the morning we work from nine (1) ____ one. Then we have a break (2) ____ lunch. We start again (3) ____ two and work (4) ____ six. At least, we should be finished by six but sometimes I am not finished (5) ____ six-thirty.

▶ Complete these answers. Note that the tenses vary.

☐ You started on Monday, I suppose? ~ No, I *didn't start till Tuesday.*

6   You finish at six, I suppose? ~ No, I ____ seven.

7   He rang you at once, I suppose? ~ No, he ____ the next day.

8   You're starting this week, I suppose? ~ No, I ____ next week.
9   They arrive early, I suppose? ~ No, they ____ midnight.

▶ Put in *for* or *since*:
He has had a number of jobs (10) ____ he left school. He worked in a car factory (11) ____ a year; then he worked as a car salesman (12) ____ two years. Then he went abroad. He's working in Paris at the moment. He's been there (13) ____ 1987. We've been friends (14) ____ our schooldays and I've known his fiancée (15) ____ a long time too.

▶ Put in *during* or *for*:
Tom fell asleep (16) ____ the first lecture and slept (17) ____ at least half an hour. Afterwards we went to the canteen and (18) ____ lunch he explained his problem. 'My flatmates have a baby who wakes up three or four times (19) ____ the night. Last night I only slept (20) ____ three hours. I haven't had a good night's sleep (21) ____ weeks.'

82 Travel and movement: *from, to, by, on* etc.

A   Travel *from . . . to*
     We walked/cycled/drove/flew from Paris to Rome.

     We send people or things *to*:
     She sent him to Bath.   I posted it to York.
     But for *home*, see C3 below.

B   Travel *by, on, via*

     We travel *by* sea/air, *by* bus/car/plane/train etc., *by* bicycle or *on* a bicycle, *on* foot, *on* horseback.

     We go *by* or *via* a certain place or route:
     We went by bus.   We went by the coast road.
     This bus goes from London to Banbury via Oxford.

C   Arrive *at, in*, get *to*

1   We arrive *in* a country or town; *at* or *in* a village; *at* any other place:
     They arrived in Spain/in Madrid.
     I arrived at the airport/at my hotel/at the bridge.

2   We get *to* any type of place:
     He got to Berlin/to the airport at 10.30.

3 We get/go/return *home*, or send somebody *home*, without a preposition:
> *He got **home** before me.   I sent him **home**.*

but we use *to* if *home* is preceded by an article, adjective etc.: *She returned **to** her parents' **home**.*

D Get *in, into, off, on, onto, out, out of*

1 We usually get *on* and *off* large vehicles such as buses and trains, and also horses and bicycles. We can use *on* or *off* with or without a noun.
> *Get **on** (the bus) here.*
> *You can't get **off** (the bus) except at the bus stop.*

We usually get *into* and *out of* any vehicle:
> *He got **into** the car and drove away.*

We use *in* and *out* without a noun:
> *He got **in** and drove away.*

but *into* and *out of* need nouns.

2 We can also get *into* and *out of* buildings (or *in* and *out*) when it is difficult to enter or leave:
> *How are we going to get **in** without a key?*

Exercise 82

▶ Put in *at, by, from, in, on* or *to*:
We went (□) *to* Paris (1) _____ air and took the train (2) _____ the airport (3) _____ the Paris air terminal. We arrived (4) _____ Paris at 6 o'clock but didn't get (5) _____ our hotel till 8 o'clock because we decided to go (6) _____ foot and we got lost. Tom and Ann came (7) _____ train. Their train didn't get (8) _____ till 11 o'clock so they didn't arrive (9) _____ our hotel till nearly midnight.

▶ Put in *into, on, onto, out* or *off*:
Tom: You can't get (10) _____ (= board) these new buses between stops because the doors are shut. You can't get (11) _____ (= leave) them between stops either. I used to get (12) _____ at these traffic lights and (13) _____ at the traffic lights near my office, but now I can't.
Bill: Well, tomorrow I'm giving you a lift, so you can get (14) _____ the car at your front door and get (15) _____ anywhere you like.

83   Giving directions

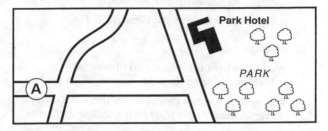

Imagine that you are at point A and somebody asks for directions.

Could you please tell me how to get to the Park Hotel? ~
*Go (straight) **on to** the end of this road* or
*Go **on till** you get to the park. Then turn left and you'll find it on your right.*

Note that you can say *Go on to* + the name of a place but not *Go on till* + the name of a place. But you can say *Go on till you get to* + the name of a place.

84   Place: *at, in, into, on, onto*

A   *at, in*

We can be *at* home/work/the office/school/university/ an address or a certain point such as a bus-stop/a bridge.

We can be *in* a country/a town/a village/a street/room/ a wood/a field or any place which is enclosed.

We can be *at* or *in* a building. *at* means 'inside or just outside'. *in* means 'inside' only.

We can be *at* or *in* the sea/a river/a lake/a swimming pool. *at* means 'near/beside'. *in* means actually in the water. *at sea* means 'on a ship'.

B   *in, into*

We normally use *in* for place:
*He keeps his savings **in** an old biscuit-tin.*
and *into* for movement or entrance:
*They climbed **into** the lorry.*

But with the verb *put* we can use either *in* or *into*:
He put his hands in/into his pockets.

in can also be an adverb: *Come in. Get in.*

C   *on, onto*

We use *on* for both place and movement:
She was sitting on the sofa.   Snow fell on the hills.

We use *onto* for movement when there is a change in level:
People climbed onto their roofs to escape the floods.

on can also be an adverb: *Come on. Go on.*

Exercise 84

▶ Put in *at* or *in*:
Mary is (□) *at* home, but she isn't (1) ____ the house; she's
(2) ____ the garden. Bill's (3) ____ work but he isn't (4) ____
his office at the moment. It's his lunch hour and he's (5) ____ a
travel agent's, looking at holiday brochures. John, their son, is
usually (6) ____ school at this time, but he has a bad cold so
his mother has kept him (7) ____ home and told him to stay
(8) ____ bed.

85   Prepositions/adverbs

We use many words as either prepositions or adverbs:
He got off the bus at the corner. (preposition)
He got off at the corner. (adverb)

The most important of these words are:

about	below	near	round
above	beneath	off	since
across	besides	on	through
along	by	opposite	under
before	down	over	underneath
behind	in	past	up

▷ For adverbs, see 34–51. For phrasal verbs, see 259–260.

Exercise 85

▶ Put in *about, before, behind, below, down, on* or *up*:
'I know the best way (□) *up* the mountain,' said Tom, 'as I'v
climbed it (1) ____. So I'll go first. Keep close (2) ____ me.

Don't stop to take photos (3) ____ the way (4) ____ ; when we get to the top you can walk (5) ____ and take photos. You'll get marvellous views of the valleys (6) ____ . We'll have our lunch (7) ____ the top and come (8) ____ the mountain by another route. (9) ____ starting (10) ____ , check that you haven't left any rubbish (11) ____ you.'

86 Place: *above, over; below, under*

A *above* and *over*

1 *above* and *over* can both mean 'higher than'.

When two things are quite close to each other we can use either:
> Flags waved **above/over** our heads.

But we use *above* when there is more space between two things:
> The plane flew **above** the clouds.
> High **above** us a lark was singing.

Note that *above* need not mean 'directly above', so we can say *the hills **above** the town*.

We use *over* when one thing is very close to or covering another:
> We put nets **over** the strawberry plants.
> She put a rug **over** him. (She covered him with a rug.)

2 *over* can also mean 'across' and 'from one side to another':
> There's a bridge **over** the river.
> The plane flew low **over** the town.

Note also *all over*, meaning 'in every part of':
> He has friends **all over** the world.

3 Both *above* and *over* can be adverbs:
> I climbed **over** the wall; Tom jumped **over**.

B *below* and *under*

below and *under* both mean 'lower than'. Often we can use either:
> Let's hang the clock here and the calendar **under/below** it.

But *below* need not mean 'directly below', so we can say:
> We camped in a field **below** the town.

When two things touch each other or are close, we usually use *under*, not *below*:

*He wore a thick sweater **under** his coat.*
*Only small boats can go **under** that bridge.*

Exercise 86

▶ Complete the sentences, using *above, over, below* or *under*:

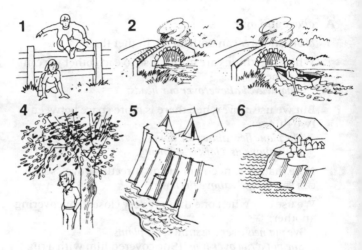

☐   Tom is jumping *over the fence.*

1   Ann has crawled ____.
2   There is a bridge ____.
3   Bill is rowing ____.
4   Mary is sheltering ____.
5   We camped ____.
6   There is a lake ____.

87   Place: *beside, between, behind, in front of, opposite*

A   *beside, between, behind, in front of*

Imagine two rows of seats in a theatre:

Stage		
Tom	Ann	Bill
Mary	Bob	Jane

We can say:
*Tom is **beside** Ann; Mary is **beside** Bob.*
*Ann is **between** Tom and Bill; Bob is **between** Mary and Jane.*
*Mary is **behind** Tom; Tom is **in front of** Mary.*

B   *in front of, opposite*

We say:
*Tom sat **in front of** Mary at the theatre.* (He sat with his
back to her).   BUT
*Tom sat **opposite** Mary at the table.* (He sat facing her.)

However, *Tom stood **in front of** Mary* can mean 'facing
her' or 'with his back to her'.

We say:
*Where's the car park? ~ **In front of** the hotel.*
but people living on one side of a street call the houses
on the other side *the houses **opposite** us*.

Exercise 87

▶ Six people are sitting round a table. Joan is sitting between
George and Bill, and opposite Tom.

Give the position of (1) Ann (2) Tom and (3) Mary, using
beside, between, opposite.

4   Mr Jones and Mr Smith are at the theatre. Give their
positions:

Mr Jones is ___ Mr Smith. Mr Smith is ___ Mr Jones.

88 Some uses of *with*

A *with* can mean 'in the company of':

*He lives **with** his aunt.   I went **with** Bill.*

and 'having' or 'carrying':

*He married a widow **with** six children.*
*A waiter came in **with** a plate of sandwiches.*

Note also: *I haven't got my passport **with** me* OR *on me.*

B We often use *with* in short descriptions:

*the man **with** red hair   a girl **with** a bad cough*
*the man **with** his back to us*

C We can use *with* with the instrument or means used to do something:

*He walks **with** a stick.   Cut it **with** scissors.*
*She writes **with** her left hand.*

D We can argue/quarrel with . . . or fight (*with*) . . .

*She quarrelled **with** everybody.*
*He fought (**with**) all the other boys.*

E We can fill a container *with* . . . We can cover something with . . .

*They filled the sacks **with** sand.*
*The hills are covered **with** trees.*

F Note also the phrases *with thanks, with pleasure*.

Exercise 88

▶ Complete the following phrases:

Which of them is:

☐ your secretary? ~ The girl *with glasses.*
1 your uncle? ~ The man _____.
2 the mathematics professor? ~ The man _____.
3 his wife? ~ The woman _____.

89   *but* and *except*

These words have the same meaning.

A *but* often follows *nobody/no one/none/nothing/nowhere* etc.
when these words begin the sentence:
*   **Nobody but** Alex knows the way.
*   **Nothing but** the best is sold in our shops.

B *except* is more usual when its noun comes later in the
sentence:
*   Nobody knew the way **except** Alex.

and after *all/everybody/everyone/everything/everywhere* etc.

C We can use either after *anybody/anyone/anything/*
anywhere etc., but *but* is more emphatic than *except*:
*   You can park anywhere **but/except** here.

90   Prepositions after adjectives and verbs

A We use particular prepositions after certain adjectives
and participles. Some of the most useful adjective +
preposition combinations are:

afraid of	*interested in*	*ready for*
fond of	*keen on*	*sorry about/for*
good/bad at/for	*proud of*	*tired of*

*   He's **good at** golf.   This book says that coffee is **bad for** you.
*   Are you **ready for** the next course?

B We use particular prepositions after certain verbs.
Useful verb + preposition combinations are:

accuse somebody of	*believe in*	*object to*
ask for (237)	*care for* (223)	*succeed in*
approve of	*insist on*	*wait for*

*   He **accused me of** opening his letters.
*   She doesn't **approve of** him. She **objects to** his long hair.

▷ For phrasal verbs, see 259–260; for *by* with passive
verbs, see 213 D; for verbs + *to*, see 77–78. See also any
good dictionary for adjectives/verbs + prepositions.

Exercise 90

▶ Put in words from the list. Use each phrase once.
afraid of, fond of, good at, good for, interested in, keen on, proud of, tired of

Ann's eldest boy was very (□) *fond of* football (= he liked football very much). He was very (1) ____ it (= he played well) and was in his school team. Ann was very (2) ____ him. The other boys were not (3) ____ games. They were much more (4) ____ motor cycles. Ann made her daughter, Mary, take swimming lessons. 'Swimming is (5) ____ you (= healthy),' she said. But Mary soon got (6) ____ swimming up and down the pool; she didn't want to swim in the sea either. She was (7) ____ the sea.

▶ Fill the spaces, using the correct form of *care for, insist on, object to, succeed in, wait for* in the correct tense:

We're (8) ____ Tom. He has gone out to get a taxi. Tom always (9) ____ going to the station by taxi. He says he doesn't (10) ____ (like) queuing for buses. I don't (11) ____ (mind) queuing but it's never any use arguing with Tom. Oh, here he is at last! He has (12) ____ getting (managed to get) a taxi.

---

10   Introduction to verbs

91   Ordinary verbs and auxiliary verbs

A Ordinary verbs are verbs like *to answer, to phone, to travel, to wait, to work* etc. (140–182).

B Auxiliary verbs are of three kinds.
1 Principal auxiliaries: *to be, to have, to do* (103–111)
2 Modal auxiliaries (modals): *can/could, may/might, must, ought, shall/should, will/would* (97 A)
3 Semi-modals: *to dare, to need, used* (97 B)

C We use the auxiliary *do* with the infinitive of ordinary verbs to form the negatives and interrogatives of the simple tenses:

    *I **do not/don't** work.*   ***Did** they/**Didn't** they wait?*

D We use the auxiliaries *be* and *have* with the present or
past participle of ordinary verbs, and *will/shall*, *would/
should* with the infinitive, to form the compound tenses:
>   He **is** working.   They **were** waiting.   We **have** phoned.
>   He **will** answer.   They **would** phone.

E We also use *be, have, do, need* and *dare* as ordinary verbs:
>   She **is** a policewoman.   They **have** a dog.   He **did** nothing.
>   Do you **need** more money?

(For *be*, see 105; for *have*, see 108; for *do*, see 111; for
need, see 130 D; for *dare*, see 137 D.)

92 Affirmative contractions of auxiliaries

A We often contract auxiliaries:
>   *'m = am*   *'ve = have*   *'ll = will*
>   *'re = are*   *'s = has*   *'d = would*
>   *'s = is*   *'d = had*

Note that *'s* can be *is* or *has*:
>   He**'s** going. = He is going.   It**'s** gone. = It has gone.

and that *'d* can be *had* or *would*:
>   He**'d** paid. = He had paid.   She**'d** like it. = She would like it.

can, could, must, shall, should, was and *were* have no
written contractions but we often shorten them in speech.

B We use contractions chiefly after personal pronouns
(*I, you, he, she, it, we, they*). But we can also use them
after *here, there, this, these, that, those*, after proper names
and sometimes other nouns:
>   Here**'s** the bus.   Tom**'s** got £5. ~ That**'ll** be enough.
>   Peter**'ll** help us.   Our guests**'ve** arrived.

We do not use affirmative contractions at the end of a
sentence or clause:
>   He isn't ready but we are.   I'll go if you will.

Exercise 92

▶ Write the words in CAPITALS in contracted form:
>   □ I AM still in London.   *I'm*
>   1 BILL IS still here too.
>   2 But PAUL HAS gone back to York.

3   WE ARE living in Chelsea.
4   THAT IS a very expensive area.
5   Yes, it is. WE HAVE spent £1,200 already.
6   WE WOULD like some more money.
7   Very well. I WILL send you £600.
8   THAT WILL only last us a month.
9   When YOU HAVE spent that YOU WILL have to come home.

93 Negatives

A We form the negative of auxiliaries by adding *not*:
  He **is not** waiting for a bus.   You **must not** be late.
  We **have not** bought tickets.   You **need not** hurry.
  I **could not** sleep.

We form the negative of simple tenses of ordinary verbs
with *do + not*:
  They **do not** work.   She **does not** cook.   We **did not** wait.

B We often use these contractions:

aren't	=	are not	*mightn't*	=	might not
can't	=	cannot	*mustn't*	=	must not
couldn't	=	could not	*needn't*	=	need not
daren't	=	dare not	*oughtn't*	=	ought not
didn't	=	did not	*shan't*	=	shall not
doesn't	=	does not	*shouldn't*	=	should not
don't	=	do not	*wasn't*	=	was not
hadn't	=	had not	*weren't*	=	were not
hasn't	=	has not	*won't*	=	will not
haven't	=	have not	*wouldn't*	=	would not
isn't	=	is not			

Note also:

'm not	=	am not	*'ve not*	=	have not
're not	=	are not	*'d not*	=	had not OR
's not	=	is not OR			would not
	=	has not	*'ll not*	=	will not

We use *'s not* and *'ve not* mainly in perfect tenses.

We can use these contractions after any noun or pronoun
subject, and they can come at the end of a sentence:
  Bill passed the exam but Tom **didn't**.

C An English clause can have only one negative expression. Two negative expressions give the clause an affirmative meaning: *Nobody did nothing* means 'Everybody did something'. So we use an affirmative verb with negative expressions such as *no* (adjective), *none, nobody, no one, nothing, hardly, hardly any, hardly ever, never*:

> *He didn't say anything* OR *He said **nothing**.*
> *We didn't see anybody* OR *We saw **nobody**.*

D When *think* introduces a negative statement, we usually make *think* negative and use an affirmative verb in the statement. So instead of *I think he isn't coming* we say:

> *I **don't think** he's coming.*

We do the same with the verbs *believe, expect, imagine* and *suppose*. So instead of *I believe he can't swim* we say:

> *I **don't believe** he can swim.*

and instead of *I suppose he isn't coming* we say:

> *I **don't suppose** he's coming.*

Exercise 93

▶ Write the words in CAPITALS in contracted form:

  □ We ARE NOT going to the seaside this summer.   *aren't*
  1 Ann DOES NOT like the sea.
  2 Tom and I DO NOT like it either.
  3 We CANNOT swim; THAT IS the trouble.
  4 They DID NOT teach us at school.
  5 And we HAVE NOT tried to learn since then.
  6 Bill can swim but he WILL NOT teach us.
  7 He says IT WOULD be a waste of time.

▶ Rewrite the words in CAPITALS in contracted form where possible:

  □ Bill HAS NOT got a car but I HAVE.   *hasn't*   *I have*
  8 He passed his last driving test but I DID NOT.
  9 But he DOES NOT drive as well as I DO.
  10 I drive much better than HE DOES.
  11 I CANNOT drive you to Gatwick but he could.
  12 But he COULD NOT take my car.
  13 It IS NOT insured.
  14 So YOU WILL have to take a train.
  15 HERE IS a timetable.
  16 You could take a taxi but IT WOULD be expensive.

▶ Replace the words in CAPITALS by the word in brackets, and
make a new sentence with the same meaning. Sometimes the
order of the words has to change.

   □ He doesn't trust ANYBODY. (nobody) *He trusts nobody.*
  17 He doesn't go out OFTEN. (never)
  18 He doesn't eat ANY meat. (no)
  19 He doesn't write letters OFTEN. (hardly ever)
  20 He doesn't talk to ANYBODY. (nobody)
  21 He doesn't do ANYTHING. (nothing)

94 Interrogatives: form

A We can form the interrogative of auxiliaries by putting
the subject after the auxiliary:
   Is he waiting for a bus?   Have you answered the letter?
   Can you see it?   Must we go?   Would Bill like to come?

We form the interrogative of simple tenses of ordinary
verbs with *do* + subject + infinitive:
   Do they work here?   Does he live at home?
   Did they write to you?

B We can contract *am, are, is, have, has, had, will, would*
after *how, what, who, where, why*:
   *Where is/**Where's** he living now?*
   *Who would/**Who'd** you like to see?*
and we can contract *is* and *will* after *when*:
   *When is/**When's** Tom going?*
   *When will/**When'll** he be back?*

(For contractions, sce also 92.)

Exercise 94

▶ Write the words in CAPITALS in contracted form:
   □ WHAT IS wrong? *What's*
  1 WHAT HAS happened?
  2 WHY IS Bill so angry?
  3 WHERE HAVE you left the car?
  4 WHAT WILL Tom do now?
  5 WHERE WOULD you like me to go?
  6 WHO IS on the phone?

95 Interrogatives: use

A We use interrogative forms

in *yes/no* questions: *Does he smoke?*

in *wh-* and *how* questions: *Where do you live? How are you?*

in question tags: *You don't smoke, do you?*

for requests: *Could you help me (to) carry this?*

B We also use the interrogative forms with an affirmative meaning in certain constructions:
> *Tom drank coffee and so did I.*
> *Never have I seen such marvellous roses.*

C We do not use interrogative forms

in questions about the identity of the subject: *Who lives here?*

in indirect questions: *He asked who lived there.*

when the question follows a phrase such as *Can you tell me? Do you know? Have you any idea? Do you think? I wonder*:
> *Do you know where Tom lives?*
> *I wonder if you could lend me £5?*

96 Negative interrogatives

A We form negative questions with a contracted negative auxiliary + subject:
> *Hasn't he paid you?   Why aren't you coming?*
> *Why didn't you phone?*

But note that the first person singular contraction here (*aren't I?*) is irregular: *I'm right, aren't I?*

B We use these forms

for questions about a negative action or statement:
> *He isn't going.* ~ *Why isn't he going?*

in *yes/no* questions when the speaker hopes for or expects an affirmative answer:
> *I can wait ten minutes.* ~ *Can't you wait a little longer?*

in question tags after an affirmative statement:
> *He arrived late, didn't he?*

Exercise 96

▶ Ask the reason for each of the following statements. Use the negative interrogative as shown:

☐ I can't phone them. ~ *Why can't you phone them?*

1 I can't start tonight. ~ _____?
2 I haven't got my ticket. ~ _____?
3 The travel agents haven't sent it. ~ _____?
4 My cheque didn't reach them in time. ~ _____?
5 I didn't send it first class. ~ _____?

97 Modals and semi-modals

A Modals

These are *can, could, may, might, must, ought, shall, should, will* and *would.*

Modal verbs have no final *s* in the third person singular:
   he can   she may   it must

They always form their negative and interrogative according to the auxiliary pattern:
   He will not/won't help us.   When can you come?

They have no proper past tenses. Four past forms exist (*could, might, should, would*) but they have only a restricted use.

Modal verbs have no infinitives or participles so we cannot use them in continuous or perfect tenses.

After all modal verbs except *ought* we use the bare infinitive:
   You should wait BUT *You ought to wait.*

A modal verb always requires an infinitive though sometimes this is understood but not mentioned:
   Can you do it? ~ Yes I can (do it).

(For *can, could, may, might, must, ought, should,* see 112–136. For *shall, will, would,* see 164–189.)

B Semi-modals

The semi-modals are *dare, need* and *used.*

These form the negative and interrogative either like modals or like ordinary verbs.

dare and *need* have infinitives and past forms.

used has a past form only, no present form.

(For *dare* and *used*, see 137–139. For *need*, see 130–134.)

98 Auxiliaries in short answers etc.

We often use subject + auxiliary only instead of repeating
the whole of a previously-mentioned verb (+ phrase):
Do you understand this book? ~ Yes, I do. (99)
Bill eats too much. ~ No, he doesn't! (100)
Tom hasn't written to you, has he? (101)
Ann played well and so did Peter. (102)
I earn less than she does. (25)

Negative auxiliaries used in this way are usually contracted:
I'm going but he isn't.

Affirmative auxiliaries here are not contracted:
He's not going but I am.

99 Short answers

We usually answer questions which require the answer
'yes' or 'no' by *yes* + subject (pronoun) + affirmative
auxiliary or *no* + subject (pronoun) + negative auxiliary:
Can you swim? ~ Yes, I can OR *No, I can't.*
Does Tom speak Spanish? ~ Yes, he does OR *No, he doesn't.*

Note answers to *must I?/need I?* questions:
Must you go?/Need you go? ~ Yes, I must OR *No, I needn't.*

Exercise 99

► Answer the following in the affirmative or negative as shown:
  □ Did you go to an estate agent? ~ Yes, *I did.*
  1 Are you buying a new house? ~ Yes, _____.
  2 Have you sold your old house? ~ No, _____.
  3 Is your new house nearer the coast? ~ Yes, _____.
  4 Does your wife like it? ~ Yes, _____.
  5 Did you look at houses together? ~ Yes, _____.
  6 Can you see the sea from the new house? ~ No, _____.
  7 Will your carpets fit the new rooms? ~ No, _____.

100 Agreement and disagreement with statements

A Agreement with affirmative statements

Here we use *yes* + subject (pronoun) + affirmative auxiliary. If there is an auxiliary in the statement we repeat this auxiliary:

It's cold today. ~ *Yes, it is.*
We've missed our bus. ~ *Yes, we have.*

If there is no auxiliary, we use *do/does/did*.

Instead of a simple present tense we use *do/does*:

Tom always goes by train. ~ *Yes, he does.*

Instead of a simple past tense we use *did*:

The police caught the murderer. ~ *Yes, they did.*

B Disagreement with affirmative statements

Here we use *no* or *oh no* + subject (pronoun) + negative auxiliary. This auxiliary is stressed:

The price has gone up. ~ *No, it ˈhasn't.*
I paid you yesterday. ~ *Oh no, you ˈdidn't.*
Bill works hard. ~ *No, he ˈdoesn't.*

C Agreement with negative statements

Here we use *no* + subject (pronoun) + negative auxiliary:

The exam wasn't difficult. ~ *No, it wasn't.*
The roads won't be crowded. ~ *No, they won't.*

D Disagreement with negative statements

Here we use *yes* or *oh yes* + subject (pronoun) + negative auxiliary. This auxiliary is stressed:

You haven't paid me. ~ *Oh yes, I ˈhave.*
Bill wasn't at the party. ~ *Yes, he ˈwas.*

Exercise 100

▶ Agree or disagree with the following affirmative statements:
  □ It's very late. ~ Yes, *it is.*
  1 We must go soon. ~ Yes, ___.
  2 Our train leaves at eight. ~ Yes, ___.
  3 It's two miles to the station. ~ Yes, ___.

4   We could walk there. ~ No, ____!
5   We'd be there in half an hour. ~ No, ____!
6   Then we'll have to take a taxi. ~ Yes, ____.
7   There are plenty of taxis. ~ Yes, ____.
8   But taxi fares have gone up recently. ~ No, ____!

► Now agree or disagree with these negative statements:
   □ It isn't raining heavily. ~ No, *it isn't.*
9   The rain hasn't stopped yet. ~ No, ____.
10   You haven't got an umbrella. ~ Yes, ____!
11   It isn't a big umbrella. ~ No, ____.
12   We needn't start just yet. ~ Yes, ____!
13   Tom won't mind waiting for us. ~ Yes, ____!

101 Question tags

These are short additions to statements, asking for
agreement or confirmation.

A   After negative statements we use auxiliary + subject
     (pronoun), i.e. the ordinary interrogative form for
     auxiliary verbs:
     *I'm not late, **am I?**   Ann doesn't eat meat, **does she?**
     The postman hasn't come yet, **has he?***

     Note that statements containing negative words such as
     no (adjective), *none, no one, nobody, nothing, never, hardly
     ever* etc. are considered as negative statements:
     *Bill never goes to parties, **does he?***

B   After affirmative statements we use a negative auxiliary
     + subject (pronoun), i.e. a negative interrogative form.
     We repeat the previously-mentioned auxiliary or use *do/
     does/did* as shown in 110 B:
     *He's living in France now, **isn't he?**
     Tom writes regularly, **doesn't he?***

Exercise 101

► Add question tags as shown:
   □ The flat's too small for them, *isn't it?*
1   They're living in a flat now, ____?
2   Tom should buy a house, ____?
3   It would be cheaper in the end, ____?
4   House prices will go up soon, ____?

5   He could get a mortgage fairly easily, ____?
6   There's a house for sale in your area, ____?
7   It has a garden, ____?
8   Children need a garden to play in, ____?

▶   Add question tags as shown:
   □   He doesn't co-operate, *does he?*
   9   He hasn't answered your last letter, ____?
   10 He didn't answer your previous letter, ____?
   11 He doesn't always open letters, ____?
   12 It isn't much use writing to him, ____?

102   Additions to remarks

Here the subject of the auxiliary can be either a noun or
a pronoun. This subject is usually stressed.

A   Affirmative additions to affirmative remarks

We make these with *so* or *and so* + auxiliary + subject,
in that order:
   Bill has written to her and so has Tom.
We could also say *and Tom has too* but the *so* construction
is more usual.

We use *do/does/did* as shown in 110 B.
   My brother wants a job in London and so do I.

B   Negative additions to affirmative remarks

We make these with *but* + subject + negative auxiliary:
   Ann can type but Mary can't.
   George knows Italian but Peter doesn't.

C   Affirmative additions to negative remarks

We make these with *but* + subject + affirmative
auxiliary:
   Bill didn't like the programme but I did.
   Ann hasn't got a driving licence but Mary has.

D   Negative additions to negative remarks

We make these with *neither/nor* + auxiliary + subject,
in that order:
   I can't swim and neither can you.
   Bill doesn't know the way, nor does Jack.

We could also say:

> *I can't swim and you can't either.*
> *Bill doesn't know and Jack doesn't either.*

But the *neither/nor* construction is more usual.

Exercise 102

► Complete the sentences using the word or phrase in brackets:

□ Tom will be promoted and so *will Jack.* (Jack)
□ John will be promoted but *Bill won't.* (Bill)
1 Tom is always well dressed and so ____. (Bill)
2 He plays polo and so ____. (his brother)
3 He has been to Mexico but ____. (we)
4 He can afford holidays abroad but ____. (we)

□ Bill didn't see the cyclists in time. Neither *did Ann.* (Ann)
□ He wasn't going fast but *they were.* (they)
5 Bill wasn't wearing a seat belt but ____. (Ann)
6 The first cyclist had no lights. Neither ____. (the second)
7 Bill couldn't stop in time, nor ____. (cyclists)
8 The first cyclist hasn't recovered yet but ____. (the second one)

11   *be*

103   Form

Participles: present *being*, past *been*.

Present tense

AFFIRMATIVE	NEGATIVE
I am/I'm	*I am not/I'm not*
you are/you're	*you are not/you aren't/you're not*
he is/he's	*he is not/he isn't/he's not*
she is/she's	*she is not/she isn't/she's not*
it is/it's	*it is not/it isn't/it's not*
we are/we're	*we are not/we aren't/we're not*
they are/they're	*they are not/they aren't/they're not*

Interrogative: *am I? are you? is he?* etc.
Negative interrogative: *aren't I? aren't you? isn't he?* etc.

Past tense

AFFIRMATIVE	NEGATIVE
I was	I was not/I wasn't
you were	you were not/you weren't
he was	he was not/he wasn't
she was	she was not/she wasn't
it was	it was not/it wasn't
we were	we were not/we weren't
they were	they were not/they weren't

Interrogative: *was I? were you? was he?* etc.
Negative interrogative: *wasn't I? weren't you? wasn't he?* etc.

104 *be* as an auxiliary verb

A   We use *be* to form some tenses of other verbs.

Continuous active tenses:
*He **is** reading.   She **was** singing.   They **will be** waiting.*

Simple and continuous passive tenses:
*He **is** employed by the bank.*
*He **was** followed.   He **was being** followed.*

B   We use *be* + infinitive for orders or instructions.

The speaker may be giving the order:
*You **are** to wait here. You're not to leave this room.*
or passing on orders received from someone else:
*You **are** to report to Mr Jones.*

We often use *be* + passive infinitive in notices and
written instructions:
*Books **are** to be returned within a fortnight.*

C   We use *be* + infinitive to express a plan:
*The new bus service **is** to start next week.* (This is the plan.)
*He **was** to leave that night.* (This was the plan.)

It is common in newspapers:
*The Prime Minister **is** to make a statement tomorrow.*

In headlines the verb *be* is usually omitted to save space:
Prime Minister to make statement tomorrow.

We use *was/were* + perfect infinitive for plans not
carried out. This is rather formal.
*He **was** to have left that night.* (The plan was made but not
carried out. He didn't leave.)

D *am/are/is* + *about* + infinitive show that the action
expressed by the infinitive will take place very soon:
*We **are about** to open a new branch in your area.*

When the action will take place immediately, we can
add *just* to emphasize this:
*The concert's **just about** to start. Hurry!*

was/were + *about* + infinitive is used for past:
*He was just **about** to dive when he saw the shark.*

Exercise 104

▶ Put these sentences into (a) negative (b) interrogative:
   □ He is working.   (a) *He isn't working.*   (b) *Is he working?*
   1 She was cooking.
   2 They are waiting for us.
   3 He's employed by the bank.
   4 The house is being watched.
   5 He has been arrested.

▶ Express the following as plans, using *is/are/was* + the
infinitive of the verb in brackets.
   □ The minister *is to open* (open) the new airport. (This is the
      plan.)
   6 We _____ (have) lunch at the airport. (This is the plan.)
   7 There _____ (be) a party after the ceremony. (This is the
      plan.)
   8 The minister's plane _____ (land) here but was diverted to
      Gatwick. (unfulfilled plan)
   9 The ceremony _____ (start) at 2 o'clock, but will now start at 3.

105 *be* as an ordinary verb

A *be* + adjective can be used to express a physical or
mental condition:
*I **am** hot/cold/hungry/thirsty.   You **are** right/wrong.*
*They **were** afraid/frightened.   She **will be** angry/pleased.*

With some adjectives, for example *clever, foolish, stupid, polite, noisy, quiet* we can use *am/are/is being* to show that the subject is behaving in this way at this time:

> The children **are being** very quiet today.

But the simple tense *am/are/is* is also possible here:

> The children **are** very quiet today.

B *be* is used for the following.

1 Age:

> How old **are** you? ~ I'**m** ten (years old). (Not *I'm ten years.*)
> The tower **is** 400 years old. (*years old* is necessary here.)

2 Height, depth, length, width, weight, distance:

> How tall **are** you?/What's your height? ~ I'**m** 1.56 metres.
> How deep **is** the pool?/What's the depth of the pool? ~
> It's two metres deep.
> What do you weigh?/What's your weight? ~ I'**m** 55 kilos.
> How far **is** it to York? ~ It's not far. It's 20 kilometres.

3 Date, time, temperature, weather:

> What date **is** it/What's the date? ~ It's 1 April.
> What time **is** it?/What's the time? ~ It's 3 p.m.
> What **was** the weather like? ~ It **was** wet and windy.

4 Price:

> How much **is** this melon? ~ It's £1.
> How much **are** the lemons? ~ They're 16p each.

C *there is/are, there was/were* etc.

1 Instead of saying, for example, *A stamp is in that drawer*, we normally use *there + be + noun + . . .*

> **There is** a stamp in that drawer.

If the noun is plural we need a plural verb:

> **There are** stamps etc.

Different tenses are, of course, possible:

> **There was** a cheque in the envelope.

2 *there is/are* etc. can also be used when *be* means 'exist', 'happen', 'occur' or 'take place':

> **There's** a new by-pass. (A new by-pass exists.)
> **There's been** an accident. (An accident has happened.)
> **There'll be** delays. (Delays will occur.)
> **There was** a meeting. (A meeting took place.)

3 *there is/are* can be used with pronouns of quantity:
    *Are **there** any matches in the house?* ~
    *Yes, **there are** some in that box* OR *No, **there aren't** any.*

4 *there is/are* can be used with *someone/anything/nobody* etc.
    ***There's** someone on the phone for you.*
    ***There'll be** nobody at home now.*

D   *it is* and *there is* compared

1 *it is* + adjective, *there is* + noun:
    It is foggy OR *There is a fog.*
    It was very wet OR *There was a lot of rain.*

2 *it is, there is* of distance and time:
    It is a long way to York.
    There is a long way still to go. (We have many miles
    still to go.)
    It is time to go home. (We always start home at six and
    it is six now.)
    *There is time for us to go home and come back again before
    the film starts.* (That amount of time exists.)

3 *it is,* used for identity, and *there is* + noun/pronoun:
    There is someone at the door. I think it's your brother.

4 *it is,* used in cleft sentences, and *there is*:
    It is the grandmother who makes the decisions.
    (the grandmother, not any other member of the family)
    *. . . and there's the grandmother, who lives in the granny-
    flat.* (The grandmother exists.)

▷   For *it is*, see also 64.

Exercise 105

▶ Complete these sentences. Use the correct form of *be* with a
suitable adjective from the list:

afraid, cold, hot, hungry, thirsty, tired

    ☐   He has worked hard all day, so now he *is tired*.
    1   They had eaten nothing all day, so now they ____.
    2   Ann is standing on a chair. She ____ of mice.
    3   I wanted a drink of water; I ____.
    4   I ____. ~ Well, put on a coat.
    5   It ____ in here. I'd better turn down the heating.

▶ Put in the correct form of *be*:

6   There ___ usually a long queue for this bus.
7   There ___ thirty people in the queue yesterday.
8   Well, there ___ (not) anybody there now.
9   But we've just missed a bus. There ___ (not) another for some time.
10 There ___ a lot of broken glass on the road. ___ there ___ an accident?

▶ Put in *it* or *there* with a form of *be*:

11 Was it very wet last night? ~ Yes, ___ a lot of rain.
12 How far ___ to Dover? ~ ___ 100 kilometres.
13 ___ time for a meal before we start tonight?
14 Have you got a map? ~ Yes, ___ one in my bag.
15 ___ someone standing by our car.
16 I think ___ a traffic warden.
17 I'd better move the car. ___ a car park behind the station and ___ (not) full; ___ plenty of spaces.

12   *have*

106 Form

A Participles: present *having*, past *had*.

Present tense

AFFIRMATIVE	NEGATIVE
I have/I've	I have not/I haven't/I've not
you have/you've	you have not/you haven't/you've not
he has/he's	he has not/he hasn't/he's not
she has/she's	she has not/she hasn't/she's not
it has/it's	it has not/it hasn't/it's not
we have/we've	we have not/we haven't/we've not
they have/they've	they have not/they haven't/they've not

Interrogative: *have I? have you? has he?* etc.
Negative interrogative: *haven't I? haven't you? hasn't he?* etc.

Past tense

Affirmative: *had/'d* for all persons.
Negative: *had not/hadn't* for all persons.
Interrogative: *had I? had you? had he?* etc.
Negative interrogative: *hadn't I? hadn't you? hadn't he?* etc.

B We can also form the negative and interrogative with *do/does/did*:

he doesn't have	*we don't have*	*they didn't have*
does he have?	*do you have?*	*did they have?*

Sometimes we can use either these forms or the forms in A above. Sometimes we can use only one form (108 A3).

C We can sometimes add *got* to *have/has/had, have not/has not/had not* and to *have you? has he? had he?* etc. (108).

107 *have* as an auxiliary verb

A *have* used to form perfect tenses

Present perfect: *I have/I've sold my house.*
Past perfect: *He said that he had/he'd sold his house.*
Future perfect: *By next year he will/he'll have paid his debts.*
Perfect conditional: *He would/He'd have paid earlier if . . .*

Perfect infinitive (*to have done, to have gone* etc.):
   He isn't here. He must have gone out. He should have left a note.
Perfect participle (*having done, having gone, having been* etc.):
   Having damaged his own car, he asked me to lend him mine.

B *have* something *done*

have and *had* here are not contracted.
Their negative and interrogative are formed with *do*:
   He doesn't have his hair cut. He cuts it himself.
   Why did you have the lock changed?

He had his house painted means 'Someone painted it for him' or 'He paid someone to paint it'.

It is essential to keep the word order, *have* + object + past participle, as otherwise the meaning and time change. *He had painted his house* would mean that he painted it himself in the past, before the time of speaking.

have here can be used in the continuous forms:
> She's **having** her hair done. (present action)
> I'm **having** the piano tuned tomorrow. (future arrangement)

C *had better (do)* something

1 *had better* is followed by a bare infinitive. The negative is *had better not*:
> You **had**/You'**d better not** drink any more. You're the driver.

In conversation *had* contracts to '*d* and often cannot be heard.

2 *had* here is an unreal past. Its meaning is present or future:
> He **had**/He'**d better** come today/tomorrow.

You had better . . . is a useful way of giving advice:
> You'**d better** go home at once. (I advise you to go home.)

With other persons *had better . . .* means 'This would be a good/wise thing (for me/him etc.) to do':
> I'**d better** hurry or I'll miss my train.
> He'**d better** book early or he won't get a seat.

3 Instead of *had better* we can say *ought to* or *should*:
> You'**d better** go now. = You **ought to**/**should** go now.

Exercise 107

▶ Answer these questions as shown. Use the correct form of *have* in each case.

□ Do you wash your car yourself? ~ No, I *have it washed*.
□ Did you translate the documents yourself? ~ No, I *had them translated*.
1 Do you develop your own films? ~ No, I ____.
2 Are you typing the report yourself? ~ No, I ____.
3 Did you build the garage yourself? ~ No, ____.
4 Is she making the curtains herself? ~ No, ____.
5 Do you clean your own carpets? ~ No, ____.

▶ Using the *had better* form, advise your friend:
to insure his luggage/to hurry/to be early/to book a seat in a non-smoker/not to travel on a Bank Holiday/ to get some traveller's cheques.

Choose a suitable phrase each time. (Use 'd for had.)

☐   My train goes in ten minutes. ~ You'd better hurry.

6   I'm going abroad next week. ~ You'd better ____.

7   I hate cigarette smoke. ~ Then you ____.

8   I hear that luggage often gets lost. ~ Yes, you ____.

9   There'll be long queues at the ticket office. ~ Probably.
      You ____.

10   I hate crowds. ~ Then you ____.

108 *have* as an ordinary verb

A   *have* meaning 'possess'

1

	AFFIRMATIVE	NEGATIVE	INTERROGATIVE
PRESENT	*have (got)*	*haven't (got)* *don't have*	*have you (got)?* etc. *do you have?* etc.
PAST	*had*	*hadn't (got)* *didn't have*	*had you (got)?* etc. *did you have?* etc.

2   Examples

> I *have*/I've *got* a new bicycle.
> You *have*/You've *got* a lovely flat.
> We *had*/We'd *got* plenty of time.
> He *had*/He'd *got* enough money.

Similarly with words for pain and illness:

> I *have*/I've *got* a headache.   I *have* headaches very often.

When there is an idea of habit, as in the last example, we do not add *got* and do not contract *have*.

3   In negative and interrogative sentences we use the *do* forms when there is an idea of habit:

> *Do* you *have* headaches often? ~ *No, I don't/Yes, I do.*

When there is not an idea of habit we can use either the *have (got)* or *do* forms, i.e. we can say:

> I *haven't (got)* time to do it OR I *don't have* time to do it.
> *Have* you *(got)* a visa? OR *Do* you *have* a visa?
> He *hadn't (got)* a work permit OR
> He *didn't have* a work permit.
> *Had* he *(got)* a ticket? OR *Did* he *have* a ticket?

4 We can add *got* to the *have* forms, as shown above. *got* makes no difference to the meaning.

When followed by *got*, *have/has/had* and *have/has/had not* are usually contracted:

> *I've got an idea.*   *He's got a bad temper.*
> *You'd got a temperature.*

The stress falls on *got*. The *'ve*, *'s* or *'d* often cannot be heard.

We do not add *got* in short answers, question tags etc.:

> *Have you got a timetable?* ~ *Yes, I have/No, I haven't.*
> *She's got a big family, hasn't she?* ~ *Yes, she has.*

5 *have* meaning 'possess' is not used in the continuous forms.

B *have* for actions

1 *have* can have a number of meanings:

> *have* a meal/something to eat/a drink/a cigarette/a bath/
> a rest/a day off
> *have* (= give) a party; *have* friends to dinner etc.
> *have* (= attend/take part in) a lesson/lecture/concert/
> meeting/an exam etc.
> *have* (= take part in) a conversation/an argument/
> a discussion/quarrel/row etc.
> *have* difficulty/trouble/an adventure/an accident/
> a dream/nightmare/good or bad days/nights/weeks etc./
> journeys/trips/weather etc.
> *have* (= undergo) treatment/operations etc.
> *have* an idea; *have* (= bear) a baby; *have* a look; *have* a go
> (= make an attempt)

2 When we use *have* for actions, we form the negative and interrogative with *do*; we do not use *got*; and we can use the continuous forms:

> *You have a month's holiday every year, don't you?*
> *Did you have a good journey?* ~
> *Not very. We had an accident on the M1.*
> *We are having supper with Tom tonight.*
> *Mrs Jones is having lunch with a client at the moment.*

3 We can say *I've got a party/lesson/exam* etc., but *have got* here has more the meaning of obligation:

> Pianist: *I've got a concert next week. I must practise.*

Exercise 108

▶ Put in a suitable form of *have (got)* in the present tense:

   □ *I've got/I have a headache.*

1   I'm sorry you ____ a headache. ____ you often ____ them?

2   I ____ (not) them in the holidays. But I ____ them in term time.

3   ____ you ____ a good reading lamp?

4   I ____ a lamp but it ____ (not) a very strong bulb.

▶ Put in a suitable form of *have*:

   □ *What's the noise? ~ My neighbour's having a party.*

5   ____ he often ____ parties? ~ Yes. I went to the last one.

6   We ____ champagne at his last party. I think they ____ champagne tonight too.

7   ____ you ____ a good time at the last party?

8   Oh yes. Everyone always ____ a great time at his parties.

9   But just now I ____ (not) time for parties. We ____ a test next week.

10   How often ____ you ____ tests? ~ We ____ one every two months.

13   do

109   Form

A   *do* as an auxiliary verb

Participles: present *doing*, past *done*.

Present tense

AFFIRMATIVE	NEGATIVE
I do	*I do not/I don't*
you do	*you do not/you don't*
he does	*he does not/he doesn't*
she does	*she does not/she doesn't*
it does	*it does not/it doesn't*
we do	*we do not/we don't*
they do	*they do not/they don't*

Interrogative: *do I? do you? does he?* etc.
Negative interrogative: *don't I? don't you? doesn't he?* etc.

Past tense

Affirmative: *did* for all persons.
Negative: *did not/didn't* for all persons.
Interrogative: *did I? did you? did he?* etc.
Negative interrogative: *didn't I? didn't you? didn't he?* etc.

B *do* **as an ordinary verb**

The affirmative forms are as shown above. For the negative and interrogative we add the auxiliary *do* to the main verb *do*:

*What **do** you **do** in the evenings?* ~
*I **don't do** anything. I relax.*

We can use the continuous forms of *do* here:
*What's he **doing**?* ~ *He's writing a letter.*

110 *do* **as an auxiliary verb**

A We use *do* to form the negative and interrogative of the simple present and past tenses of ordinary verbs:

*He **doesn't** eat meat.* ~ ***Does** he eat eggs?*
*He **didn't** write.* ~ ***Did** he phone?*

We can use *do* in the affirmative

to add emphasis:

*You think he doesn't understand but he **does** understand.*
*I **did** read it, honestly!*

with an imperative to make a request or invitation more persuasive:

***Do** help me* is more persuasive than *Help me*.
***Do** come with us* is more persuasive than *Come with us*.

in answer to a suggestion or a request for permission when we want to show approval or encouragement:

Shall I tell him? ~ *Yes, **do** OR **Do**.*

B We can use *do* to avoid repeating the same verb or phrase

in short answers (99):

Did he write to you? ~ *Yes, he **did**/No, he **didn't**.*

in short agreements and disagreements (100):
He drives too fast. ~ *Yes, he does/No, he doesn't.*

in question tags (101):
You don't take sugar, do you?   You saw him, didn't you?

in additions to remarks (102):
Bill didn't like the film, but I did.

in comparisons (39 D):
He works harder than she does.

in if-clauses (188 E):
He says he knows four languages. ~
If he really does, he'll be useful.

in time clauses (255):
He says he'll ring back. ~
When he does, let me know, will you?

Exercise 110

▶ Interrupt the first speaker with a negative statement as
shown:
   □ When he pays his taxes . . . ~ *But he doesn't pay* his taxes!
   1 When he answered your letter . . . ~ ____ my letter!
   2 When you make a mistake . . . ~ ____ mistakes!
   3 When I wrote to you . . . ~ ____ to me!
   4 When she does her homework . . . ~ ____ her homework!

▶ Put in the correct form of *do*:
   □ Ann doesn't work here, but Tom *does*. (= Tom works
     here.)
   5 Did he come by car? ~ Yes, he ____.
   6 He swims better than I ____.
   7 They earned more than we ____.
   8 You don't smoke, ____ you?
   9 I hope you'll win. If you ____ we'll have a party.
  10 I'll accept his offer. ~ Before you ____, read the
     conditions again.

111 *do* as an ordinary verb

A   *do* is mostly used to mean 'perform' (an action), 'occupy oneself with' (something):

He's in Alaska. ~ *What's he **doing** there?*
*What's Ann **doing**?* ~ *She's **doing** the washing-up.*
*What **are** you **doing** tonight?* (What plans have you made?) ~ *I'm not **doing** anything.* (I'm not going out.)
*What **does** he **do** for a living?* ~ *He is an architect.*
*What **were** they **doing**?* ~ *They were playing chess.*
'DIY' stands for 'Do It Yourself'. (Do your own redecoration/repairs etc.)
*You can **do** what you like but I have to **do** what I'm told.* (I have to obey orders.)

B   Other uses of *do*

*How **do** you **do**?* is a formal greeting. When two people are introduced, each says *How do you do?* It is in the form of a question but there is no answer. Do not confuse it with *How are you?*, which is a question about the other person's health.

*The treatment is **doing** me good.* (I am benefiting from it.)
*He **did** well at school.* (He was successful.)
*She **does** her best.* (She works as well as she can.)
*Would a knife **do**?* (Would a knife be suitable/adequate?) ~ *No, it wouldn't. I need scissors.*
*Would £5 **do**?* (Would £5 be enough?) ~ *No, it wouldn't.*

Exercise 111

▶ Put in the correct form of *do*:

□   What *is* he ***doing*** now? ~ He*'s doing* his homework.

1   What ____ they usually ____ in the evenings? ~ They watch TV.

2   What ____ you ____ tonight? ~ We're going to the theatre.

3   ____ you still ____ exercises every morning? ~ I ____ if I have time. I ____ (not) them regularly.

4   The pills ____ (not) him any good, so he stopped taking them.

5   He's out of work. ~ What ____ all day? ~ He ____ (not) anything.

6   (at a political demonstration) ____ demonstrations ____ any good? ~ Sometimes they ____ .

14 Permission: *can* and *may*

112 Forms

A *can* and *may* are modal verbs and have no infinitive or participles.

AFFIRMATIVE	*can/may* for all persons in the present and future. *could/might* for the past and conditional.	
NEGATIVE	*cannot/can't* *could not/couldn't*	*may not/mayn't* *might not/mightn't*
INTERROGATIVE	*can I?* etc. *could I?* etc.	*may I?* etc. *might I?* etc.
NEGATIVE INTERROGATIVE	*can I not/can't I?* etc.? *could I not?/ couldn't I?* etc.	*may I not?* etc. *might I not?/ mightn't I?* etc.

The above forms are the same for all persons, and are followed by the bare infinitive: *He can swim.*

Other forms are made with *allow/be allowed*:
   *Since her last accident her husband **hasn't allowed** her to drive the car.* (115)

113 *can* or *may*

A *can* expresses permission informally.

I can means 'I am allowed to':
   Child: *I **can** buy coke in a shop but I **can't** buy it in a bar.* (I am not allowed to buy it in a bar.)

you can means 'you are allowed to' or 'I allow you to':
   Child to friend: *You're lucky. You **can** watch TV till ten.*
   Teacher: *You **can** use your dictionaries for this test.*

he/they can means 'he is/they are allowed to':
>   Teacher: *Parents **can** visit the school at any time.*
or 'I allow him/them to':
>   Mother to child: *Your puppy **can** sleep in your room.*

B   *may* expresses permission more formally.

I may for permission is not usual, but *may I?* is quite common (114 A–B).

you may usually means, 'I allow you to'. It is more formal than *you can*:
>   Examiner: *You **may** use a calculator if you wish.*

he/they may usually means 'he is/they are allowed to'. It is more formal than *he/they can*:
>   Extract from school prospectus: *Parents **may** visit the school at any time.*

Exercise 113

▶ Rewrite these sentences using *can* or *can't*:
□   In Britain you ARE ALLOWED TO buy weapons in shops.
     In Britain you can buy weapons in shops.
1   But you AREN'T ALLOWED TO carry them in the streets.
2   So I'M NOT ALLOWED TO carry a knife, AM I?
3   No, you AREN'T (allowed to).
4   IS my sister ALLOWED TO carry her umbrella?
5   Oh yes, SHE'S ALLOWED TO carry her umbrella.
6   If someone tries to mug her, IS she ALLOWED TO hit him with her umbrella?
7   She ISN'T ALLOWED TO hit him first, but if he hits her, she IS ALLOWED TO hit back.

▶ Now rewrite these sentences. Use *may* or *may not* or *can* or *can't*:
8   (exam regulations) Candidates who finish early ARE ALLOWED TO leave the hall.
9   But candidates who leave ARE NOT ALLOWED TO return.
10   (student to friend) If we finish early we ARE ALLOWED TO leave the hall.
11   But we AREN'T ALLOWED TO return.

114 Requests for permission

A   *can I?/could I?/may I?* and *might I?* are all possible.
         can I? is the most informal.

could I? is the most generally useful. We can use it for informal or fairly formal requests.
may I? is more formal than *could I?*
might I? is still more formal and indicates greater uncertainty on the part of the speaker about the answer.

B Note the choice of *can/could* etc. in each situation and the answers to these forms:

1 ***Can** I have another sweet?* ~ *Yes, you **can**/No, you **can't**.*
2 ***Could** I use your phone?* ~ *Yes, of course you **can**.* (not *could*)
3 Policeman: ***Could** I see your driving licence, please?*
4 (In a crowded restaurant) ***May** I share your table?* ~ *Yes, of course (you **can**).*
5 *I've left my camera at home. **May** I/**Might** I borrow yours?* ~ *Yes, you **may**.* (not *might*)

C We can use *can't I?* and *couldn't I?* to show that we hope for an affirmative answer:

Child: ***Can't** I come with you?* ~ *No, (you **can't**,) not today.*
I want it done today. ~ ***Couldn't** it wait till tomorrow?*

Exercise 114

▶ Decide what you would say in these situations. Choose the most suitable phrase: *can I?, could I?, may I?* or *might I?*

☐ (in a shop) You want to try on a swimsuit. *May I try it on?*
1 You want to borrow a friend's timetable.
2 You want to use your neighbour's phone. (You don't know him well.)
3 You are a child and you want to go out and play. (Ask your mother.)
4 (on the train) You want to have a look at another traveller's newspaper. (He isn't reading it. Use *your paper*.)
5 You want to photocopy a page of a book. (Ask the librarian. Use *this book*.)

115 *allow*

A For perfect and continuous tenses we have to use *allow*:
*I **have** always **allowed** my children to eat what they like.*
*I haven't got a work permit yet, but they**'re allowing** me to work temporarily.*

B *could* can express general permission in the past:
> *After tea the children* ***could*** *do what they liked.* (They were allowed to do what they liked.)

But for a particular permission we use *was/were allowed to*:
> *It was after hospital visiting hours, but I* ***was allowed*** *to visit him.* (I did visit him.)

couldn't, however, can be used more widely:
> *We arrived late and* ***couldn't*** *get in/weren't allowed in till the interval.* (particular refusal of permission)
> *Patients* ***couldn't*** *smoke in the wards.* (general refusal of permission)

Exercise 115

▶ Put in *could* or *was/were allowed to*. Often both forms are possible.
    ☐ Non-residents *could* (or *were allowed to*) have meals in the hotel restaurant.
    1   But they ____ (not) use the residents' lounge.
    2   Guests ____ (not) bring dogs into the hotel.
    3   But Tom brought in his guide dog. He ____ bring him in.
    4   Guests ____ (not) park in front of the hotel.
    5   But sometimes disabled guests ____ park there.

15   Possibility: *may/might* and *can/could*

116   *may/might*

A Form

may/might for all persons in the present and future.
might after verbs in the past tense and in the conditional.
Negative: *may not, might not/mightn't.*
Interrogative: see D below.

B *may/might* + present infinitive can express possibility in the present or future:
> *I rang him but got no answer.* ~ *He* ***may/might*** *be away.* (Perhaps he is away.)

*The price **may/might** go up.* (Perhaps the price will go up.)
*He **may/might** not believe you.* (Perhaps he doesn't/
won't believe you.)

We can use either *may* or *might* here. *might* slightly
increases the doubt.

C We use *might*, not *may*, when the sentence is introduced
by a verb in a past tense:
*He said he **might** not have time for a meal.*
and in conditional type 2 sentences (185 D2):
*If you paid your staff more they **might** work better.*

D In the interrogative, we normally use *do you think?*:
Do you think he believes/will believe you?
or *be + likely + infinitive*:
*Is he **likely** to believe you?   Are prices **likely** to go up?*

Exercise 116

► Tom wants to have a barbecue party in the garden. Ann and
Bill are not sure that it is a good idea. Rewrite these sentences
using *may* or *might*. Sometimes both forms are possible.

☐ Bill: PERHAPS it WILL rain.   *It may (or might) rain.*
☐ Ann: And if it was very wet PERHAPS people WOULDN'T
come.   *And if it was very wet people mightn't come.*
1 Bill: PERHAPS it WILL be windy.
2 Ann: And if it was windy PERHAPS people WOULDN'T
want to eat out of doors.
3 Bill: PERHAPS your brother WILL bring his dogs.
4 Tom: Yes, he said that PERHAPS he WOULD bring them.
5 Bill: If other people bring their dogs PERHAPS there'LL be a
dog fight.

117 *may/might + have done* etc.

A We use this form in speculations about past actions:
*He **may/might have missed** the train.* (Perhaps he
missed/has missed it.)
*He **may/might** not **have received** the letter.* (Perhaps he
didn't receive/hasn't received it.)

But we need *might* after a past tense:
*She said that he **might have missed** the train.*

B We can use *might* (not *may*) + *have* + past participle for an action which was possible but didn't happen:
*Why did you leave the matches there? The children **might have started** a fire.* (But they didn't start one.)

C We can use *might* + *have* + past participle in conditional sentences, type 3 (186 C3):
*If you had tried again you **might have passed**.* (Perhaps you would have passed.)

Exercise 117

► An old man died and left his gold watch to his daughter. But she cannot find the watch, and she and her husband are wondering what has happened to it. Complete the sentences, using *may* or *might* with the past participle of the verb in CAPITALS. Sometimes both *may* and *might* are possible.

☐ Perhaps he LOST it. ~ Yes, he *may/might have lost* it.
☐ Perhaps he SOLD it. ~ Yes, if someone had made him a good offer for it he *might have sold* it.
1 Perhaps he LENT it to someone. ~
Yes, he ____ it to Peter, who collects gold watches.
2 Perhaps he SENT it to be repaired. ~
Yes, if it had stopped working, he ____ it to a jewellers'.
3 Perhaps he GAVE it away. ~
Yes, he ____ it to George. George was always asking for it.
4 Perhaps he FORGOT he'd promised it to you. ~
Yes, he had a bad memory. He ____.
5 Perhaps he HID it somewhere. ~
Yes, if he had wanted to keep it safe, he ____ it.

118 *could* instead of *may/might*

A We can use *could be* instead of *may/might be*:
*What kind of tree is this? ~ I'm not sure. It **could be** a maple* OR *It **may/might be** a maple.*

But we cannot do this in the negative because there is a difference in meaning. Compare:
*It **may/might not be** a maple* means 'Perhaps it isn't a maple'.
*It **couldn't be** a maple* means 'That is impossible.' (Perhaps because maples don't grow in the area.)

B We can use *could* + *have* + the past participle of any verb instead of *may/might* + *have* + past participle:
> *She **could/may/might** have paid by cheque.* (Perhaps she paid by cheque.)

As above, there is a difference of meaning in the negative. Compare:
> *She **may/might not have paid** by cheque.* (Perhaps she didn't.)
> *She **couldn't have paid** by cheque. She hasn't got a bank account.* (It was impossible for her to pay by cheque.)

Exercise 118

▶ Two men are wondering how a burglar got into a house. Complete the sentences, using *may/might/could have* or *couldn't have* with the past participle of the verb in brackets.

☐ He *may/might/could have opened* (open) the back door. The lock isn't very strong.

☐ No, he *couldn't have opened* (open) it. It was bolted inside.

1 The downstairs windows are all locked, so he _____ (get) in that way.

2 He _____ (get) in through an upstairs window. The upstairs windows aren't locked.

3 But he _____ (reach) the upstairs windows without a ladder. It's just not possible.

4 There is a ladder in the garage. He _____ (use) that.

119 *can*

A Subject + *can* can mean 'it is possible' or 'circumstances permit':
> *You **can** get to the top of the mountain by cable car.* (It is possible to do this.)

The past form is *could*:
> *You **couldn't** drink the water; it was polluted.*

B *can* in the affirmative can also express an occasional possibility:
> *Strikes **can** last for a long time.* (They sometimes last . . .)

The past form is *could*:
> *These demonstrations **could** be very violent.* (They sometimes were . . .)

16 Ability: *can* and *be able*

120 Forms

Affirmative: *can* for all persons in the present, *could* for all persons in the past (but see 121 B) and conditional.
Negative: *cannot/can't, could not/couldn't.*
Interrogative: *can he?* etc., *could he?* etc.
Negative interrogative: *can he not/can't he? could he not?* etc.
After *can* we use the bare infinitive: *I can pay by cheque.*

Other forms made with *be able*

Perfect tenses:
> *I've been able to read since I was five.*
> *He said he'd been able to read since he was five.*

Infinitive: *to be able*
> *It's nice to be able to pay by credit card.*

Gerund: *being able*
> *Being able to buy things by mail order is very convenient.*

Exercise 120

► Bill and Tom are reading information about a sailing school.
Put in *can, can't, will be able to, have/has been able to* or *be able to.*
□ Bill: It says here that all students must *be able to* swim.
1 Tom: But I ____ (not) swim. ____ you swim?
2 Bill: Yes. I ____ swim since I was six.
3 Tom: You're like my brother. He ____ swim since he was four.
4 Bill: But you ____ learn to swim at any age. If you start lessons now, you ____ swim in a week's time.
5 Tom: Are you sure that I ____ swim after only a week's lessons?

121 Use

A For present ability we use either *can* or *am/are/is able.*
can is more common.
> *I can't read a word of Russian. Can you?*
> *His foot is still in plaster, but he is able to walk a little now.*

B For the past, we use *could* or *was/were able*.

For ability only we use *could*:
> *He **could** speak six languages.*

But for ability + a particular action we use *was/were able*:
> *The plate broke but I **was able** to mend it.* (I managed to mend it and I did mend it.)

Similarly in the interrogative:
> ***Were** you **able** to mend the plate?*

But we can use *could* for a particular action with verbs of the senses and in the negative:
> *I **could** hear him shouting.*
> *I looked for it but I **couldn't** find it.*

C For the future we normally use *will/shall be able*:
> *He**'ll be able** to swim after a few more lessons.*

D For the conditional we can use either *could* or *would be able*:
> ***Could** you carry your luggage yourself if you had to?*
> (Would you be able to . . .)

E For *could you/couldn't you* in requests, see 219 A.

F Instead of *not able*, we often use the adjective *unable*:
> *I **am unable** to see anything without my glasses.*

Exercise 121

▶ Put in *could, couldn't* or *was/were able to*. Use *was/were able to* only when necessary.
Last month I had a fire in my kitchen. I (□) *couldn't* (not) put it out and I (1) _____ (not) phone the Fire Brigade from my house but I (2) _____ wake my neighbour and ask if I could use her phone. She (3) _____ see smoke pouring out of my window so she said, 'Of course'. My hands were shaking but I (4) _____ dial 999 and give my address. The Fire Brigade came quickly and (5) _____ put the fire out. But for a week afterwards you (6) _____ still smell smoke.

122   *could* + *have done* etc.

We use this form to show that the subject had the ability to do something but did not do it:

*Why didn't you ask Tom? He **could have lent** you the money.*

or when we don't know whether he did it or not:

I wonder who told her the news. ~
*Bill knew. He **could have told** her.*

(But we don't know whether Bill told her or not.)

Exercise 122

► Put in *could have* with the past participle of one of these verbs: *ring, save, write, walk*

   □ A: I couldn't come to work. There was a bus strike.
        B: But it's only three miles. You *could have walked*.

1   A: I didn't save any money last year.
       B: But you have a good salary. You ____ more than £1,000.

2   A: I didn't know your phone number.
       B: But you knew my address. You ____ to me.

3   A: I rang once but got no answer.
       B: You ____ again.

17   Obligation: *ought to, should, must, have to* and *need*

123   *ought to* and *should*: forms

A We can use *ought to* or *should* for all persons

in the present or future:

*You **ought to** tell OR **should** tell him today or tomorrow.*

after a past tense:

*He thought I **ought to** go OR **should** go at once.*

with the perfect infinitive:

*You **ought to** have OR **should** have paid him at once.*

B   After *ought* we use the full infinitive: *You ought to ring him*. This is why we call the form *ought to*.

After *should* we use the bare infinitive: *You should ring him*.

124   *ought to* and *should*: use

ought to and *should* here have the same meaning, but *should* is more often used. We can use *ought to/should*:

to express the subject's obligation or duty:
> *You **ought to** write to your mother.*
> *Ann **should** take more exercise.*

to indicate a correct or sensible action or arrangement:
> *There **ought to** be more buses on this route.*
> *He **should** insure his house.*

to express advice (221 A):
> *You **ought to** book a seat.*
> *You **should** keep a copy of the letter.*

▷   For *ought to/should* for assumption, see 136.
For other uses of *should*, see 222 D, 236 B, 240, 250 E.

Exercise 124

►   A father is complaining about his son's behaviour. The boy's mother agrees tactfully. Write what she says. Use *should* or *shouldn't* and the words in brackets.

   □   He only shaves once a week. ~ (Yes/more often)
      Yes, he should shave more often.
   □   He wears ear-rings! ~ (Yes)
      Yes, he shouldn't wear ear-rings.
   1   He only cuts his hair once a month. ~ (Yes/more often)
   2   He doesn't get up till 10. ~ (Yes/earlier)
   3   He borrows my shirts. ~ (Yes/your)
   4   He uses my razor. ~ (Yes/your)
   5   He isn't trying to find a job. ~ (Yes)

125   *ought to/should have done* etc.

A   If we say *You ought to have written*, we mean 'You didn't write and this was wrong' or 'You didn't write and this

was foolish'. Similarly *He shouldn't have left her* means
'He left her, and this was wrong or foolish'.

B Contractions are usual in colloquial speech:
ought to have, ought to've   ought not to have, oughtn't to've
should have, should've   should not have, shouldn't've

C Compare *ought to/should have done* and *could have done.*
If we use *ought to/should* here we show that we think
that the subject acted wrongly or foolishly. So we are
criticizing him or blaming him. If we use *could* we are
not criticizing or blaming. We are merely pointing out a
possible (alternative) action.

Exercise 125

▶ Tom spent a night at an expensive hotel and was not satisfied.
He complains to the travel agent who booked the room for
him. The agent is sympathetic. Imagine you are the agent and
make comments as shown. Use *should've*.
  □ Tom: You booked me a room with a bath but they gave
    me one with a shower.
  That was bad. They should've given you a room with a bath.

1 Tom: They didn't carry my luggage up. ~
2 Tom: The central heating wasn't on. ~
3 Tom: They said breakfast was at 7.30 but it wasn't served
    till half past eight. ~
4 Tom: I asked them to call me at 7 but they didn't call me till
    8. ~

126 *must*: form

A We use *must* for all persons in the present and future.
Negative: *must not/mustn't.*
Interrogative: *must I?* etc.
Negative interrogative: *mustn't I?* etc.

must has no past tense, so we use *had to* here.

B After *must* we use the bare infinitive:
  Policeman: *You **must move** your car, sir.*
but *have* needs a full infinitive:
  *We **had to move** the car.*

127 *must* or *ought to/should* for obligation

A We use *must* when the speaker has the authority to give an order:

Ann's father: *You **must** be in by 10.30.*

With *ought to* and *should* there is usually no authority. It is usually a matter of conscience and good sense:

Ann's friend: *You **ought to** be in bed. You've got a bad cold.*

B We also use *you must* and *you ought to/should* for advice. *you must* here is more emphatic than *you ought to/should*:

*It's a marvellous book. You **must** read it.*
*It's quite an interesting book. You **should** read it.*

128 *have to*: form

A Present: *have (got) to*.
Past: *had to*.
Future: *will/shall have to*.

For negative and interrogative forms, see 132 A, 133 A.

B After *have* we use a full infinitive for obligation:

*We'll **have to** wait till the fog lifts.*

C *have to* and *have got to*

For a single action we can use either form:

*I **have to** go now* OR *I've **got to** go now.*

For habitual obligations *got* is less usual:

*I **have to** write an essay every week.*

have got to is usually contracted:

*He's **got to** wait. We've **got to** wait with him.*

129 *must* or *have to*?

A Affirmative forms

Future: *must* or *will/shall have to*.
Present: *must* or *have (got) to*.

There is only one past form: *had to*.

B   We use *must* when the speaker has the authority to give
the order:
   Airport regulations: *Passengers **must** check in an hour
   before their flight.*

We use *have to* when somebody else, not the speaker,
has the authority. We call this 'external authority'.
   Tom: *Passengers **have to** check in an hour before their
   flight, so you'll **have to** check in at 9.30, Ann.* (The air
   company, not Tom, is the authority here.)

We also use *have to* when the action is necessary for
other reasons:
   *Everybody **has to** eat.*

C   Present and future: examples of *must* and *have to*

1   Second person
   Manageress of launderette to new customer: *You **must**
   wait till the machine stops.* (speaker's authority)
   Old customer to new customer: *You **have to** wait till
   the machine stops.* (external authority/necessity)

2   Third person
   London Underground regulations: *All passengers **must**
   have a ticket.* (speaker's authority)
   *My son **has to** wear uniform at school.* (external authority)
   *People often **have to** queue at the ticket office.* (necessity)

3   First person

   We can use either *I/we must* or *I/we have to*.

   must is better when the obligation is urgent or seems
   important to the speaker:
   *Look at the time! I **must** run!*
   *I **must** catch the 8.30 train tomorrow.* (*will have to* is
   possible but would be less emphatic.)

   have to is better for habitual obligations, or necessity:
   *I **have to** catch the 8.30 train every morning.*
   *I usually **have to** stand all the way.*

D   Past

   Here we have no problem as there is only one form, *had to*:
   *There was no oil; I **had to** cook it in butter.*

Exercise 129

▶ A tour guide is giving directions to his group. Tom and Ann listen and make quiet comments. Put in *must* or a *have to* form.

☐ Guide: You *must* be ready by eight tomorrow morning.

1 Tom: Poor tourists. They ___ get up early tomorrow.

2 Ann: But people on bus tours always ___ get up early.

3 Guide: You ___ keep together. It's easy to get lost.

4 Tom: Some of them *will* get lost and he ___ go and look for them.

5 Ann: And the others ___ wait till he finds them.

6 Guide: Lunch is paid for at the Swan Hotel. But you ___ remember to pay for your drinks.

7 Tom: They ___ pay a lot for drinks at the Swan Hotel.

130 *need*: forms

The verb *need* has both modal forms and ordinary verb forms. We use it chiefly in the negative and interrogative.

A Modal forms

We use *need* for all persons in the present and future.

Negative: *need not*.
Interrogative: *need I?* etc.
Negative interrogative: *need I not/needn't I?* etc.

After *need* formed as above, we use the bare infinitive:
   You **needn't cook** it; we can eat it raw.

B Ordinary verb forms

Future	Negative:	*will not/won't need to*
		shall not/shan't need to
	Interrogative:	*shall I/will he* etc. *need to?*
Present	Negative:	*do not/don't need to*
		does not/doesn't need to
	Interrogative:	*did he* etc. *need to?*

After *need* formed as above, we use the full infinitive:
   I **don't need to work** on Saturdays. (see also 132)

C We use the above forms to express absence of obligation. We can use *have* forms instead of the *need* forms in B above.

D We can also use *need* as an ordinary verb meaning 'require'. It then has all the usual forms and tenses except the present and past continuous.

Present: *I/you/we/they need, he/she/it needs.*
Past: *needed* for all persons.

Other forms are as in B above.

We can use *need* with a noun/pronoun object or with a gerund or passive infinitive:
  *We **need** more time.*
  *The windows **need** cleaning/to be cleaned.*

131   *must not* and *need not*

A *must not* expresses negative obligation and the speaker's authority:
  *You **must not** go* means 'I order you not to go'.
  Railway notice: *Passengers **must not** cross the line except by the footbridge.*

We can also use *must not* for emphatic advice:
  *You **mustn't** use a very hot iron on this shirt.*

B *you/he/they need not* in the present or future also expresses the speaker's authority, but here the speaker is giving someone permission not to do something, or saying that something is not necessary:
  Examiner: *You **needn't** make a long speech. Just talk for two minutes on one of these topics.*
  *You **needn't** pay me now. Next week will be soon enough.*

Exercise 131

▶ An exam supervisor is giving instructions to the candidates. Put in *must not* or *need not*.
  □ You *must not* talk during the exam.
  1 You ＿＿ attempt all the questions. Answer any six.
  2 You ＿＿ copy another candidate's answers.
  3 You ＿＿ write very long answers. One page for each question is plenty.
  4 You ＿＿ do the questions in any particular order.
  5 You ＿＿ look at your text books during the exam.

132 Absence of obligation

A   Forms

	SPEAKER'S AUTHORITY	EXTERNAL AUTHORITY
PRESENT	*need not*	*do/does not need to* *do/does not have to* *have/has not got to*
FUTURE	*need not*	*will/shall not need to* *will/shall not have to*
PAST		*did not need to* *did not have to* *had not got to*

B   Difference between *need not* and the other forms

need not expresses the speaker's authority:
> Mother to child: *You **needn't** eat it all.*
> Employer to typist: *You **needn't** finish it today.*

The other forms express external authority:
> *The children **don't have to** walk to school. There's a school bus.*
> *We **didn't have to** pay. The car park was free.*

With the first person we can often use either form:
> *I **needn't** go tomorrow* OR *I **won't have to** go.*
But for habitual actions *don't need to* or *don't have to* are more usual.

C   *haven't got to* and *don't need to/don't have to* compared

We use *haven't got to* chiefly for single actions:
> *We **haven't got to** decide now. We can decide later.*

But we can use *don't need to/don't have to* for both single and habitual actions:
> *We **don't need to/have to** decide now.* (single action)
> *He **doesn't need to/have to** pay rent.* (habitual action)

There is a similar difference between the past forms, so *didn't need to/didn't have to* is more useful than *hadn't got to*.

Exercise 132

▶ Bill, the manager, is telling a new employee, Fred, about the job. Bill's secretary, Mary, is there too. Put in *needn't* or *don't have to*.

☐ Bill: You *needn't* call me 'sir'. We use first names here, don't we, Mary?

1 Mary: Oh yes, you ____ call him 'sir'. He's Bill.

2 Bill: You ____ work 9 to 5; if you prefer you can work 10 to 6 or 8 to 4, like Mary.

3 Mary: If you work 8 to 4 you ____ travel in the rush hour.

4 Bill: You ____ do overtime unless you wish.

5 Mary: This means that you ____ work on Saturdays.

6 Bill: Oh, and you ____ go out for lunch. We have a very good canteen.

133   *need, must* and *have to* in the interrogative

A Forms

	ASKING THE AUTHORITY	ASKING SOMEONE ELSE
PRESENT	*need I?*	*do I?/does he need to?*
	must I?	*do I/does he have to?*
		have I/has he got to?
FUTURE	*need I?*	*will I need to?*
	must I?	*will I have to?*
PAST	*did he need to?*	
	did he have to?	
	had he got to?	

B *need I?* and *must I?*

Note possible answers to *need I/must I* questions:
    Need I go? ~ *Yes, you **must*** OR *No, you **needn't**.*
    Must I go? ~ *Yes, you **must*** OR *No, you **needn't**.*

C Note answers to the other forms:
    Will he have to pay? ~ *Yes, he **will*** OR *No, he **won't**.*

134 *needn't have done*

We use this form to show that an action which was done was unnecessary:

I've brought sandwiches. ~ *You **needn't have brought** them. We're going to have lunch at a hotel.*

Sometimes we combine this *needn't have* construction with *could* + perfect infinitive:

I walked all the way. ~ *You **needn't have walked**. You **could have taken** a bus.*

Exercise 134

▶ Complete these replies in a similar way to the example. In each case the second speaker thinks that the first action was unnecessary.

  □ I've typed it again. ~ You *needn't have typed* it again. I'd made a photocopy.

  1 I've ironed my shirt. ~ You ____ it. It's a drip-dry shirt.
  2 I've put 50p in the parking meter. ~ You ____ in any money. Parking is free on Sunday.
  3 I've ordered a taxi. ~ You ____ one. We can go by bus.
  4 He boiled the water first. ~ He ____ it. The water here is quite safe.
  5 They bought a new one. ~ They ____ a new one. They could have repaired the old one.
  6 I've brought my sleeping bag. ~ You ____ it. We're going to stay in a hotel.

18   Deduction and assumption

135 *must* and *can't/couldn't* for deduction

A We use *must* + present infinitive (*must be, must have, must know* etc.) for deduction about the present:

*He **must be** very rich. He has just bought a second Rolls Royce.*
I asked Ann Jones. ~ *Who's Ann Jones?* ~ *You **must know** Ann; she works in the canteen.*

You must know Ann means 'I feel sure that you know her'.

B We use *must* + perfect infinitive (*must have been, must have had, must have known* etc.) for deduction about the past:

> *Tom was the only one who knew how to open the safe. ~ But now Ann knows. ~ Then Tom **must have told** her.*
>
> *He **must have come** by taxi. There are no buses today.*
>
> *Where's my umbrella? I had it when I got into the bus. ~ You **must have left** it on the bus, then.*

C We use *can't/couldn't* + present infinitive for negative deduction about the present:
> *I'm tired. ~ You **can't be** tired already. We've only walked two miles.*

We can normally use either *can't* or *couldn't* here. But *couldn't* is necessary after a past tense:
> *He said she **couldn't be** tired already.*

D We use *can't/couldn't* + perfect infinitive for negative deduction about the past:
> *Perhaps Bill repaired it himself. ~ Bill **can't/couldn't have repaired** it. He knows nothing about cars.*

As above, *couldn't* is necessary after a past tense:
> *She knew that he **couldn't have carried** it by himself. It was much too heavy.*

Exercise 135

▶ Put in *must* + one of the verbs from the list: *spend, have, drive, know*

☐ I'm 65 and I've lived here all my life. ~ You *must know* the area very well.

1 She always looks very elegant. ~ She _____ a lot of money on clothes.

2 Which of us has the keys? ~ I haven't got them, so you _____ them.

3 He says that the journey only takes him half an hour by car. ~ He _____ very fast.

▶ Put in *must* + perfect infinitive of one of the verbs from the list: *switch, have, let, know*

    4   They didn't break in. ~ Then someone ____ them in.

    5   The alarm wires weren't cut. ~ Someone ____ the alarm off.

    6   They opened the safe without damaging it. ~ They ____ keys.

    7   When they came out the police were waiting for them. ~ The police ____ that there was going to be a bank raid.

▶ Put in *can't/couldn't* + the present infinitive of a verb in the previous sentence:

    ☐   Is it a scorpion? ~ No, it *can't/couldn't be* a scorpion. We don't have them in this country.

    8   He gets a good salary, I suppose? ~ He ____ a good salary yet; he's only a junior.

    9   Does he know the town well? ~ He ____ it well. He's only been there twice.

    10   Does she still have time to play tennis? ~ She ____ much time for tennis now. She has a large family to look after.

136 *will* and *should* for assumption

A For assumptions about the present we use *will/should* + present or continuous infinitive.

1 *will* + present infinitive (of non-deliberate actions only):
    He'll know the address. (I'm sure that he knows it.)
    Similarly:
    He won't know it. (I'm sure that he doesn't know it.)

2 *will* + continuous infinitive:
    He'll be waiting for us. (I'm sure he is waiting for us.)

3 *should*, affirmative, or *shouldn't be* + adjective is possible also. But assumptions with *should* are less confident than assumptions with *will*:
    They'll be on the beach by now. (I'm sure that they are on the beach.)
    They should be there by now. (I expect that they are.)

B For assumptions about the past we use *will/should* + perfect infinitive:
    The plane will have landed by now. (I'm sure that it has landed.)

*The plane **should have landed** by now.* (I expect that it has
We can use *will* and *should* here with deliberate actions.

C *ought* could replace *should* in A and B, but is less usual.

Exercise 136

▶ Replace the clause in CAPITALS by *will* or *should* + infinitive.
(Sentence 3 requires a perfect infinitive; sentence 5 requires a
continuous infinitive.)
- □ (Midnight on Sunday) Don't ring now. I'M SURE HE'S in
  bed.   *He'll be in bed.*
- □ (8 a.m. on Monday) Ring now. I EXPECT HE'S up by now.
  He should be up by now.
1 (6 p.m.) I'M SURE TOM IS NOT at home now.
2 I'M SURE HE'S STILL in his office.   (put *still* before *be*)
3 (7 p.m.) Do you think he's still in his office? ~
  No, I EXPECT HE HAS FINISHED by now.
4 HE'S PROBABLY on the train home.
5 I'M SURE HIS WIFE IS WAITING at the station with the car.

19   *dare* and *used*

137   *dare*

A *to dare* means 'to have the courage (to do something)':
*She **didn't dare** to interrupt him.* (She hadn't the
courage to interrupt him.)

We use it chiefly in the negative. The interrogative is
less common and the affirmative is hardly ever used
except as shown in C1 below.

B The form is *dare* for all persons in the present, *dared* in
the past. For negative and interrogative we can use
modal forms with a bare infinitive:
*He **dare not/dared not** complain.*
*How **dare** you read my diary!* (see C below)
or ordinary verb forms with full infinitive:
*He **doesn't/didn't dare** to complain.*
***Did** anyone **dare** to object to your scheme?*

But we often omit the '*to*' of the infinitive, especially with a negative verb:

*He **didn't dare** complain.*

Similarly with *will/would + dare*:

*He **wouldn't dare** (to) tell the truth.*

C Some special uses

1 *I dare say* (or *I daresay*)

This can mean 'I suppose':

*I **daresay** they'll serve lunch on the plane.*

or 'I accept what you say (but it doesn't make any difference)':

Patient: *But I clean my teeth twice a day!*
Dentist: *I **daresay** (you do) but you don't clean them properly.*

2 *How dare you!*

We seldom use *dare* + subject except in *how dare you/he/ they!*, which is an expression of indignation.

***How dare you** open my letters!* (I am angry with you for opening them.)

D *dare* (= challenge)

to dare someone to do something means 'to challenge him to do it'. The action always requires courage:

*Why did he try to cross the river when the ice was so thin? ~ Another boy **dared** him to do it.*

Exercise 137

▶ Ann and Tom are talking about a friend who is unhappy in his job but doesn't want to lose it. He is rather a timid character. Ann does not know this. Imagine you are Tom. Answer Ann, using *doesn't* or *didn't dare to*.

☐ Ann: *He applied for promotion, I suppose.*
  Tom: *Oh no, he didn't dare to apply for promotion.*

1 He asked for a rise, I suppose. ~ *Oh no, he____.*
2 He complained, I suppose. ~ *____.*
3 He refused to do overtime, I suppose. ~ *____.*
4 He goes home early sometimes, I suppose. (omit 'sometimes') ~ *____.*
5 He takes a weekend off occasionally, I suppose. (omit 'occasionally') ~ *____.*

138 *used to*

A Form

used to has past forms only. It has no present tense.

The affirmative is *used* for all persons. The negative is
used not/usedn't. But *did* forms are also possible in speech:
> *he didn't use to   did he use to?   didn't he use to?*

After all *used* forms we use the full infinitive.

B Use

1 To express a discontinued habit/routine or a past
situation which contrasts with the present:
> *He **used to** cycle to work. Now he drives.*
> *We **used to** have a railway station. But they closed it down.*

2 To describe someone's routine or pattern of action
during a certain period in the past:
> *Every morning the campers **used to** rush down to the river
> for a swim. Then they **used to** cook an enormous breakfast.*

would can replace *used to* in the examples above:
> *the campers **would** rush . . .   they **would** cook . . .*

Remember that *used to* has no present tense. So for
present habits or routines we must use the present
simple tense of the main verb.

Exercise 138

▶ Ann is talking to Bill about Tony, who was once very rich. Bill
also is much poorer than he used to be. Imagine you are Bill.
Answer in the way shown.
> ☐ Ann: Tony gave marvellous parties, didn't he?
>   Bill: *Yes, he did. I used to give marvellous parties too.*
1 Tony drank champagne every night, didn't he? ~ _____.
2 He drove a Rolls Royce, didn't he? ~ _____.
3 He went to the Bahamas every year, didn't he? ~ _____.

▶ Replace the verbs in CAPITALS by *would* (*'d*) + infinitive:
When the children were young we used to spend two weeks
every year at a holiday camp. We (☐) WENT/*would go* there by
train and the holiday camp bus (4) MET/_____ us at the
station. The children loved it. They (5) SWAM/_____ every
morning and in the afternoon the camp staff (6) ORGANIZED/
_____ games for them. Sometimes we (7) PLAYED/_____
tennis; sometimes we (8) SUNBATHED/_____.

139 *be used to* and *to use*

Do not confuse the form *used to*, described above, with

1 *be used to* + noun/pronoun/gerund (see also 203):
     *I am **used to** queues/to standing in queues.* (I have done this a good many times so I don't mind it/it doesn't annoy me.)

2 the ordinary verb *to use* (= make use of):
     *We **use** natural fertilizers, not chemicals.*

20   The present tenses

140 Present continuous: form

A We form this tense with *am/are/is* + present participle.

AFFIRMATIVE	NEGATIVE
I am/I'm working	*I am/I'm not working*
you are/you're working	*you are not/you aren't/you're not working*
he is/he's working	*he is not/he isn't/he's not working*
she is/she's working	*she is not/she isn't/she's not working*
it is/it's working	*it is not/it isn't/it's not working*
we are/we're working	*we are not/we aren't/we're not working*
they are/they're working	*they are not/they aren't/they're not working*

Interrogative: *am I working? are you working? is he working?* etc.
Negative interrogative: *aren't I working? aren't you working? isn't he working?* etc.

In conversation we often contract *is* and sometimes *are* after *how? what? where? who? why?*:
What's he doing?   Who're you meeting?

B The present participle is infinitive + *ing*:
help + ing = helping   see + ing = seeing

But note some spelling changes:

love, loving; drive, driving	We drop a final single *e*.
run, running; stop, stopping	We double a final consonant after a single vowel.
be\gin, beginning	We do the same with longer verbs when the last syllable is stressed.
\enter, entering	But we make no change when the last syllable is unstressed.
travel, travelling	We double a final *l* after a single vowel.

(See also 265–266, 269.)

C When we have two actions by the same subject we can express the second action by a participle only:
*He is singing and **dancing** in the new show.*

Exercise 140

▶ Write the present participles of these verbs:

☐ agree   *agreeing*

1	carry	7	marry	13	shop	19	swim
2	cry	8	permit	14	sit	20	take
3	eat	9	play	15	stand	21	travel
4	forget	10	prefer	16	stare	22	win
5	have	11	quarrel	17	steal		
6	like	12	see	18	stop		

141 Present continuous: use

A For an action happening now:
*Tom's **watching** television.*

B For an action happening around now but not
necessarily at the moment of speaking:
> *I'm painting* the door. (But I'm not painting at the
> moment. I'm having a rest.)

C With *always* for a frequently repeated action:
> *He's always taking* exams. (He takes exams very often/
> too often.)

or for an action which appears to be continuous:
> *He's always studying*. (He spends a lot of time/too
> much time studying.)

These actions usually annoy the speaker or seem unreason-
able to him. If we use the first person, *I'm always losing my
keys*, it is often an accidental action.

D For a definite arrangement in the near future:
> *I'm playing* tennis next Sunday.

This is the most usual way of expressing immediate
plans (see also 166).

Exercise 141

▶ Put the verbs into the present continuous:
- □ Where *is Ann working* (Ann/work)?
- 1 Ann ____ (work) in a travel agent's at the moment.
- 2 Where ____ (you/work)?
- 3 I ____ (not/do) anything at the moment. I ____ (look) for a job.
- 4 Jack and Jill ____ (wait) to hear their exam results.
- 5 Meanwhile they ____ (help) their father in his shop.
- 6 He ____ (not/pay) them very much.
- 7 Why isn't Tom here? What ____ (he/do)?
- 8 He ____ (talk) to Ann on the phone. He ____ (make) arrangements for tonight.
- 9 They ____ (go) to a concert together.
- 10 But he ____ (not/pay) for her. She ____ (pay) for herself.

142 Verbs we don't normally use in the continuous tenses

We use the continuous tenses chiefly for deliberate
actions. With some verbs, therefore, we don't normally

use continuous forms. Instead we use the simple forms:
the present simple instead of the present continuous, the
past simple instead of the past continuous, etc.

We can group these verbs as follows.

A Verbs of the senses (involuntary actions)

feel, hear, see, smell; also *notice*

*Do you **hear** anything? ~ Yes, I **hear** footsteps.*

But note that *see* (meaning 'meet by appointment'), *see
about, see to,* and *see* someone *home/off/out* are deliberate
actions, so we can use them in the continuous:
*Where's Tom? ~ He's **seeing** Ann home.*

Note also that *feel* (= touch), *listen, look* and *watch* are
deliberate actions, so we can say:
*Bill's **watching** a match on TV.*

B Certain link verbs

appear, feel, look, seem, smell, sound, taste

*Your case **feels** heavy.   The salad **looks** good.*
*The milk **smells** sour.   The soup **tastes** salty.*

But all except *seem* can also be deliberate actions and
then used in the continuous:
*I'm just **tasting** the soup to see if it's hot enough.*

C Verbs expressing emotions and feelings

care, care for (= like), *dislike, fear, hate, like, love, mind*
(= care), *want, wish*

*I **don't care** for murder stories. ~ Oh, I **like** them.*

But we can use *long for* (= wish for) and *enjoy* in the
continuous: *I'm **longing for** the holidays.*

D Verbs of mental activity

agree, believe, expect (= think), *feel* (= think), *forget,
know, mean, remember, see* (= understand), *think* (=
have an opinion)

*Do you **believe** him? ~ Yes, I **think** he's telling the truth.*

But we can use *think* in the continuous when we are not
giving or asking for an opinion:
   Tom *is thinking* of emigrating.

We can also use *expect* (= wait for) in the continuous:
   I'm *expecting* a letter.

E Verbs of possession

   belong, own, owe, possess

   Who *does* the house *belong* to? ~ The bank *owns* it.

F The auxiliaries, except *be* and *have* in some uses

G Certain other verbs

   concern, consist, contain, hold (= contain), *keep*
   (= continue), *matter, need*

   Our tinned fruit *contains* no preservatives.
   The soup *doesn't need* any more salt.

> **Exercise 142**

▶ Put the verbs into the present continuous or the present
   simple:
   □ Bill: Lunch will be ready in a minute: We *are having*
      (have) soup.
   1 Mary: It ____ (smell) good.
   2 Bill: Ann ____ (just / taste) it to see if it ____ (need) more
      salt.
   3 Bill: I'm afraid she ____ (think) it does. She ____ (look)
      for the salt.
   4 Mary: I ____ (not / like) too much salt so I'll have mine
      now, please.
   5 Mary: Thanks. It ____ (look) lovely. It ____ (taste) good
      too.
   6 Bill: Ann, it really ____ (not need) any more salt!

143 Present simple: form

A The affirmative form is the infinitive with *s* added in
   the third person singular.
   Negative: *do/does not* + infinitive.
   Interrogative: *do I? does he?* etc. + infinitive.

AFFIRMATIVE	NEGATIVE
I work	I do not/I don't work
you work	you do not/you don't work
he works	he does not/he doesn't work
she works	she does not/she doesn't work
it works	it does not/it doesn't work
we work	we do not/we don't work
they work	they do not/they don't work

Interrogative: *do I work? do you work? does he work?* etc.
Negative interrogative: *don't I work? don't you work?*
doesn't he work? etc.

B Note the spelling of the third person singular. We add *es*,
instead of *s* alone, to verbs ending in *ss, sh, ch, x* and *o*:
  I kiss, he kisses   *I push, he pushes*   *I watch, he watches*

With verbs ending in a consonant + *y*, we change the *y*
to *i* and add *es*:
  I carry, he carries   *I fly, he flies*

But verbs ending in a vowel + *y* follow the usual rule:
  obey, obeys   *say, says*

Exercise 143

▶ Put the verbs in brackets into the present simple. Watch the
spelling.
Every day Bill (□) *goes* (go) home by train and usually (1) ____
(catch) the 6.15. He always (2) ____ (hurry) to the station
because if he misses the 6.15, he (3) ____ (have) to wait an
hour for the next train. When he (4) ____ (get) home he
(5) ____ (relax) with a drink and (6) ____ (watch) a TV programme. He (7) ____ (say) that this is the best part of the day.

144 Present simple: use

A For habitual actions:
  *Post offices **sell** stamps.   Bees **make** honey.*

This does not mean that the action is happening at the
moment of speaking. If we want to make this clear we

must add a verb in the present continuous:
  *Bill usually **walks** to work, but he **isn't walking** today
  because it's raining.*

We often use time expressions here, like *always, never,
sometimes, usually, every day/week, once/twice a year* etc.:
  *He **always** gets up early.   **On Mondays** she goes shopping.*
and also time clauses:
  ***When(ever)** he needs money he asks me.*

B In newspaper headlines for past events:
  *CAR BOMB **KILLS** TWO*

C To describe the actions in a book, play etc.:
  *In the film the murderer **hides** the body in a cellar.*
  and in radio commentaries when describing events:
  *McEnroe **serves** to Lendl. Lendl **returns** it . . .*

D For a planned future action or series of planned future
  actions:
  *We **fly** to Venice and **join** our ship there. The ship **sails** . . .*

E When giving or asking for information from books,
  notices etc. or from very recently received letters:
  *What **does** that notice **say**? ~ It **warns** people not to light
  fires.*
  *I've just got a letter from Tom. ~ Oh, what **does** he **say**?*

F Instead of the continuous tense with verbs which
  cannot be used in the continuous: *I **know** what he **wants**.*

▷ For the use of this tense in time clauses, see 255 B, C2;
  in conditional clauses, see 184.

  Exercise 144

▶ Put the verbs in brackets into the present simple or present
  continuous:
  Tom and I both (□) *belong* (belong) to a big engineering firm.
  I (1) ____ (work) in the design section; Tom (2) ____ (work) in
  the sales section. He often (3) ____ (go) abroad on business. At
  the moment he (4) ____ (travel) round America, and next
  month he (5) ____ (meet) a customer in Toronto. He (6) ____
  (like) travelling and (7) ____ (enjoy) his present trip, but he
  always (8) ____ (feel) happy to get back home.

21   The past and perfect tenses

145   Past continuous: form

We form this tense with *was/were* + present participle.

AFFIRMATIVE	NEGATIVE
I was working	*I was not/I wasn't working*
you were working	*you were not/you weren't working*
he was working	*he was not/he wasn't working*
she was working	*she was not/she wasn't working*
it was working	*it was not/it wasn't working*
we were working	*we were not/we weren't working*
they were working	*they were not/they weren't working*

Interrogative: *was I working? were you working? was he working?* etc.
Negative interrogative: *wasn't I working? weren't you working? wasn't he working?* etc.

(For the spelling of the present participle, see 140 B, 265–266, 269.)

146   Past continuous: use

A   We use this tense chiefly for past actions which continued for some time but whose exact limits are not known and are not important. We can show this in a diagram by:

where ——— indicates the action and ━ ━ ━ ━ ━ the uncertainty about times of starting and finishing.

B   We can use it without a time expression to indicate gradual development:
   *It **was getting** darker.*   *The wind **was rising**.*

C   We can use it with a point in time to indicate an action
which began before that point and probably continued
after it:
At 8 o'clock he was having breakfast.

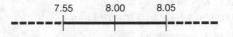

This implies that he had started breakfast before 8.
If we say *At 8 o'clock he had breakfast* we mean that he
started breakfast at 8.

D   If we replace the time expression with a verb in the past
simple, *When I arrived he was watching TV*, we mean that
the action in the past continuous started before the action
in the past simple and probably continued after it.

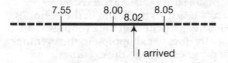

Compare this with a combination of two past simple tenses:
When he saw me (first action), *he turned off the TV*
(second action).

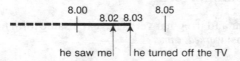

E   We use the past continuous tense in descriptions. Note
the combination of description (past continuous) with
narrative (past simple):
*Tom was reading, Ann was knitting. Suddenly the doorbell
rang. They both looked up.*

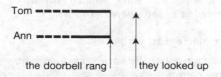

F   We also use this tense as a past equivalent of the present continuous:

> *He said, 'I'm living in Rome.'*
> *He said that he **was living** in Rome.*

> *'I'm packing. I'm leaving tonight.'*
> *He **was packing**. He **was leaving** that night.*

> *He is always complaining.*
> *He **was** always **complaining**.*

G   Some verbs cannot be used in the continuous tenses (142).

Exercise 146

▶   Make negative comments on the statements and then ask questions as shown:

    □   He usually reads in the evenings.
       He wasn't reading when I saw him yesterday.
       Was he reading when you saw him yesterday?

1   He usually practises the piano in the evenings.
2   They usually play chess in the evenings.
3   She usually does her shopping in the evenings.
4   He usually goes home in the evenings.
5   They usually watch TV in the evenings.
6   She usually writes letters in the evenings.

147   Past simple: form

A   Regular and irregular verbs have the same form for all persons: *worked, came*.

B   Affirmative of regular verbs

We add *ed* to the infinitive: *work, worked; start, started*. But we add only *d* to infinitives ending in *e*: *love, loved*.

Examples of spelling changes when *ed* is added:
> *stop, stopped; travel, travelled* (140 B)
> *per'mit, per'mitted* BUT *'enter, 'entered* (140 B)
> *carry, carried* BUT *obey, obeyed* (143 B)

C   Affirmative of irregular verbs

Here the past tense usually varies: *give, gave; go, went*. For a list of some common examples, see inside covers.

D Negative of all verbs

We form this with *did not/didn't* + infinitive:
he stopped, he didn't stop   they went, they didn't go

E Interrogative of all verbs

We form this with *did* + subject + infinitive:
did he stop?   did they go?

Exercise 147

▶ Write the past simple of these verbs. Make spelling changes where necessary.
☐ answer   *answered*

1 apply	6 enter	11 obey	16 signal
2 bury	7 fit	12 occur	17 stay
3 cry	8 grab	13 play	18 stop
4 die	9 hurry	14 quarrel	19 travel
5 drop	10 knit	15 refer	20 try

▶ Now write the past simple of these irregular verbs:
☐ begin   *began*

21 break	26 cut	31 hear	36 put
22 bring	27 drink	32 keep	37 see
23 buy	28 feel	33 leave	38 shut
24 come	29 get	34 lie	39 wake
25 choose	30 go	35 pay	

148 Past simple: use

A We use the past simple for an action completed in the past at a definite time.

We may give the time:
*They **left** on Monday.   I **bought** it yesterday.*

Monday	Tuesday	Wednesday	Thursday (NOW)
↑ they left		↑ I bought it	

or ask about the time:
*When **did** you **see** him?*

    or it may be clear that the action happened at a definite time
    *Where **did** you **buy** your watch?   I **took** these photos in Seville.*
    or the time may be indicated by a statement in the
    present perfect:
    *I've just been for a walk. ~ **Did** you **go** along the river?*

B We use the past simple for an action which occupied a
    period of time now finished:
    *He **played** for our team for two years.* (He doesn't play now.)

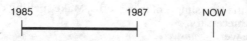

    or occurred at a moment in a period of time now
    finished:
    ***Did** you ever **see** Maria Callas? ~ Yes, I **saw** her once.*

    (Here ——— represents the lifetime of Maria Callas and
    ↑ represents the action.)

C We use the past simple for past habits:
    *He never **ate** meat.* (See also *used to*, 138.)

▷ For the use of this form in conditional sentences, see
   185; after *as if/though, it is time*, see 217; after *I wish, if only*,
   see 228 C; and after *I would sooner/rather*, see 226 B.

Exercise 148

▶ Put the verbs into the past simple:
   □ John: I've lost my car keys.
       Liz: When *did you see* (you/see) them last?
  1 John: I ____ (have) them when I ____ (come) in last night.
  2 I ____ (take) them out of my pocket.
  3 I ____ (put) them on the table.
  4 Liz: Why (you/____ not hang) them on the hook as usual?
  5 John: Well, Bill ____ (ring) just then and ____ (want)
      advice about his car.

▶ Now put the verbs in brackets into the past continuous or past simple:
When I first (6) _____ (meet) Tom, he (7) _____ (work) in a bank and (8) _____ (share) a flat with his brother Paul. But Paul (9) _____ (get) married six months ago and (10) _____ (move out). Tom (11) _____ (ring) me last week and (12) _____ (tell) me this. He also (13) _____ (say) that he (14) _____ (look) for a smaller flat and (15) _____ (try) to find something in Chelsea. I (16) _____ (advise) him to try Battersea.

149 Present perfect: form

We form this tense with *have/has* + past participle.
In regular verbs the past participle has the same form as the past simple (147 A–B). In irregular verbs the past participles vary (see inside covers).

AFFIRMATIVE	NEGATIVE
I have/I've worked	*I have not/I haven't/I've not worked*
you have/you've worked	*you have not/you haven't/you've not worked*
he has/he's worked	*he has not/he hasn't/he's not worked*
she has/she's worked	*she has not/she hasn't/she's not worked*
it has/it's worked	*it has not/it hasn't/it's not worked*
we have/we've worked	*we have not/we haven't/we've not worked*
they have/they've worked	*they have not/they haven't/they've not worked*

Interrogative: *have I worked? have you worked? has he worked?* etc.
Negative interrogative: *haven't I worked? haven't you worked? hasn't he worked?* etc.

We can contract *have* and *has* after *how? what? where? why?*:
    Where've you been?   What's happened?

150 Present perfect: use with *just* for a recently completed action

We use this form chiefly in the affirmative:
*He has **just** gone out.* (He went out a few minutes ago.)

just must come after *have/has*.

Exercise 150

▶ Write answers to these questions. Use the present perfect.
□   Did Tom tell you this a long time ago? ~
    No, *he's (he has)* ~~only~~ *just told me.*
1   Did they go out some time ago? ~ No, ____ .
2   Did the train leave some time ago? ~ No, ____ .
3   Did Tom buy the house some time ago? ~ No, ____ it.
4   Did you send the letter some time ago? ~ No, ____ it.

151 Present perfect: use for past actions whose time is not definite

A   We use the present perfect chiefly for recent actions:
    *I've lost my watch. **Have you seen** it anywhere?*

    But if we give the time we must use the past simple:
    *I **lost** my watch yesterday.*

    Note possible answers to questions in the present
    perfect:
    Has** the plane **landed**? ~ Yes, it **has**/No, it **hasn't BUT
    *Yes, it **landed** ten minutes ago.* (past simple)

B   We can also use the present perfect for actions which
    occurred some time ago, provided that there is still a
    connection with the present, that is, provided the
    action could be repeated:
    *Bill **has won** several races on this horse.*

    We can use this tense if Bill and the horse are still
    running in races. But if the horse has stopped racing or
    Bill has stopped riding we would say:
    *Bill **won** several races on this horse.*
    Here we use the past simple because we are thinking of
    a completed period.

▶ **Exercise 151**

George is in a lift which is stuck between the fourth and fifth floors of an office block. Luckily a cleaner hears him shouting. Put the verbs into the present perfect or past simple.

☐ Cleaner: How long *have you been* (you/be) here?
1 George: I ____ (be) here for an hour!
2 Cleaner: ____ (you/try) the emergency bell?
3 George: Yes, I ____ (try) it at once but I ____ (not/hear) anything. I don't think the bell works.
4 Cleaner: The last time this ____ (happen) I ____ (get) the engineer. But I think he ____ (leave) the building already.

152 Present perfect: use with *this morning* etc.

We can use the present perfect with *this morning/ afternoon/week/month, today* etc. when we use these expressions to mean an incomplete period.

A *this morning* can be a complete or incomplete period. *this morning* indicates an incomplete period only when it is still morning at the time of speaking. Up to 12 noon we can say *I haven't seen Tom this morning*. After 12 noon we will say *I didn't see Tom this morning*. We use the past simple here because *this morning* is now a completed period.

Similarly with *this afternoon*. Up to about 5 p.m. we can say *He hasn't phoned this afternoon* but after 5 p.m. we must say *He didn't phone this afternoon*.

B We use the present perfect with an incomplete period of time chiefly for an action which took place at some undefined time during this period.

If we are thinking of a certain moment or of a certain part of our period we use the past simple. Imagine that my alarm clock usually goes off at 6 a.m. If one day it doesn't go off, I might say at breakfast *My alarm clock didn't go off this morning*.

Similarly if our postman usually comes between 8 and 9 a.m. we can, up to 9 a.m., say *Has the postman come this morning?* But after 9 a.m. we must say *Did the postman come this morning?*

C   We use the present perfect in this way mainly in the
    negative and interrogative.

    For single affirmative statements + *this morning/today*
    etc. we more often use the past simple:
        He **left** this morning.   They **arrived** today.

    But we can use the present perfect for repeated actions:
        I've **written** six letters this morning.

Exercise 152

▶   Put the verbs into the present perfect or past simple:
    ☐   Tom and Bill *haven't been* (not/be) to any lectures this week.
    1   They ____ (not/go) to any lectures last week either.
    2   It's 11.30. Bill ____ (not/open) a book this morning.
    3   Bill ____ (not write) to his parents this week.
    4   It's 3 p.m. Tom ____ (not/hand in) his essay this morning.
    5   Tom ____ (not/pay) this month's rent yet.

153   Present perfect: use with *ever, never, always*

A   We can use the present perfect with *ever, never* and
    always when these adverbs refer to an incomplete
    period.

    Imagine we are talking to the pilot of our plane. We
    might ask him:
        Have you **ever fallen** asleep at the controls?
    But if we are talking to a retired pilot we would use the
    past simple:
        Did you **ever fall** asleep at the controls?

B   We can use the present perfect with *always* and *never* for
    habitual actions:
        I've **always arrived** on time. I've **never missed** my train.

C   Note also the use of the superlative with the present
    perfect + *ever*:
        This is the **worst** storm we've **ever had**. (24 C)

Exercise 153

▶ Put the verbs in brackets into the present perfect or past
simple. Use *have* or *did* to fill the other spaces.

□ Bill and Tom are talking about John, who *has just won*
(just/win) a big competition.

1 Bill: ____ (you/ever/see) him play?
2 Tom: Yes, I ____ . I ____ (see) him at Wimbledon last year.
3 Bill: I ____ (never/be) to any of his matches but I ____
    (see) him on TV.
4 Tom: His sister ____ (play) in competitions till she ____
    (get) married. She ____ (not play) at all since then.
5 Bill: ____ (you/ever/see) her play?
6 Tom: I ____ once.

154 Present perfect: use for an action which lasts throughout an incomplete period

We can use the present perfect with time expressions
like *for, since* (81 B–C), *all day/night, all the time, always*.

A The action begins in the past and usually continues
after the time of speaking in the present:
*He **has lived** here for six years.* (He is still here.)

```
    1   2   3   4   5   6 (NOW)
    |   |   |   |   |   |
────┼───┼───┼───┼───┼───┼──────
```

Compare this with: *He **lived** here for six years.*

```
1982                    1988   NOW
|                        |      |
├────────────────────────┤      
```

which means that the action has finished. (He went
away or died.)

B Sometimes, however, the action finishes at the time of
speaking:
Ann: *Hello, Tom! I **haven't seen** you for ages.*
But the period of 'not seeing Tom' finished at the time
of speaking.

C We can use *think* and *know* as shown in A above:
*I **have known** Tom for years.*

But with actions of the type shown in B above we use
the past simple:
*Hello, Tom! I haven't seen you for ages. I **thought** you were
abroad* OR *I **didn't know** you were in London.*

D Questions and answers of the type:
*How long **have** you **been** here? ~ I've **been** here six months.*
may be followed by questions in the present perfect.
The answers will be in the present perfect if no time is
given; if the time is given the answers will be in the
past simple:
*Have you **been** to any concerts? ~ Yes, I **have**/No, I **haven't***
OR *Yes, I **went** to the Festival Hall last night.*

Exercise 154

► Comment on these statements in the way shown:
  ☐ (It's Friday.) I've got a headache. It started on Monday.
    So you've had a headache for four days.
  ☐ (It's 1989.) I last saw a doctor in 1983.
    So you haven't seen a doctor for six years.
  1 (It's 1987.) I'm a vegetarian. I began this diet in 1985.
  2 (It's August.) I wear glasses. I began wearing them in May.
  3 (It's the last week of May.) I last took sleeping pills during
     the first week of May.
  4 (It's 1990.) I last smoked a cigarette in 1985.

155 Present perfect: use with *for* and *since*

A *for* + a period of time (*for two days, for a week* etc.)

We use *for* with the present perfect for an incomplete
period of time:
*I **have taught** here for five years.* (I am still teaching here.)

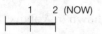

```
    1    2    3    4    5  (NOW)
    |    |    |    |    |
```

or for a period which continues up to the time of speaking:
*I **haven't ridden** a horse for two years.* (But I'm riding now.)

```
    1    2  (NOW)
    |    |
```

We use *for* with the past simple for a complete period:
    *He **typed** his own letters **for** a week.* (Then he engaged a
    secretary.)

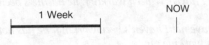

We don't use *for* before expressions beginning with *all*:
    *I've **been** here all day.*

B   *since* + a point in time (*since five o'clock, since then* etc.)

since + a point in time means 'from that point to the
time of speaking'. We always use it with a perfect
tense, except as shown in C below.
    *He **hasn't ridden since** his accident/**since** he broke his arm.*

since then is often useful:
    *He had a bad fall. He **hasn't ridden since then**.*

C   *it is* + a period of time + *since*

The following four sentences all mean the same:
    *It is two years **since** I've played the piano.*
    *It is two years **since** I (last) played the piano.*
    *I haven't played the piano **for** two years.*
    I last played the piano two years ago.
Note that we use an affirmative verb in the first two
sentences.

Exercise 155

▶ Put in *for* or *since*:
    ☐   I've been standing here *since* 2 o'clock.
  1   The man behind me has been waiting ____ longer than I
       have.
  2   And it's been raining ____ the last ten minutes.
  3   Buses have been running late ____ they introduced the
       new timetable.
  4   Fares have gone up twice ____ March.
  5   Regular passengers have been complaining ____ quite a
       long time.

156 Present perfect continuous: form

We form this tense with *have been* + present participle.
Affirmative: *I have/I've been working, he has/he's been working* etc.
Negative: *I have not/I haven't been working, he has not/he hasn't been working* etc.
Interrogative: *have I been working? has he been working?* etc.
Negative interrogative: *haven't I been working? hasn't he been working?* etc.

157 Present perfect continuous: use

We use this tense for an action which begins in the past and is still continuing:

I've been looking for a job for two years.

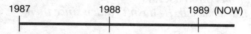

or has just finished:

Oh, here's my key! I've been looking for it all day!

We can use this tense with or without a time expression.

Certain verbs, *know, hate, love* etc. (142), cannot be used in the continuous forms. But we can use the present perfect continuous with *hear* and *want*.

158 Present perfect or present perfect continuous?

A For actions which last throughout an incomplete period we can, with certain verbs, use either form. We can say:
    *He **has played** for our club for two years* OR
    *He **has been playing** for our club for two years.*

Verbs we can use in this way include: *expect, hope, learn, lie, live, look, play, rain, snow, stand, study, teach, wait, want, work.*

B We can sometimes replace a repeated action in the simple present perfect by the continuous form. We can say:

*I've **written** three letters this morning* OR
*I've **been writing** letters.*

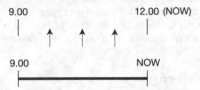

Note that the action in the second sentence appears to be a continuous action. We do not use the present perfect continuous if we mention the number of actions or the number of objects etc.

C There is a difference between a single action in the present perfect and an action in the present perfect continuous. *I've painted the door* means that I did this fairly recently, but *I've been painting the door* is an action of the type shown in 157 above. Perhaps I'm still painting. Perhaps I have just finished painting it.

So the present perfect stands for a completed action; the present perfect continuous expresses an action which may be complete or incomplete.

Exercise 158

▶ Make questions about the statements. Use the present perfect or present perfect continuous.

- □ I've been writing letters. ~ How many *have you written?* ~ Six letters.
- □ Bill's been in the kitchen. ~ What *has he been doing?* ~ He's been washing the glasses.
1. I've been telling people about the party. ~ How many ____? ~ About five people.
2. Bob's been picking strawberries. ~ How many ____? ~ About three boxes.
3. Ann's been in the kitchen. ~ What ____? ~ She's been making mayonnaise.
4. Mary's been grilling sausages all morning. ~ How many ____? ~ About a hundred.

▶ Put the verbs in brackets into the present perfect or present perfect continuous:
  □ I *'ve mended* (mend) the broken plates. Here they are.
  □ I *'ve been mending* (mend) the broken plates. I haven't quite finished.
  5 I ____ (write) to Ann. Here's the letter.
  6 I ____ (write) to Ann. I'll finish it after tea.
  7 He ____ (paint) the seat. But he hasn't finished it yet.
  8 We ____ (cut up) the onions. You can start frying now.

159 Past perfect: form

A We form this tense with *had* + past participle.
Affirmative: *I had/I'd worked, he had/he'd worked* etc.
Negative: *I had not/I hadn't worked, he had not/he hadn't worked* etc.
Interrogative: *had I worked? had he worked?* etc.
Negative interrogative: *hadn't I worked? hadn't he worked?* etc.

B The past perfect is the past equivalent of both the present perfect and the past simple:

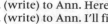

present simple: *work/works*

present perfect: *have/has worked*

past simple: *worked*

past perfect: *had worked*

160 Past perfect: use as a past equivalent of the present perfect

A *Tom's just left.* (150)
When I arrived Tom had just left.

B *We can't get into the house. I've lost the key.* (151)
We couldn't get into the house. I'd lost the key.

C *We've waited for weeks.* (We are still waiting). (154 A)
We had waited for weeks. (We were still waiting.)

*He **has lived** here all his life.* (But he is now leaving.) (154 B)
*He **had lived** there all his life.* (But he was now leaving.)

D We can use the past perfect with or without a time
expression.

Exercise 160

▶ Put the verbs in brackets into the past perfect:
  □ When I last met Paul he was feeling very depressed
    because recently everything *had gone* (go) wrong.
  1 His wife ____ (leave) him.
  2 He ____ (quarrel) with his son.
  3 He ____ (lose) his job.
  4 He ____ (crash) his car.
  5 He ____ (broke) his watch.
  6 His landlord ____ (put up) the rent.

161 Past perfect: use as a past equivalent of the past simple

When talking or writing about past events we normally
use the past simple tense. But we use the past perfect
tense when, from a time in the past, the speaker or
narrator looks back to an earlier action. This action may
occupy a period of time:

  *As a young man he **had been** a sailor and he liked talking
  about those days.*

or it may be a single action or a number of actions:

  *Bill was in hospital. He **had broken** his leg in a skiing accident.*

162 Past perfect continuous: form and use

A We form this tense with *had been* + present participle:
Affirmative: *I had/I'd been working, he had/he'd been
working* etc.
Negative: *I had not/I hadn't been working, he had not/he
hadn't been working* etc.
Interrogative: *had I been working? had he been working?* etc.
Negative interrogative: *hadn't I been working? hadn't he
been working?* etc.

B   We use this tense for an action which began before a time in the past and continued up to this point or beyond it:

> She **had been living** alone for many years.

Exercise 162

▶ Answer the questions:

□   When you first met her, had she just started to give lectures? ~
> *No, she'd been giving lectures for quite a long time.*

1   Had she just started to paint portraits? ~ ____.
2   Had she just started to sell her paintings? ~ ____.
3   Had she just started to diet? ~ ____.
4   Had she just started to look for a house? ~ ____.

163   Past perfect or past perfect continuous?

The relationship between these two forms is the same as the relationship between the present perfect and the present perfect continuous (158).

A   For actions of the type shown in 158 A, we can normally use either form. We can say:

> We expected him to speak French fluently, for he **had studied** it for six years OR he **had been studying** it for six years.

B   We can replace a series of actions in the past perfect by an apparently continuous action in the past perfect continuous (158 B):

> He **had made** six speeches and he was tired.
> He **had been making** speeches and he was tired.

C   There is a difference between a single action in the past perfect and an action in the past perfect continuous (158 C

> He **had painted** her portrait. He showed it to us. (The portrait was completed some time before he showed it.
> He **had been painting** her portrait. (He had only just finished or had not yet finished the portrait.)

22   The future

164   Future forms

A   There are a number of ways of expressing the future:
1 The present simple (165)
2 The present continuous (166)
3 *be going to* (167–169)
4 The future simple (170–171)
5 *will* for intention (172–174)
6 The future continuous (175)
7 The future perfect (176)
8 The future perfect continuous (177)

B   The meaning of 'future with intention'

When the subject wishes to do something and decides to do it, we express this wish + decision by a 'future with intention' form: *will* or *be going to*.

Other forms show future without intention. They merely state that an action will happen. We don't know whether or not the subject made the decision and we don't know what he thinks about it.

165   Present simple + a time expression

We use this form mainly for impersonal statements about future actions:
    School programme: *Next term starts on 12 September.*
    Museum attendant: *The museum closes in ten minutes.*

For personal statements we more often use the present continuous (166), but we sometimes say:
    I've got a job! I start on Monday.
and for a series of future actions, the present simple is neater:
    We leave at six and arrive in Paris at nine. We spend two days there and then fly on to Athens.

Exercise 165

▶ Put the verbs in brackets into the present simple tense. The meaning here is future.

Travel arrangements for a coming tour:

☐ The coach *leaves* (leave) Victoria at 8 a.m. tomorrow.
1 It ____ (arrive) in Dover at 9.30.
2 The coach then ____ (return) to London.
3 The passengers ____ (embark) on the ferry.
4 The ferry ____ (sail) at 12.00
5 and ____ (dock) in Calais at 1.00.
6 Then the passengers ____ (disembark) and ____ (board) the Paris train.

166 Present continuous + a time expression

A We use this form mainly for a definite arrangement in the near future:
    He's flying to Rome tomorrow. (He has booked his seat.)

B With certain verbs, for example *come, go, stay, do* and *have* (food/drink), we can use this form for a decision/plan only, without any definite arrangement:
    What are you doing this weekend? (What are your plans?) ~ *I'm not doing anything. I'm staying at home.*

C We do not use this form with verbs of the senses (*see* etc.) or with verbs such as *have* (= possess), *know* and *understand* (142). With these we must use *will/shall*:
    You will have time to do it tomorrow.

But *see* can also have other meanings (142 A). With these we can use the continuous tense:
    I'm seeing (= meeting) *the director tomorrow.* (We've arranged this.)
    Tom is seeing (= escorting) *Ann home after the party.* (He's arranged this.)

We can also use *have* for actions (108 B) in this way:
    I'm having a party next week.
and the *have* + object + past participle construction:
    We're having the piano tuned tomorrow.

(For *will* and the present continuous, see 172 B).

Exercise 166

▶ Imagine you are Tom, and this is your diary for next weekend:

Saturday
  9.00   Take children to zoo
 11.00   Golf with Bill
 11.30   Ann has driving lesson
  7.30   Concert in Festival Hall

Sunday
a.m.   Drive to Sevenoaks
       Lunch with Ann's parents
p.m.   Bill and Mary to supper

On Friday evening someone says, 'What are you both doing this weekend?' Answer, using the information from the diary.

☐ At 9 on Saturday we're taking the children to the zoo.
1 At 11 I ____.
2 At 11.30 Ann ____.
3 At 7.30 we ____.
4 On Sunday morning we ____.
5 We ____ with Ann's parents.
6 Bill and Mary ____.

167 *be going to*

A The form is *am/are/is going* + the full infinitive:
   I'm going to take some photographs.
   Are you going to repair it yourself?
   He isn't going to study Greek.

B We use this form for premeditated intention (168) and for prediction (169).

168 *be going to* for premeditated intention

A We use this form when the speaker mentions an intended future action, but the subject made the decision some time before the time of speaking:
   Ann (putting up a step-ladder): *I'm going to hang my new curtains.*
   Tom's bought a building site. *He's going to build a house.*

B   When we use this form we normally expect the action to happen fairly soon. We can use *be going* with or without a time expression.

C   We can use this form instead of the present continuous (166 A), i.e. Tom could say:
   I'm meeting Ann at Heathrow at 7.30 OR
   I'm going to meet Ann at Heathrow.
But if he says 'I'm meeting Ann' we know that he has arranged this with Ann. If he says 'I'm going to meet Ann' we are not certain. Perhaps Ann will be surprised.

D   We don't normally use *be going to* with the verbs *come* and *go*; we use the present continuous: *I'm coming, I'm going.*

▷   For comparison with *will* for intention, see 173.

169   *be going to* or *will* for prediction

A   We can use *be going to* when the speaker feels quite sure that an action will happen very soon. There are usually signs which make the speaker confident:
   Look at those clouds! It's going to rain.

We can also use *will* when we believe that an action will happen (171).

B   With impersonal statements we can often use either form:
   It's going to be/It will be difficult to finish on time.

But note the following examples. Before a race Tom says:
   Jack's the best runner. He'll win.
During the race Bill says:
   Look at Jack out in front! He's going to win!
Tom says *Jack will win* because he has previous knowledge of Tom's ability. Bill says *Jack is going to win* because he sees him out in front.

C   With *will* here there are no time limits. The action may happen soon or not for some time:
   Wife (reading a note from her husband): *He's left me!*
   Friend: *He came back last time. He'll come back this time too.* (But we don't know when.)

Exercise 169

▶ Put the verbs in brackets into the *be going to* form:

☐ That girl's very white; I think she *is going to faint* (faint).

1 The car's making a very strange noise; I think it ____
    (break down).

2 That metal box is ticking; I think it ____ (explode).

3 The bridge doesn't look very safe; I think it ____ (collapse).

4 The sky's very dark; I think we ____ (have) a storm.

5 There's more smoke than usual above the crater; I think
    the volcano ____ (erupt).

170 Future simple

A Form

AFFIRMATIVE	NEGATIVE
I will/I'll work OR *I shall work*	*I will not/I won't work* OR *I shall not/I shan't work*
you will/you'll work	*you will not/you won't work*
he will/he'll work etc.	*he will not/he won't work* etc.
we will/we'll work OR *we shall work*	*we will not/we won't work* OR *we shall not/we shan't work*
they will/they'll work	*they will not/they won't work*

Interrogative: *will I/shall I work? will you work? will he work?* etc.

Negative interrogative: *won't I work? won't you work? won't he work?* etc.

We do not contract *shall* in the affirmative.

B *I/we will* or *I/we shall*

We can use *I/we will* for intention:

    *I **will** send you a cheque.*

and we can use *I/we shall* when there is no intention:

    *We **shall** know tomorrow.* (It will be in the papers.)

But *will/'ll* is much more usual:

    *We **will** know tomorrow.*

We use *I/we shall* in the interrogative.

Note the useful *shall* tag after *let's*: *Let's go, **shall we?*** (For examples of *shall?*, see 236.)

Sometimes in formal announcements you may see or hear *I/we shall* used for determination, but *will* is more common.

Exercise 170

▶ Put in *will* or *shall*. Sometimes you can use either. Use a contracted form (*'ll/won't/shan't*) where possible.
  □   *Shall* we walk home?
  1   But if we walk, it _____ take us two hours.
  2   We _____ (not) get home till 8.
  3   We _____ miss our TV programme.
  4   Let's take a taxi, _____ we?
  5   We _____ find taxis in the square.
  6   We _____ have to pay by cheque.
  7   But perhaps the taxi driver _____ (not) mind.

171 Future simple: use

A We use the future simple to express what the speaker believes/expects/fears/hopes etc. will happen:
    *Don't worry about Tom. He'**ll come** back sooner or later.*

We can introduce statements of this kind by *I'm sure/I'm afraid/I expect/suppose/hope* etc. We can use this form with or without a time expression.
    *(I'm sure) he'**ll come** back soon.*
and we can add *perhaps, possibly* or *probably*:
    *(Perhaps) it **will be** a better day tomorrow.*

B We also use the future simple for

future habitual actions:
    *These birds **will come** back next spring.*

with conditional and time clauses (but not in them – see 184, 225):
    *If you drop it, it **will break**.* (conditional)
    *When it gets warmer the snow **will start** to melt.* (time clause)

with the type of verbs listed in 142:
    *I'm going to tell him the truth. ~ He **won't believe** you.*

in newspapers and news broadcasts for formal announcements of future events and for weather forecasts:

*The President **will open** the new Olympic stadium tomorrow.*

On the radio: *Fog **will** soon **clear** in all areas.*

But in conversation we would say *The President is opening/is going to open the new Olympic stadium* and *The fog is going to clear soon.*

C   We also use *will* for intention (172), so *He won't help us* can mean either 'I don't think he will help us' or 'He doesn't intend to help us/He refuses to help us'.

Exercise 171

▶ Put the verbs in brackets into the future simple:

    □   His wife hopes he *'ll change* (change) his mind about emigrating.

1   She doesn't think that he ____ (like) Australia.

2   She is afraid that the climate ____ (not suit) him.

3   But I don't suppose that he ____ (take) her advice.

4   If he goes I'm sure that he ____ (be) back in a few years' time.

5   And then he ____ (have) to start looking for another job.

172 *will* for unpremeditated intention

A   We use this form when the speaker makes a decision and tells another person immediately or almost immediately:

    Child: *My balloon's burst!*

    Mother: *Never mind. I'**ll get** you another one.*

    Ann: *I'm not going by air. I can't afford it.*

    Tom: *I'**ll lend** you the air fare.*

Note that if the speaker or the other person mentions the intended action again (before it has happened) he or she will use the present continuous:

    Ann: *I'm flying after all. Tom is lending me the fare.*

B   Examples of *will* and the present continuous

Bill is in a restaurant. He looks at the menu and says to the waiter *I'**ll have** the trout, please.* But if, before the trout

has come, Tom joins Bill, Tom will probably say *What **are** you **having**, Bill?* and the conversation may continue:
  *I'm **having** the trout. It's always good here.* ~
  *Oh, well, I'll **have** it too.*

Ann is phoning Tom from Paris.
  Ann: *My plane gets to Heathrow at 7.30.*
  Tom: *Good. I'll **meet** you there.*
But before the plane lands Ann may say:
  *Tom **is meeting** me at Heathrow.*

Exercise 172

▶ A group of friends are going to give a party. Ann asks for help.

Someone will have to:
  □ get the food.   Alice: *I'll get the food.*
  1 buy the wine. Bill: ____.
  2 hire glasses. Tom: ____.
  3 open the bottles. George: ____.
  4 make the coffee. Mary: ____.

▶ Now, imagine that after the above conversation a friend asks Ann about the preparations for the party. Write Ann's replies to her questions.

What about:
  □ the food?   Ann: *Alice is getting the food.*
  5 the wine?   7 the bottles?
  6 the glasses?   8 the coffee?

173 *will* or *be going to* for intention

A We can use *will* here for unpremeditated intentions, and *be going to* for premeditated intentions:
  Ann: *My door needs painting.*
  Jack: *I'll **paint** it for you if you like.*

On the following Saturday Jack leaves his flat carrying a pot of paint:
  Bill: *What's the paint for, Jack?*
  Jack: *I'm **going to paint** Ann's door.*

B We can use *will* for actions in the near future or the more remote future. *be going to* usually refers to actions in the near future.

C We use *will* mainly with the first person. We can use *be going to* with all persons. In the negative, however, we can use *will not (won't)* for all persons.

won't is much more emphatic than *not going to*:
   Mother to small boy: *Give the ball back to your sister*.
   Small boy: *No, I won't*. (I refuse to.)

Exercise 173

▶ A group of friends are staying at a country hotel. Some have already decided how to spend the day; others haven't. Use *will('ll)* or *be going to*.
   □ Bill: *I'm going to take* (I/take) some photographs of the countryside.
      Mary: I wanted to take some photographs but I forgot to bring my camera.
      Bill: *I'll lend* (I/lend) you mine, if you like.
   1 Tom: Why are you wearing your climbing boots? ___ (you/climb) a mountain?
   2 John: Well, ___ (I/climb) the hill behind the hotel.
   3 Tom: What a good idea! ___ (I/come) too!
   4 Paul: There's Charles with his fishing rod. Where ___ (you/fish) Charles?
   5 Charles: ___ (I/fish) in the lake. I need someone to row me. What about you?
   6 Paul: OK, ___ (I/row) you.
   7 Ann: What ___ (you/do) Alice?
   8 Alice: ___ (I/sit) here in the garden and relax.
   9 Ann: That's rather a good idea. I think ___ (I/do) the same.

174 *will* or *want/wish/would like*

Do not confuse *will* with *want/wish/would like*. *will* can express a wish to do something + a decision to do it: *I'll help you*. *want/wish/would like* merely express a wish or desire. They do not tell us anything about future actions.

Note, however, that *I'd like* + noun is often an alternative to *I'll have/take* + noun. We use this mostly in shops or restaurants:
   Customer: *I'll have/I'd like a pound of grapes, please*.
   Diner: *I'll have/I'd like a tomato juice please, and* . . .

Exercise 174

▶ Put in *will ('ll)* or *want(s) to*:
  □ Ann (on the phone to Mary): All right, Mary, if you *want to* meet me in Edinburgh, *I'll* come to Edinburgh.
  1 Ann (to Tom, afterwards): I ____ (not) go to Edinburgh but I ____ have to go because Mary says it's urgent.
  2 I don't even know why she ____ see me. She wouldn't tell me.
  3 Tom: I ____ drive you if you like.
  4 Ann: No thanks, Tom. I ____ (not) spend too long on the journey.
  5 I'd better take a train. I ____ try to catch the 9 a.m. train.

175 Future continuous

A Form

We form this tense with the future simple of *be* + the present participle.
Affirmative: *I will/shall be working, he will be working* etc.
Negative: *I will/shall not be working, he will not be working* etc.
Interrogative: *shall I be working? will he be working?* etc.
Negative interrogative: *won't you be working?* etc.

will contracts to *'ll, will not* to *won't, shall not* to *shan't*.

B Use

1 We can use the future continuous for an action which will continue for some time in the future. We may mention the period but this is not essential:
  Next week we'll be rehearsing for the concert.

If we mention a point in future time, the action will start before this time and probably continue after it:
  This time tomorrow I'll be playing golf.

2 We can use this form to express future without intention.

Compare it with the other future forms. If Tom says *I'm helping Ann on Monday*, he has arranged this with Ann. If he says *I'll help Ann on Monday* or *I'm going to help Ann on Monday*, he is expressing his intention. But if he says *I'll be helping Ann on Monday* he hasn't made the arrangement and he isn't expressing an intention. He is

merely stating that this will happen. Perhaps it is a matter
of routine; perhaps he always helps Ann on Mondays. We
very often use this form for routine actions.

3 Note the difference between *won't do* and *won't be doing*.

won't could indicate refusal. *Tom won't help us* could mean
'He refuses to help us'. But *He won't be helping us* merely
states the fact. It tells us nothing about Tom's feelings.
Perhaps he will be away or doing some other job.

Exercise 175

▶ Five friends usually go to Bath at weekends. Peter or George
usually drive. Put the verbs in brackets into the future
continuous or the *will* +infinitive form.

☐ Sue: Peter *won't be driving* (not/drive) us tomorrow. He's
   still in hospital.

1 Bill: And George _____ (not/come) because he's got an
   exam.

2 Sue: Then I _____ (ask) Ann to drive us.

3 Bill: Remember that Ann _____ (not/drive) on the M1. She
   says it's dangerous.

4 Sue: But we _____ (not/go) along the M1. We _____ (go)
   along the M4.

5 Bill: But Ann _____ (not/go) on the M4 either. That's
   where Peter had his crash.

176 Future perfect

A Form

This tense has the same form as the future simple,
except that instead of the present infinitive we use the
perfect infinitive, *have* + past participle: *have worked*,
have seen etc.

Future simple: *will work, will see*.
Future perfect: *will have worked, will have seen*.

B Use

We use the future perfect with *by* + a point in future
time: *by then, by the end of May* etc. We use it for an action
which at this point in future time (PFT) will be in the past.

The action may occur in the period between the time of speaking (TS) and the PFT:

*Come next week. Tom **will have gone** by then.*

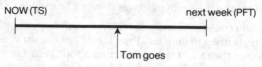

or may begin at or before the TS and continue right through the period:

*By the end of May I'll **have worked** here for 25 years.*

Exercise 176

▶ Make comments on these New Year resolutions as shown:

    □ I plan to watch two educational programmes a week. ~
    So by the end of the year you'll have watched 104 educational programmes.

I plan:

1   to write 1,000 words a day.
2   to run five miles every day.
3   to lose ½ kilo a month.
4   to learn 50 new words a month.

177 Future perfect continuous

A Form

We form this tense with the future perfect of *be* + the present participle: *I will/shall have been working, he will have been working* etc.

B Use

We use this form with *by* + a point in future time.

We can use it instead of the future perfect when the action is continuous. So instead of *I'll have worked* in

176 B2 above, we could say *I'll have been working*. (See also the present perfect continuous, 158 A).

We can also use it instead of a series of actions in the future perfect. Instead of *By the end of the year he will have painted 100 pictures* we could say *By the end of the year he'll have been painting for twenty years*. The action here appears as a continuous action. We can't mention the number of actions or objects (see 158 B).

23 *would* + infinitive

178 *would* + present infinitive

Form

The same form is used for all persons:
Affirmative: *he would/he'd work*.
Negative: *he would not/he wouldn't work*.
Interrogative: *would he work?*
Negative interrogative: *wouldn't he work?*

Main uses

1 In conditional sentences, type 2 (185).
2 For 'future in the past' (179–180).
3 For past routine (181).
4 For requests and invitations (219–220).

179 *would* for 'future in the past'

We can use *would* for an action or state which, at a time in the past, appeared as a future action or state:
   *She hoped that he **would** come to her party.*
   *I thought that he **would** refuse the invitation.*

Note this use of *would* in reported speech (231 C):
> He said, 'I'm afraid that I will be late.' →
> He said he was afraid that he **would** be late.

Exercise 179

▶ Complete the following, using *would* + infinitive and
pronouns instead of nouns.
- □ Tom's wife didn't come to the party. ~ No, I didn't think
  she would come.
1   Tom came to the party. ~ I thought ____.
2   He said he'd got the job he applied for. ~ I'm glad. I hoped
  ____.
3   He likes his new employers. ~ I knew ____.
4   His wife objected at first. ~ I was afraid ____.
5   She didn't want to move house. ~ I didn't think ____.

180   *would/would not* for past intention

We can use *would not*. It can be the main verb:
> She **wouldn't** help me. (She refused to help me.)
> The car **wouldn't** start. (It refused to start.)

But we cannot use *would* (affirmative) for past intention
as a main verb. We can use it only in indirect speech or
in a clause after *hoped/knew/was sure/thought* etc.:
> I said I **would** help him.   I knew they **would** wait for me.

▷ For the use of *will* for intention, see 172–174.

181   *would* for a past routine

We can use either *used to* (138) or *would* for a past
routine. *would ('d)* is the more usual form:
> At weekends we **would** cycle to the beach. We**'d** take our lunch
> with us and (**would**) eat it on the sands. Afterwards we**'d** swim,
> or fish from the rocks. We**'d** come home tired and sunburnt.

In the above sentences, *used to* could replace *would ('d)*.

But note that when *used to* is used for a discontinued
habit, it is not replaceable by *would*.

▷ For *would* in requests, see 219; in invitations, see 220.

182 *would* + **perfect infinitive**

Form

The same form is used for all persons:
Affirmative: *he would have worked/he'd have worked.*
Negative: *he would not have worked/he wouldn't have worked.*
Interrogative: *would he have worked?*
Negative interrogative: *wouldn't he have worked?*

Main use

In conditional sentences, type 3 (186).

▷ For *would have liked*, see 225 D.

24   Conditional sentences

183 Introduction

A   Conditional sentences have two parts: the *if*-clause and
the main clause. Consider the sentence:
    If you drop the glass, it will break.
If you drop is the *if*-clause and *it will break* is the main
clause. The main clause can come first:
    It will break if you drop it.

B   There are three types of conditional sentence:
    Type 1: *If I find your passport, I'll post it to you.* (184)
    Type 2: *If I knew his number, I would ring him.* (185)
    Type 3: *If I'd had enough money, I would have bought it.* (186)

184 Conditional sentences, type 1

A   Form

The verb in the *if*-clause is in the present tense and the
verb in the main clause is in the future simple:
    If I see Tom tomorrow, I'll give him your message.

Note that the *if*-clause usually refers to the future, but the verb is in the present tense.

B Use

We use type 1 conditional sentences when we think the action or situation in the *if*-clause is possible or probable.

Type 1 conditionals often refer to the future (*If I see him tomorrow, . . .*) but can refer to the present:
If you feel cold (now), I'll shut the window.

C Variations of the basic form

1 In the *if*-clause, instead of the present simple, we can use the present continuous:
If you're looking for Tom, you'll find him upstairs.
or the present perfect:
If you've finished your homework, we'll watch TV.

2 In the main clause, instead of *will*, we can use *may/can* for permission:
If you eat all your dinner, you can have a chocolate.
or *may/might/could* for possibility:
If it's foggy tonight, the plane may be late.
or *can/could* for ability:
If the ice is thick, we can walk across. (we'll be able to walk across)
or any expression of command, advice, suggestion or request:
If you are tired, sit down (command/advice) OR
you should sit down/you had better sit down (advice) OR
why don't you sit down? (advice or suggestion)
If you aren't too busy, would you help me with this? (request)

3 We can also use two present simple tenses to express automatic or habitual results:
If you press this button, the light goes on. (automatic result)
If you argue with him, he gets angry. (habitual result)
or to make a statement more dramatic:
If he comes, I go!

Exercise 184

▶ Combine each pair of sentences into one. Begin *if*; omit *perhaps* and *then*.

☐ Perhaps my firm will move to London. Then I'll have to find a new place to live.
If my firm moves to London, I'll have to find a new place to live.

1 Perhaps I'll get a house in the suburbs. Then I'll have a garden. *If I get _____ .*

2 Perhaps I'll rent a flat in the centre. Then I'll be able to walk to work.

3 Perhaps I'll be able to walk to work. Then I'll save money.

▶ Put in the phrases from the list:
ask, you can, could you, you had better, why don't you

☐ If you want information about the engine, *ask* my brother. (advice)

4 If you can't afford a new car, _____ buy a second-hand one. (advice)

5 If you are thinking of a second-hand car, _____ have a look at mine? (advice/suggestion)

6 If you have time at the weekend, _____ take it for a test drive if you like. (permission)

7 If you decide to buy it, _____ give me a ring on Sunday night? (request)

185 Conditional sentences, type 2

A Form

The verb in the *if*-clause is in the past simple tense and the verb in the main clause is *would* + infinitive (178):
If he had a garden, he would grow roses.
If I won £50,000, I'd give up my job.

Type 2 conditional sentences refer to the present or future. The past tense in the *if*-clause doesn't indicate past time. It is an 'unreal past' and indicates unreality or doubt (217).

B Use

We use type 2 conditional sentences as follows.

1 When the statement in the *if*-clause is contrary to known fact. *If he had a garden, . . .* means that he doesn't have a garden. The *if*-clause here refers to the present.

2 When the action in the *if*-clause is improbable. If someone says, *If I won £50,000, . . .* we know that he doesn't expect to win so much. The *if*-clause here refers to the future.

3 Sometimes when we are considering possible actions:
I'll go by bus. ~ If you went by train, you'd get there sooner.

But it is easier for the student to use the type 1 construction here:
If you go by bus, you'll get there sooner.

C The use of *were*

1 Instead of *if* + *was*, we can use *if* + *were*:
If I was/were rich, I'd build a house.

Note the form *If I was/were you, I'd . . .* :
If I were you, I'd buy a car.
This is a useful way of expressing advice.

2 When the *if*-clause expresses an improbable action (B2 above) we can replace a past simple form by *were* + infinitive:
If I were to win £50,000, I'd give up my job.
This is a fairly formal construction.

D Variations of the basic form

1 In the *if*-clause, we can use the past continuous:
I'm going by bus. If I were going by car, I'd offer you a lift.

2 In the main clause we can use *might* or *could* to express a possible result or ability:
If you wrote to him, he might answer. (possible result)
If I knew his address, I could write to him. (ability)
Compare with the basic form, in which *would* expresses a certain result:
If you wrote to him, he would answer.

3 We can use *would* + continuous infinitive (= the continuous conditional):
If I were on holiday now, I'd be skiing.

4 We can also use two past tenses for automatic or habitual results in the past:
If anyone tried to break in, the alarm went off.
If you dismissed one man, the others went on strike.

Exercise 185

▶ Read about Mary and then complete the sentences:
Mary works late and getting home is a problem. It's a long way; there isn't a late bus and taxis are expensive. She hasn't got a bicycle and doesn't use her car because she can't park near the office. Hitch-hiking is rather dangerous.
- ☐ I'd walk home, *if it wasn't so far.*
- ☐ I'd go by bus, *if there was a late bus.*
- 1   I'd take a taxi, _____ so _____.   3   I'd cycle home, _____.
- 2   I'd use my car, _____.   4   I'd hitch-hike, _____.

▶ Put the verbs in brackets into the correct tense:
- ☐ Bill: I've got tickets for the big match. Get the day off and come too.
  Tom: If my boss *was* (be) like your boss, there would be no problem.
- 5   Tom: If he _____ (like) rugby, he might give me the day off. But he doesn't like rugby.
- 6   Tom: He likes golf. He said yesterday, 'If you _____ (belong) to a golf club, Tom, you would be more useful to the firm.' But I don't play golf.
- 7   Tom: He thinks that if I _____ (play) golf with clients, I could talk business at the same time.
- 8   Bill: Offer to take up golf and then ask for a day off.
  Tom: No. If I _____ (offer) to take up golf, he'd make me do it, and I don't like golf.

186   Conditional sentences, type 3

A   Form

The verb in the *if*-clause is in the past perfect tense (*had* +past participle) and the verb in the main clause is *would* +perfect infinitive (182):
    *If he **had been** in his office, I **would have seen** him.*

B   Use

We use type 3 conditional sentences when we refer to the past and to an action or situation that did not happen:
    *If I **had seen** him, I **would have warned** him.* (But I didn't see him, so I didn't warn him.)
    *If you'd **spoken** politely, he **wouldn't have been** angry.* (But you didn't speak politely and he was angry.)

C Variations of the basic form

1 In the *if*-clause we can use the perfect continuous:
   *You were driving too fast. If you **had been going** more
   slowly, you'd have been able to stop.*

2 We can put *had* first and omit the *if*. But this is a very
   formal construction:
   ***Had** the Minister **known** all the facts, he would have acted
   differently.*

3 In the main clause we can use *might* or *could*:
   *If you'd asked him, he **might** have helped you.* (possibility)
   *If you'd asked him, he **could** have helped you.* (ability)

Exercise 186

▶ Complete these sentences in the way shown:
   □ You didn't tell her! ~ I didn't see her. *If I'd seen her, I'd
      have told her.*
   1 You didn't ring her! ~ I didn't know her number. If ___
   2 You didn't write to him! ~ He didn't give me his address
      If ___ .
   3 You didn't pay the bill! ~ They didn't send me a bill.
      If ___ .
   4 You didn't help her! ~ She didn't ask for help. If ___ .

▶ Read about Arthur and then put the words in brackets into th
   correct tense:

   He overslept so he got up late and had no time for breakfast.
   He left the house late and missed his train and was late for
   work. His boss was annoyed. He had to work through his
   lunch hour so he didn't go out to lunch and he felt very
   hungry in the afternoon.

   □ If he hadn't overslept, he *wouldn't have got up* (not/get up)
      late.
   5 If he'd left the house earlier, he ___ (catch) his train.
   6 If he'd caught his train, he ___ (be) in time for work.
   7 If he'd been in time for work, his boss ___ (not/be)
      annoyed.
   8 If he hadn't had to work through his lunchtime, he ___
      (go out) to lunch.
   9 If he'd had lunch, he ___ (not/feel) so hungry in the
      afternoon.

187 Special uses of *won't* and *would* in *if*-clauses

A We can use *if* + *won't* + infinitive instead of *if* + *refuse/ refuses* +infinitive:
*If they **won't take** cheques, we'll have to pay cash.* (If they refuse to take cheques, we'll have to pay cash.)

B *if* + *would like/care* can replace *if* + *want* (225):
If you'd like to go to the concert, I'll get you a ticket.
(If you want to go to the concert, I'll get you a ticket.)

188 Other conditional expressions

A *unless* + affirmative verb is similar to *if* + negative verb:
***Unless** I hurry, I'll miss my bus.* (If I don't hurry, I'll miss my bus.)

B *otherwise* means 'if we don't do this/if he didn't do this/if I hadn't done this' etc.:
*He must take the pills. **Otherwise** he won't get well.*
*You had to be early. **Otherwise** you didn't get a seat.*
*We took a taxi. **Otherwise** we'd have missed the plane.*

C *provided (that)* means 'on condition that' and emphasizes a restriction:
*You can park here, **provided** you leave before six.*

D *if* + auxiliary

An auxiliary can represent a previously mentioned verb (+ phrase):
*Do you want to eat out? If you **do**, let's book a table.*

Instead of *If you do* above, we could say *If so*, and instead of *If you can't* we could say *If not*.

E *if so/not*

so or *not* here can represent a previously mentioned clause:
*Do you want this job? **If so** (= If you do), you can have it. **If not** (= If you don't), I'll offer it to Ann.*

Exercise 188

▶ Rewrite these sentences, using *unless*:
  □ If he doesn't hurry, he'll miss his plane.
    Unless he hurries, he'll miss his plane.
  1 If he doesn't put money in the meter, he may get a parking ticket.
  2 If he doesn't pay his telephone bill, they'll cut him off.
  3 They won't employ you, if you don't speak French.
  4 If you don't book at once, you won't get a seat.
  5 Don't ask for help, if you don't need it.

▶ Complete these sentences as shown:
  □ Are you ready? If *you are*, we can go now.
  □ Have you read this book? If *you haven't* (not), you can borrow it.
  6 Are you coming by train? If ____, we'll meet you at the station.
  7 Would you like to climb a mountain? If ____, you can join Peter's party.
  8 Have you got climbing boots? If ____ (not), we can lend you some.
  9 Can you swim? If ____, we'll go to the deep pool.
  10 Do you ride well? If ____ (not), we'll find you a quiet horse.

189 *in case* and *if*

A *in case* clauses and *if*-clauses appear similar, but they are not the same. An *in case* clause gives the reason for the action in the main clause:
  1 *She doesn't let the little boy play by the river **in case** he **falls** in.* (She is afraid that he will fall in.)
  Similarly in the past:
  2 *She didn't let him play by the river **in case** he **fell** in.* (She was afraid that he would fall in.)

B Note that after *in case* in (1) above we use the present, not a future tense, and that in (2) we use the past, not the conditional.

C Note the difference between an *in case* clause and an *if*-clause. Compare:
  1 *I'll give him another blanket **in case** he is cold* AND
  2 *I'll give him another blanket **if** he is cold*.

In 1 she will give him the extra blanket. We could omit the *in case* clause without changing the meaning.

In 2 she will give him the extra blanket only if he needs it. The first action depends on the second. We cannot omit the *if*-clause without changing the meaning.

D *in case of* + noun is, however, similar to an *if*-clause:
   In case of fire . . . (If a fire breaks out . . .)

We see this chiefly in notices:
   In case of fire, break this glass.

Exercise 189

▶ Combine these pairs of sentences into one sentence, using *in case*:
   □ Take an umbrella. It may rain.
      Take an umbrella in case it rains.
   1 Take some sandwiches. There may not be a café at the station.
   2 Take a coat for Bob. It may turn cold.
   3 Take a spare pair of gloves for him. He may lose one of his.
   4 Take the pushchair. He may get tired on the walk.

25   The infinitive

190 Infinitive forms and uses

A Examples of infinitive forms

Present infinitive	*to work*
Present continuous infinitive	*to be working*
Perfect infinitive	*to have worked*
Perfect continuous infinitive	*to have been working*

The full infinitive includes the word *to*, as shown above; but after certain verbs and in certain expressions we use the infinitive without *to*:
   *He may **need** help. We must **help** him.*
We call this the bare infinitive.

B The infinitive:

1 can be the subject of a verb:
   It was easy to get part time work. (191, also 28)

2 can follow a verb:
   He intends to cycle all the way. (192)
   or a verb + *how/what/when/where/which/who/whether*:
   He discovered how to open the safe. (193)
   or a verb + object:
   He wants you to wait for him. (194–195)

3 can follow certain adjectives like *anxious, glad, sorry*, etc.
   I was sorry to hear about your accident. (28)

4 can follow *too/enough* with adjective or adverb:
   He was too tired to walk any further. (197)

5 can follow a noun or *anything/nothing/something*:
   a book to read   something to do (70)

6 can express purpose:
   I turned on the light to see what time it was. (249)

7 can be used in certain passive constructions:
   She is said to have forty grandchildren. (214)

▷ For *be* + infinitive, see 104 B–C.

191 Infinitive as subject of a verb

A An infinitive or infinitive phrase can be the subject of
appear, be, seem and other link verbs. The infinitive can
come first:
   To lean out of the window is dangerous.
But we usually put *it* first:
   It is dangerous to lean out of the window.

Note the use of *it* with interrogatives:
   Is it possible to get there by train?

B We use this construction chiefly with adjectives (see
above and 28). But we can also use it with words like
a crime, an offence, a mistake/pity/shame/relief, a good idea:
   It's an offence to take photographs here.

C An infinitive can also be the subject of *cost* and *take*:
   It would cost millions to rebuild the palace.
   It will take ages to get there.

Exercise 191

▶ Use the words in brackets to answer the questions:
   □ Shall we cut down the trees? ~ (No/shame)
   No, it would be a shame to cut down the trees.
   1 Shall we dig up the rose bushes? ~ (No/a pity)
   2 Shall we plant rhododendrons? ~ (No/a mistake)
   3 Shall we cut the grass? ~ (Yes/a good idea)
   4 Shall we sweep up the leaves? ~ (No/a waste of time)

192 Verbs followed by the infinitive

A Some verbs are often followed by an infinitive:

agree*	determine*	manage	promise*
appear*	forget*	mean	refuse
attempt	happen	offer	remember
bother (negative)	hope*	plan	seem*
care (interrogative)	intend*	prepare	threaten
decide*	learn*	pretend*	try

   She agreed to meet me. I hope to see him soon.

   * These verbs can also be used with a *that*-clause (257 A).

   (For *intend, mean, remember, try,* see 206.)

B After *appear, happen, pretend, seem* we can also use the
   continuous infinitive (198):
   He pretended to be watching the game.

C Infinitives are also used after modal verbs (97), and can
   be used after *be* (104 B–D) and *have* (129, 132, 133).

Exercise 192

▶ Use the word in brackets to complete these sentences:
   □ He wasn't busy but (pretend) *he pretended to be busy.*
   1 He didn't help us but (offer) ____.
   2 He said he'd buy meat but (forget) ____ any.
   3 He didn't shoot the pilot but (threaten) ____ him.
   4 He didn't ring Ann but (try) ____ her.

193 Verbs followed by *how/what/when* etc. and the infinitive

A We often use *how/what/when/where/which/who/whether* + infinitive after the following:

ask	forget	see	show + object
decide	know	can't think	teach + object
discover	learn	understand	tell + object
find out	remember	wonder	

*I remembered **which** key to use.   I couldn't think **who** to ask.*

B We often use *whether* + infinitive after *want to know, don't/didn't know* and *wonder*:
*I don't know **whether to rent** a flat or buy one.*
and after *decide* and *remember* when they follow a negative or interrogative verb:
*He couldn't decide **whether to write** or phone.*

Exercise 193

▶ Use the word in brackets to reply to these commands:
  □ Put it away! (where) ~ But I don't know *where to put it.*
  1 Open the safe! (how) ~ But I don't know ____.
  2 Ask someone! (who) ~ But I don't know ____
  3 Do something! (what) ~ But I don't know ____.
  4 Choose one of them! (which) ~ But I don't know ____.

▶ Now reply to these questions:
  □ How do I repair it? ~ You must learn *how to repair it.*
  5 Which road shall I take? ~ You should remember ____.
  6 How shall I get there? ~ You must find out ____.
  7 What shall I say? ~ You must decide ____.
  8 Who shall I ask? ~ You should know ____.

194 Verb (+ object) + infinitive

A Some verbs can be followed by an infinitive or an object + infinitive:

ask	mean	wish	would love
expect	want	would hate	would prefer
intend	like	would like	

I want to go to Rome this summer, and I want you to come with me. ~ *But I would prefer to go/my mother would prefer me to go to Florence.*

B Note the difference between *ask* + infinitive and *ask* + object + infinitive:

I asked to speak to Mr Jones. (I said, 'Could I speak to Mr Jones?')

I asked Tom to speak to Mr Jones. (I said, 'Tom, would you speak to Mr Jones, please?')

C *expect* + object + infinitive often expresses an obligation:

He expects me to type his letters. (He thinks it is my duty to type his letters.)

Exercise 194

▶ Complete these sentences as shown. Use *do, listen to, read, tape, watch* or *learn how to use*.

  □   There's a very good radio programme at 6 o'clock; I*'d like you to tape it.*

1   This is a splendid book; I _____.
2   This is a very interesting tape; I _____.
3   There's an excellent TV programme on tonight; I _____.
4   This is a very useful exercise; I _____.
5   Here is our new word processor; I _____.

195   Verb + object + infinitive

A We can use an object + infinitive after:

beg	*force*	*oblige*	*train*
bribe	*get*	*order*	*teach*
compel	*hear*	*persuade*	*tell*
enable	*invite*	*remind*	*urge*
encourage	*let*	*request*	*warn*
feel	*make*	*see*	*watch*

She got the taxi-driver to carry her case into the house.
The raiders ordered the cashier to open the safe. (239 A)
He persuaded us to help him.

After *persuade, remind, teach, tell* and *warn* we can also use a *that*-clause (257).

B *hear/see/make* (in the active) and *let, feel* and *watch* take the bare infinitive:

*The teacher **made me do** the exercise again.*
*Please **let me know**.   **Let's go** now, shall we?*

But after *hear/see/make* in the passive we use the full infinitive:

*I was **made to do** it again.*

▷ For *feel, hear, see, watch*, see 208.
For *advise, allow, permit* and *recommend*, see 204.

Exercise 195

▶ Use the words in brackets and an infinitive to reply to these questions:
  □ Did you dive? ~ (Yes/teach)
     Yes, they taught us to dive.
  □ Did you eat the local shellfish? ~ (No/warn)
     No, they warned us not to eat the local shellfish.
  1 Did you go with them? ~ (Yes/invite)
  2 Did you book in advance? ~ (Yes/remind)
  3 Did you insure yourselves? ~ (Yes/persuade) (Use *ourselves*.)
  4 Did you drink the water? ~ (No/advise)
  5 Did you go out alone at night? ~ (No/warn)

196 Infinitive represented by its *to*

Instead of repeating an infinitive (+ phrase) we can sometimes use the *to* only:

*Would you like **to see** the programme? ~*
*Yes, I'd like **to** (see it) very much.*

We often add 'very much' to 'I'd like to' here. We can use *to* in this way after a number of verbs. For example:

ask + object	*intend*	*try*
be able	*mean*	*want*
be going (for future)	*need*	*would hate*
have (for obligation)	*ought*	*would like*
hope	*tell* + object	*would love*

*Would you like **to go**? ~ Yes, I'd love **to** (go).*

197 *too/enough* + **adjective/adverb** + **infinitive**

A *too* + adjective + infinitive

1 We can say:
> *He was so tired that he couldn't walk any further* OR
> *He was too tired to walk any further.*

2 We can say:
> *The case is so heavy that we can't lift it* OR
> *The case is too heavy (for us) to lift.*

Note that the *it* is necessary after *so . . . that* but that we do not put *it* after the infinitive. Note also that we can add *for* + object, as shown.

3 We can say:
> *The grass was so wet that we couldn't sit on it* OR
> *The grass was too wet to sit on.* (without *it*)

B *too* + adverb + infinitive

Examples:
> *I was sitting too far back to hear what the speaker said.*
> *You are standing too close to the picture to see it properly.*
> *It's too late (for us) to do anything.*

C Adjective + *enough* + infinitive

1 We can say:
> *He can travel alone; he is old enough* OR
> *He is old enough to travel alone.*

2 We can say:
> *The case is so light that a child could carry it* OR
> *The case is light enough (for a child) to carry.*

Note that we omit *it* here, as we do in A2 above.

3 The infinitive can also refer to the object of a preposition:
> *The floor wasn't very strong. You couldn't dance on it.*
> *The floor wasn't strong enough to dance on.* (without *it*)

D Adverb + *enough* + infinitive

Examples:
> *I was standing near enough to hear every word.*
> *She didn't ski fast enough to win a prize.*

Exercise 197

▶ Complete these sentences as shown:
  □ Let's wait here. ~ It's too cold *to wait here*.
  1 Let's play tennis. ~ It's too warm _____.
  2 Let's take photos. ~ It's too dark _____.
  3 Let's sit in the garden. ~ It's too windy _____.

  □ The ladder is so heavy that we can't carry it.
    The ladder *is too heavy to carry*.
  4 The shelf is very high. We can't reach it. The shelf _____.
  5 The wardrobe is so heavy that we can't move it.
    The wardrobe _____.
  6 The paint is so thick that we can't use it. The paint _____.

▶ This time use the adjective in brackets:
  □ She's talking about travelling alone. (old) ~
    But *is she old enough to travel alone?*
  7 She hopes to cycle 100 miles a day. (strong) ~ But _____?
  8 He talks about getting another job. (young) ~ But _____?
  9 They are thinking of joining the police. (tall) ~ But _____?

▶ Make these pairs of sentences into one sentence:
  □ The case isn't very small. You can't take it into the cabin.
    It isn't small enough to take into the cabin.
  10 The rope isn't very strong. We can't use it as a tow rope.
  11 The tent isn't very light. You couldn't carry it far.
  12 The fruit isn't quite ripe. We can't pick it yet.

198 The continuous and perfect infinitives

A Form

Present continuous infinitive	*to be working*
Perfect infinitive	*to have worked*
Perfect continuous infinitive	*to have been working*

B Present continuous infinitive and perfect infinitive

We can use these infinitives

1 after auxiliary verbs:
  *He may **be coming** by bus.* (Perhaps he is coming by bus.)
  Tom's watching TV. ~ *He shouldn't **be watching** TV; he
  should **be doing** his homework.*
  *I haven't got my key. I must **have left** it at home.* (deduction)
  *Why didn't you write to him? You should **have written**.*

2 after *appear/seem* and *pretend*:

He seems to be losing weight. (It seems that he is losing weight.)

He pretended to be working for MI5. (He pretended that he was working for MI5.)

Your grandfather seems to have been a great traveller. (It seems that he was a great traveller.)

The fire appears to have started in the basement. (It appears that the fire started in the basement.)

3 after adjectives:

It's nice to be going home again.

I'm sorry to have wasted your time.

C Perfect continuous infinitive

We can use this after auxiliary verbs and after *appear/seem*:

He may have been waiting for Ann. (Perhaps he was waiting for her.)

They got into the ten o'clock train. ~ Then they must have been going to London. It's a non-stop train. (deduction)

I was doing 160 k.p.h. ~ You shouldn't have been driving so fast.

He appears to have been living here for a long time.

Exercise 198

▶ Complete these replies as shown:

  □ Perhaps he's flying. ~ Yes, *he may be flying.*

  1 Perhaps he's coming by train. ~ Yes, ____.

  2 Perhaps he's bringing his girlfriend. ~ Yes, ____.

  3 Perhaps they're waiting at the station. ~ Yes, ____.

  □ Perhaps he forgot that we had moved. ~ *Yes, he may have forgotten.*

  4 Perhaps he lost our address. ~ Yes, ____ it.

  5 Perhaps he got lost on the way here. ~ Yes, ____.

  6 Perhaps his car broke down on the way here. ~ Yes, ____.

▶ Tom was alone in Jean and Mary's flat over the weekend. Use the word in brackets to complete what Mary says.

  □ Jean: The clock's going again! (wind)

     Mary: Tom *must have wound it.*

  7 Jean: There are some library books here. (leave)

     Mary: Tom ____.

8   Jean: There is some coffee in the thermos. (made)
     Mary: Tom _____.
9   Jean: There is cheese in the fridge. (buy)
     Mary: Tom _____.

▶   Imagine that you and Ann are watching from across the road.
     Complete these replies in the way shown:
     □   Is he parking there, on the yellow lines? ~
         Yes, *he seems to be parking there.*
     10   Is the traffic warden asking him to move? ~ Yes, she _____.
     11   Is he arguing with the traffic warden? ~ Yes, _____.
     12   Is she giving him a parking ticket? ~ Yes, _____.

26   The gerund

199 Form and use

The gerund has the same form as the present participle:
working, running.

The gerund is a verbal noun, so we can use it:
As subject of a verb: *Skiing can be dangerous.* (200)
After certain verbs: *She enjoys riding.* (201)
After prepositions: *They accused him of spying.* (202)
In noun compounds: *a swimming pool* (18)

200 Gerund as subject of a verb

A We can use a gerund as subject when we are making a
   general statement:
       Parking in the centre of Oxford is impossible.
   but if we are talking about a particular action we more
   often use an infinitive:
       It was impossible to find a parking space yesterday.

B We use the gerund in short prohibitions:
       No smoking   No parking   No fishing
   but if we want to put an object after the verb we use an
   imperative:
       Do not touch this button.   Do not fold the paper.

Exercise 200

▶ Complete the replies to these questions:
  □ Is it possible to get weekends off? ~
    Yes. *Getting weekends off is* usually possible.
  1 Is it easy to find a guest house? ~ Yes, ___ quite easy.
  2 Is it a good idea to book in advance? ~ Yes, ___ usually
    advisable.
  3 Is it dangerous to climb alone? ~ Yes, ___ very
    dangerous.
  4 Is it safer to go with a group? ~ Yes, ___ much safer.
  5 Is it essential to start early? ~ Yes, ___ usually essential.

201 Gerunds after verbs

A Some common verbs followed by gerunds:

admit*	forgive + object	object to
avoid	fancy/imagine	prevent + object
deny*	finish	risk
dislike	keep (= continue)	save
enjoy	mind (negative	suggest* (222 D)
excuse + object	and interrogative)	

  * After these verbs we can also use a *that*-clause.

  We can also use gerunds after:
    can't help (= prevent/avoid), *can't stand* (= bear/endure),
    it's no good/use and *it's not/it isn't worth*

B *excuse*, *forgive* and *prevent* + object + gerund:
    Excuse/Forgive me (for) interrupting you.
    Try to prevent him (from) doing too much.

C Note the difference in meaning between *mind* + gerund
  and *mind* + object + gerund:
    I don't mind cooking the meals. (I cook and I don't mind
    doing it.)
    I don't mind them cooking in my kitchen. (They cook and
    I don't mind.)
  object to could replace *mind* here.

D *do you/would you mind?* is a very common request form:
    Do you mind moving your bike? (Please move it.)
    Would you mind not smoking? (Please don't smoke.)

Exercise 201

▶ Complete these replies:

☐ Did he really write that article in the Guardian? ~
   Yes, he admits *writing it.*

1 My mother is very easily shocked. ~ I'll try to avoid ____.
2 It's the sixth time he's made the same mistake. ~ Imagine
   ____ six times!
3 She's going to marry that dreadful man! ~ You can't
   prevent her ____.
4 You'll have to pay for it. ~ I don't mind ____.

202 Gerunds after prepositions

A When we put a verb directly after a preposition we use
   a gerund:
   *Switch off the light **before changing** the bulb.*

B Here are some useful expressions with noun/adjective
   + preposition that are followed by the gerund:

be afraid of (206 D)	*have difficulty in*
be fond of/keen on	*in spite of*
be for/against	*there's no point in*
be good/bad at	*what about?*
be sorry for (= apologize for)	*what's the point of?*
be tired of	

   *Jane's quite **good at spelling**.*
   *We had **difficulty in getting** visas.*
   *I'm **tired of doing** it by hand. Let's get a machine.*

C We can also use gerunds after some verbs +
   prepositions/adverbs:

accuse somebody of	*give up* (= stop)
be talking of	*go on* (= continue)
be thinking of	*insist on*
be used to	*look forward to*
blame somebody for	*object to*
care for	*put off* (= postpone)
feel like	*succeed in*
fine somebody for	

*Are you **thinking of inviting** Bill to your party?*
*They can **fine you for speeding**.*
*He **gave up smoking**.   **Go on working**.*
*She **insisted on reading** the letter.*

Exercise 202

▶ Combine these pairs of sentences into one sentence as shown.
Use the words in brackets, and omit the words in CAPITALS.

   □ He ran all the way. He got there in time. (by)
      He got there in time by running all the way.
   1 He didn't wait for us. He went off by himself. (instead of)
   2 I came here. BEFORE THAT I lived in York. (before)
   3 She drove a few miles. THEN she lost her way. (after)
   4 He didn't waste any time. He set off for York. (without)
   5 He started late. BUT he arrived in time. (in spite of)

▶ Now complete these replies:

   □ Let's look for George. ~ I'm tired *of looking for George.*
   6 Let's wait for George. ~ I'm tired ____.
   7 Let's ring his home. ~ What's the point of ____?
   8 It's often difficult for him to get away on time ~ We all
      have difficulty in ____ on time.
   9 Let's give him another ten minutes. ~ I'm against ____.
   10 Perhaps we shouldn't waste any more time. ~ There's no
      point in ____.

203 *be used to* + noun/gerund and *used* + full infinitive (= *used to*)

Be careful not to confuse *be used to* and *used to*. They have
different meanings.

I used to wait for Tom means that in the past I often
waited for him but I no longer do so. It expresses a
discontinued past routine or habit (138 B). But *I'm used
to waiting for Tom* means that I have waited for him a
good many times and that I don't mind waiting (139).

Another difference is that we use *used to* for the past
only, but that we can use *be used to* in any tense.

Instead of *be* we can use *become* or *get* here:
   You'll soon get used to waiting for Tom.

27   Gerund or infinitive

204   Verbs followed by either gerund or infinitive

Some verbs can be followed by gerunds (201) but not infinitives and some can be followed by infinitives (192) but not gerunds:

> *I enjoy swimming.* (We don't say *I enjoy to swim.*)
> *I hope to see him soon.* (We don't say *I hope seeing . . .*)

But there are other verbs that can be followed by either gerunds or infinitives. Here is a list of some common ones:

advise	like (223 B)	recommend
allow	love (223 B)	regret
begin	mean	remember
continue	permit	remember
hate (223 B)	prefer	start
intend	propose	stop
		try

Also *it needs* (= requires), *can bear* in negative or interrogative, *be afraid (of)*, *be sorry (for)*.

205   Verbs followed by gerund or infinitive without change of meaning

A   *advise, recommend* and *allow, permit*

If we mention the person who is advised/recommended or allowed/permitted to do something, we use the infinitive:

> *He advised me to buy a season ticket.*
> *They don't allow us to park here.*

If we don't mention this person, we use the gerund:

> *He advised buying a season ticket.*
> *They don't allow parking here.*

B   *begin, start, continue*

After these verbs we can usually use either gerunds or infinitives:

> *The baby has started walking* OR *started to walk.*

But the infinitive is more usual after the continuous forms of the above verbs:

He's beginning to talk.

and in sentences like:

I began to understand/like/admire him.

C *it needs* (= requires)

After *it needs* a gerund is usual but a passive infinitive is also possible:

The grass needs cutting OR *needs to be cut.*

The door needed painting OR *needed to be painted.*

D *can't/couldn't bear, can/could bear*

With these we can use either gerund or infinitive:

How can you bear living/to live in such a dark room?

Exercise 205

▶ Complete these replies as shown.

He always advises:
- □ waiting for good weather. ~ Yes, *he advised us to wait for good weather too.*
- 1   starting with an easy climb. ~ Yes, _____.
- 2   getting up early. ~ Yes, _____.
- 3   climbing with a group. ~ Yes, _____.
- 4   using ropes. ~ Yes, _____.

They didn't allow us:
- □ to smoke there. ~ That's strange. They used to *allow smoking.*
- 5   to park there. ~ That's strange. They used to _____.
- 6   to swim there. ~ That's strange. They used to _____.
- 7   to fish there. ~ That's strange. _____.
- 8   to camp there. ~ That's strange. _____.

▶ Now complete these replies.
- □ Is the baby walking yet? ~ Yes, *he's beginning to walk.*
- 9   Is he talking yet? ~ Yes, _____.
- 10   Is he eating solid food yet? ~ Yes, _____.
- 11   Is his brother reading yet? ~ Yes, _____.

206 Verbs followed by gerund or infinitive with change of meaning

A *propose, mean*

propose meaning 'suggest' takes a gerund:
   I **propose starting** early.

propose meaning 'intend' usually takes an infinitive:
   I **propose to spend** a week in Paris.

mean meaning 'involve' takes a gerund:
   I want to see that film, but it will **mean standing** in a queue.
   (You can't see that film without standing in a queue.)
Note that we use *mean* here only with *it* as subject.

mean meaning 'intend' takes an infinitive:
   I **mean to see** as much of the world as I can.

B *regret, remember*

We use *regret* + gerund when we regret an earlier action:
   I **regret wasting** so much time.

We use *remember* + gerund when we remember an earlier action:
   I **remember meeting** him.

We use *regret* + infinitive when regret is the first action:
   I **regret to say** that/I **regret to inform** you that there is no news.
The infinitive here is usually *to say* or *to inform*.

We use *remember* + infinitive when *remember* is the first action:
   I **remembered to lock** the door. (I didn't forget to lock it.)

C *try, stop*

try meaning 'make this experiment' or 'do this and see if it helps' takes a gerund:
   The key won't turn. ~ **Try oiling** the lock. (Oil the lock. Perhaps the key will turn then.)

try meaning 'attempt' or 'make an effort' takes an infinitive:
   Try to get up earlier. (Make an effort to get up earlier.)

stop meaning 'finish' or 'give up' takes a gerund:
   They **stopped talking** when I came in.

stop meaning 'halt' takes an infinitive:
> *He **stopped to buy** petrol.* (He stopped his car for this purpose.)

D *be afraid*

We use *be afraid of* + gerund when the subject is afraid that the action in the gerund will happen:
> *She never eats butter. She is **afraid of getting** fat.* (She is afraid that she will get fat.)

We use *be afraid* + infinitive when the subject doesn't perform the action because he is too frightened:
> *I was **afraid to jump**.* (I didn't jump because I was afraid.)

(For *afraid* + *that*-clause, see 29 A.)

E *be sorry*

I'm sorry for + gerund usually means the same as 'I apologize for' + gerund:
> *I'm **sorry for waking** you up last night.*

The action in the gerund is usually an earlier action.

When we apologize for or regret an action that is happening now we can use *I'm sorry* + infinitive or *I'm sorry for* + gerund:
> *I'm **sorry to interrupt** you but you're wanted on the phone.*

I'm sorry + *to hear/learn/see* expresses regret, not apology:
> *I was **sorry to hear** about Tom's accident.*

Note also: *I'm sorry to say that* . . . (I'm afraid that . . .)

Exercise 206

▶ Tom and Bill are mountaineers. Tom is braver than Bill. Use the correct form of the verb in brackets.

- □ Tom: I mean *to climb* (climb) the mountain.
- □ Bill: That means *starting* (start) at 5 a.m.
- 1 Tom: I mean ____ (take) the northern route.
- 2 Bill: That means ____ (cross) the glacier.
- 3 Tom: I mean ____ (camp) on the top.
- 4 Bill: That means ____ (carry) a tent.
- 5 Bill: Going alone means ____ (risk) your life.

▶ A mother is looking at photos of her son as a child. Complete his replies.

    ☐ Mother: You were an aggressive little boy.
         Son: I don't *remember being aggressive.*

6 You used to kick your sister. ~ I don't _____.
7 You broke her toys. ~ I don't _____.
8 You stole apples. ~ Yes, I remember _____.
9 You ran away from home. ~ Yes, I _____.
10 A policeman brought you home. ~ Yes, I remember a policeman _____.

▶ Bill annoys Jack in various ways. Ann gives Jack advice. Complete her replies.

    ☐ Jack: He reads my diary! ~ Ann: Well, tell him to stop *reading your diary.*
    ☐ He rings up at 2 in the morning. ~ Well, tell him not *to ring up at 2.*

11 He reads my letters! ~ Well, tell him not _____.
12 He borrows my clothes! ~ Well, tell him to stop _____.
13 He uses my phone! ~ Why can't you stop him _____?
14 He invites his friends to my parties! ~ Well, tell him not _____.

28 | The present participle

207 The present participle: form and use

A Form

Bare infinitive + *ing*. For spelling rules, see 265–269.

B Use

We can use the present participle
1 to form the continuous tenses: *I'm working* (140 etc.)
2 as an adjective: ***dripping*** *taps,* ***running*** *water* (20 C)
3 after certain verbs (208–209)

We can sometimes use present participle phrases
4 instead of relative clauses (70 B)
5 instead of certain other clauses (210–211)
6 to introduce statements in reported speech (243 C)

208   The present participle or bare infinitive after verbs of sensation

A   After the basic verbs of sensation (*see*, *hear*, *feel* and *smell*) and after *listen to*, *notice* and *watch*, we can use object + participle:

> *I **heard** the car **stopping** and **saw** him **getting** out.*
> *Can you **smell** something **burning**?*
> *We **watched** the children **playing**.*

B   After *see*, *hear* and *watch* we can also use the bare infinitive:

> *I **heard** the car **stop** and **saw** him **get** out.*

But see 195 B for passive use.

C   There is a difference in meaning between the participle and the infinitive. An action expressed by the present participle may be either incomplete or complete. *I saw him crossing the road* may mean that I saw only part of the action (diagram 1) or that I saw the whole action (diagram 2). An action expressed by the infinitive is a complete action. *I saw him cross the road* means that I saw the whole action (diagram 2).

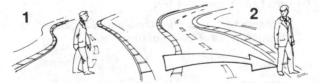

Exercise 208

▶ Reply to these questions. Use the verb in brackets and a present participle.

☐   Are you sure that he unlocked the drawer? (hear) ~ Yes, *I heard him unlocking it.*

Are you sure that:

1.   he took a document out? (see) ~ Yes, ____.
2.   he read it? (see) ~ Yes, ____.
3.   the phone rang? (hear) ~ Yes, ____.
4.   he answered it? (hear) ~ Yes, ____.
5.   he threw the document into the fire? (see) ~ Yes, ____.
6.   it burnt? (smell) ~ Yes, ____.

209 The present participle after certain verbs

A *find, catch* and *leave* + object (person or thing)

find

I **found** them **picking** apples. (They were picking apples when I arrived.)

We **found** a tree **lying** across the road.

catch

I **caught** them **stealing** my apples. (They were stealing my apples when I arrived.)

But here the action displeases the speaker or the subject:

If she **catches** you **wearing** her shoes she'll be angry.

leave

We had to **leave** the tree **lying** there.

I **left** them **talking**. (They were talking when I left.)

B *go* and *come*

With these we can use the participles of verbs of physical activity: *dancing, riding, sailing, skiing* etc., also *shopping*.

Come dancing with me on Saturday.   I'm **going shopping**.

C *spend* and *waste* + object

He **spent** a fortune **rebuilding** that old house.

I **wasted** a lot of time **standing** in queues.

D *be busy*

She's always **busy cooking** or cleaning.

Exercise 209

▶ Read the sentence in brackets and complete these sentences using an object + bare infinitive (steal) or object + present participle (stealing). Sometimes both are possible.

☐ (Last Monday he stole my neighbour's pears.)
   I caught *him stealing my neighbour's pears.*

1 (Yesterday he went up her big pear tree.) I saw _____.
2 (He climbed along a thin branch.) I watched _____.
3 (The branch broke.) I heard _____.
4 (He fell.) I saw _____.
5 (He lay at the foot of the tree.) I went out and found _____.

▶ Read the example conversation A and complete conversation
    B in the same way. (Try and do it without looking back at the
    example.)

    A   Do you sail? ~
    □   *Yes, I go sailing with Tom. We often spend the whole day sailing.*
        You must come sailing with us one day. ~ *I'd love to but my*
        family won't like it. They say I waste too much time sailing.

    B   Do you ride? ~
    6   Yes, I go ____.
    7   We often spend ____.
    8   You must come ____. ~
    9   I'd love to but my family won't like it. They say I spend
        ____.

210 A participle phrase giving the reason for
        an action

A   Instead of:
        He knew (that) it would be cold so he packed a coat.
    we can say:
        Knowing (that) it would be cold, he packed a coat.
    The participle phrase usually comes first, as shown.

    We often use *believe, expect, fear, hope, know, think* and
    find, hear, learn, notice and *see* in this way:
        Hoping for a good tip, he offered to guide us.
        Thinking (that) she hadn't heard, he asked again.
        Hearing of a job in York, Ann decided to go there.

    We can also use the participles of *be, have, need* and *feel*:
        Being a stranger, he didn't know the way. (Because he
        was a stranger . . .)
        Having plenty of time, we decided to walk. (Because we
        had plenty of time . . .)
        Feeling tired, he sat down on a bench. (Because he felt
        tired . . .)

B   In the above sentences the subject of the main verb is
    also the subject of the participle phrase. It is possible
    for the subject to come first:
        Ann, hearing of a job in York, decided to go there.

    It is also possible for the phrase to have a different subject:
        The tide being out, we were able to walk along the beach.
    The subject in this case must begin the phrase.

C   We use these phrases mainly in written English. In speech we normally use two clauses, with *so* or *as* (253).

Exercise 210

▶   Rewrite these sentences to make a new sentence with the same meaning:
  ☐   He hoped to arrange a meeting. He rang her number.
      Hoping to arrange a meeting, he rang her number.
  1   He expected to find her at home. He brought some flowers.
  2   He heard no sound. He knocked again.
  3   He thought she might be in the garden. He went round to the back of the house.
  4   He found nobody there and went away.

211 A participle phrase instead of a sentence or main clause

A   When the subject performs two actions at the same time, we can often express one of the actions by a present participle phrase:
      He drove along the street. He looked for a place to park.
      He drove along the street, looking for a place to park.
    We can put the participle phrase before or after the clause.

B   When one action immediately follows another and the subject is the same, we can often use a participle phrase for the first action. This phrase must come first.

      He ran upstairs and called his mother.
      Running upstairs, he called his mother.

      He opened the safe and took out a cashbox.
      Opening the safe, he took out a cashbox.

C   When the second action forms part of the first or is a result of it, we can express this second action by a participle phrase. This phrase must follow the main clause.
      He came in noisily, waking us all up.

D   We use the above phrases mainly in written English. In speech we normally use two clauses joined by *and*.

Exercise 211

▶ Rewrite these sentences to make new ones with the same
   meaning:

   ☐ I looked round and saw that the man was still behind me.
      Looking round, I saw that the man was still behind me.
   1 I saw a policeman and decided to report the man.
   2 I went up to the policeman and told him I was being
      followed.
   3 He took out his notebook and asked for a description of the
      man.
   4 Just then the man walked past. He nodded pleasantly
      at us.
   5 The policeman put away his notebook and said that the
      man was a plain clothes detective.
   6 I thanked the policeman and hurried on. I felt rather
      foolish. (Use two participle phrases.)

29   The passive

212   Active and passive forms

	ACTIVE	PASSIVE
Present simple	*keeps*	*is kept*
Present continuous	*is keeping*	*is being kept*
Past simple	*kept*	*was kept*
Past continuous	*was keeping*	*was being kept*
Present perfect	*has kept*	*has been kept*
Past perfect	*had kept*	*had been kept*
Conditional	*would keep*	*would be kept*
Perfect conditional	*would have kept*	*would have been kept*
Present infinitive	*to keep*	*to be kept*
Perfect infinitive	*to have kept*	*to have been kept*
Present participle/ gerund	*keeping*	*being kept*
Perfect participle	*having kept*	*having been kept*

213 Passive sentences

A We form the passive of an active tense by putting the verb *to be* into the same tense and adding the past participle of the active verb (212):

Active:	*We keep the key here.*
Passive:	*The key **is kept** here.*

Active:	*Someone stole the money.*
Passive:	*The money **was stolen**.*

Active:	*They haven't washed the car.*
Passive:	*The car **hasn't been washed**.*

To make the passive of continuous tenses we use the continuous forms of *to be*:

Active:	*They are sweeping the streets.*
Passive:	*The streets **are being swept**.*

Active:	*They were repairing the road.*
Passive:	*The road **was being repaired**.*

B To form the passive of auxiliary + infinitive combinations we use the auxiliary + passive infinitive:

Active:	*You should type the letter.*
Passive:	*The letter **should be typed**.*

Active:	*We had to count the money.*
Passive:	*The money **had to be counted**.*

C With other verb + infinitive forms we make the verb passive:

*They told him to wait.　He **was told** to wait.*

Note that we use the full infinitive:

*He **was made to wait**.*

D We can put *by* + noun/pronoun after a passive verb to show who performs the action. This person or thing is known as the 'agent':

*He was bitten **by a dog**.　The tree was struck **by lightning**. This wasn't written **by Shakespeare**.*

When we ask who or what the agent is/was/will be, we
put *by* at the end of the question:
Who was this picture painted by?
But in most passive sentences the agent is not mentioned.

E   We use an affirmative verb for questions about the
    identity of the subject of an active verb:
    Who wrote this play?
    But this type of question needs an interrogative verb in
    the passive:
    *Who **was** this play **written** by?*

    In the active we use an interrogative verb for questions
    about the identity of the object:
    What did they steal?
    But this type of question takes an affirmative verb in
    the passive:
    *What **was stolen**?*

    Other types of question need an interrogative verb in
    both active and passive:
    Active: *Where did they hide the stolen goods?*
    Passive: *Where **were** the stolen goods **hidden**?*

F   When phrasal verbs (259–260) are put into the passive,
    the preposition/adverb comes immediately after the verb:

    Active: *They will cut the tree down/cut down the tree.*
    Passive: *The tree **will be cut down**.*

    Active: *He turned the lights out/turned out the lights.*
    Passive: *The lights **were turned out**.*

Exercise 213

▶   Rewrite these sentences in the passive:
    □   We usually lock the safe.   The safe *is usually locked*.
    1   But last night someone left it open.   But last night
        it _____.
    2   And thieves stole everything in it.   And everything
        in it _____.
    3   The police don't think that they will catch the thieves.
        They don't think that the thieves _____.
    4   Are they questioning everybody in the house?   Is
        everybody _____?
    5   Have you told the bank manager?   Has _____?

▶ Complete these sentences:
  □ We'll have to answer this letter, I suppose? ~ Yes, it *will have to be answered*.
  6 We should have answered it earlier, I suppose? ~ Yes, it ____.
  7 We needn't type it, I suppose? ~ No, it ____.
  8 But we must photocopy it, I suppose? ~ Yes, it ____.
  9 We ought to post it today, I suppose? ~ Yes, it ____.

▶ Answer these questions, in the way shown. Use the verbs in brackets.
  □ What happened to the letters? (may/burn) ~ *They may have been burnt.*
  10 What happened to his passport? (may/steal) ~
  11 Why didn't our agent wake up? (must/drug) ~
  12 Why did the officials take no action? (could/bribe) ~
  13 Why hasn't our agent appeared? (might/murder) ~

214 Infinitive constructions after passive verbs

A Infinitives after *believe*, *know*, *say* and *think* in the passive

1 Sentences beginning *People believe/know/say/think* have two possible passive forms:
    *It is believed **that** he is here* OR *He is believed **to be** here.*
    *It is said **that** he is an inventor* OR *He is said **to be** an inventor.*

   Similarly in the past:
    *It was believed **that** he was a millionaire* OR
    *He was believed **to be** a millionaire.*

2 As well as the simple infinitive *to be* we can use the continuous infinitive of any verb:
    *He is said **to be living** in Paris.*

3 When the belief etc. concerns an earlier action we can use the perfect infinitive of any verb:
    *He is believed **to have been** a murderer.*
    *He is said **to have murdered** his whole family.*

B After *suppose* in the passive we can use the infinitive of any verb:
    *You're **supposed to do** the washing up.* (It's your duty.)

Exercise 214

▶ Complete these replies. Use the words in brackets.
   □ Is he working there?   (believe) ~
      Yes, *he's believed to be working there.*
   1 Is he writing another novel?   (suppose) ~ Yes ____ .
   2 Is he living in France? (say) ~ Yes ____ .
   3 Is he building a house there?   (believe) ~ Yes ____ .

▶ Now complete these replies. Use the words in CAPITALS.
   □ Do the police KNOW that he was a terrorist? ~
      Yes, *he is known to have been a terrorist.*
   4 Do they THINK that he was responsible for the plane
      crash? ~ Yes, ____ .
   5 Do they BELIEVE that he smuggled explosives into the
      plane? ~ Yes, ____ .
   6 Do they SUPPOSE that he died in the crash? ~ Yes, ____ .

215 Uses of the passive

We use the passive as follows.

A When it is not necessary to mention the agent as it is
   obvious or not important who he is/was/will be:
      *The road **has been repaired**.   Refreshments **will be served**.*

B When we don't know exactly or have forgotten who
   did the action:
      *The guard **was murdered**.   The money **was stolen**.*

C When we are more interested in the action than in the
   person who did it:
      *This book **was published** in Belgium.*
      *The flat above us **has been sold**.*

D When the subject of the active verb would be 'people':
      *He **is expected** to win.* (People expect that he will win.)

E When the speaker prefers not to mention the subject.
   An employer, instead of saying *I do not allow smoking in
   the workshop*, will probably say *Smoking is not allowed in
   the workshop*. Similarly in a private conversation, Tom,
   who suspects Bill of opening his letters, may say *This
   letter has been opened!* instead of *You have opened this letter!*

30   The subjunctive

216   The present subjunctive

A   The present subjunctive has the same form as the bare infinitive:
The Queen lives here. (present simple tense)
Long live the Queen! (subjunctive)

B   We use the present subjunctive in certain exclamations and phrases:
(God) bless you!   God save the Queen!
If need be (= if necessary) *we can lend you more money.*

217   The past subjunctive (unreal past)

A   This has the same form as the past simple except that in the past subjunctive of *to be* we can use *were* for all persons.

B   *as if/as though* + past subjunctive

The past subjunctive here shows that the statement after *as if/as though* is untrue:
He orders me about as though I were his wife! (But I'm not.)
or that we don't know whether it is true or not:
Tom talks as if he met the minister quite often. (Perhaps he does meet the minister quite often, but we are not sure.)

We can put the main verb into a past tense without changing the subjunctive:
Tom talked as if he met the minister quite often.

But if the action after *as if/as though* is earlier than the action in the main verb we normally use the past perfect, though the past tense is possible:
He talks as though he (had) built the house himself.

C *it is time* + past subjunctive

We use this when we feel the precise time when we should have done something has passed:

It's time we went. (We should have already left.)

▷ See also conditional sentences, 185; *would rather/sooner*, 226 B; *wish*, 227, 228 C. For past subjunctives in indirect speech, see 232 A.

Exercise 217

▶ Complete these sentences:

☐ He uses the car as if it *were* his own. (But it is not his own.)

1 He talks as if he _____ the managers personally. (But he doesn't know them.)

2 He behaves as if he _____ the hotel. (But he doesn't own it.)

3 He treats the hotel staff as if they _____ his own employees. (But they are not his own employees.)

4 He talks as if he _____ the hotel himself. (But he didn't build it.)

▶ Complete these replies:

☐ The children had better go to bed. ~
Yes, *it's time they went to bed.*

5 We'd better have a meeting. ~ Yes, _____.

6 We'll have to make some plans. ~ Yes, _____.

7 We must write to Tom. ~ Yes, _____.

31   Commands, requests, invitations, advice and suggestions

218   Commands

A The imperative form

1 The second person imperative has the same form as the bare infinitive:

Hurry!   Stop!   Wait!

For the negative we put *do not/don't* before the infinitive:

Don't hurry!   Don't stop.

We can show who we are speaking to by adding a noun:
*Come here, **Tom**. Be quiet, **boys**.*
But we don't usually do this.

We can add *do* for emphasis:
***Do** hurry! **Do** be quiet!*

2   The first person imperative has the form *let us/let's* +
bare infinitive:
***Let's** ask Ann. **Let's** go by bus.*

For the negative we can put *not* before the infinitive:
*Let's **not** tell anyone.*
or *don't* before *let's*:
***Don't** let's tell anyone.*

The speaker who says *Let's . . .* usually wants another
person/other people to do something with him or, in
the negative, to agree not to do it.

(For *let's* for suggestions, see 222 A.)

3   The third person imperative has the form *let him/them* +
bare infinitive:
***Let** them go by train.*
But see B and C below for more usual forms.

B   *be* + infinitive (see also 104 B–C)

We can use this form with both second and third persons:
*You **are to** wait for Tom. (These are Mr Smith's orders.)*
These orders or instructions are normally part of a
previously made plan or scheme.

C   *must*

must is more emphatic than the *be* form:
*You **must** not smoke in the laboratory.*
*Visitors to this country **must** have a visa.*

D   *no* + gerund

We often use this in notices:
No smoking.   No parking.

Exercise 218

▶ Write sentences as shown. Use the words in brackets.

☐ Peter advises selling the car. ~ (good)
   That's a good idea. Sell the car.

☐ Peter advises opening a shop. ~ (not good)
   That's not a good idea. Don't open a shop.

Peter advises:
1   buying an old bicycle.   (not good)
2   going on foot.   (good)
3   learning another language.   (good)
4   staying at home next summer.   (good)
5   borrowing money.   (not good)
6   getting more credit cards.   (not good)

219   Requests

A *could you*

> *Could you please wait a moment?*

couldn't you shows that the speaker hopes for a more favourable answer:

> *I can't wait. ~ Couldn't you wait ten minutes?*

B *would you*

This form is similar to *could you*:

> *Would you please shut the door?*

would you at the end of the phrase *Shut the door, would you?* is possible but only between friends.

C *will*

We can use *will* with the third person in notices and announcements:

> *Will anyone who saw this accident please ring 1234?*
> *Will Mr Jones, travelling to Rome, please come to the Information Desk?* (airport announcement)

For second person requests *would you* is more common than *will you*, but we can use *will you (please)* to friends.

Notice also the persuasive form *You will . . . , won't you?*

> *You'll write to me, won't you?*

D *would you mind*

> *Would you mind opening the window?* (Please open it.)

E *if you would*

This is used for polite, rather formal requests:
> *If you'd sign the register.* (Please sign it.)

We can add *just* to show that it is a very simple request:
> *If you'd just put your address on the back of the cheque.*

F *would you like*

> *Would you like to come this way?* (Please come this way.)

G *I wish you would*

We often use this when we are annoyed or impatient:
> *I wish you'd shut the door. Why do you always leave it open?*

H *you might*

This can express a very casual request to friends only:
> *You might post these letters for me.*

▷ For requests for permission etc., see 114.

Exercise 219

► You are going on holiday with your husband Tom and your children Ann and Bill. Complete these requests.

□ (You ask Tom to carry the cases down.)   Could you *carry these cases down?*

1 (You ask Bill to ring for a taxi.) Would you ____?
2 (You ask the taxi driver to wait.) Would you mind ____?
3 (You ask Ann, rather impatiently, to hurry up.) I wish you ____.
4 (You ask Bill to check that the windows are shut.) You might ____.

► Now write the offers for the situations in brackets:

5 (You offer a friend a drink.) Would ____?
6 (You offer him a cigarette.) Will ____?
7 (You invite some friends to have coffee with you tomorrow.) Could ____?

220   Invitations

A   *will you have/would you like* + noun

> *Will you have a coffee?* OR *Have a coffee.*
> *Would you like a sandwich?* ~ *Yes, please* OR *No, thank you.*

Don't use *do you want* here.

B   *would you/could you* OR *would you like to*

> *Would you/Could you have lunch with me tomorrow?*
> *I have two tickets. Would you like to come with me?*

Possible answers:
> *I'd like to very much/I'd love to* OR
> *I'd like to very much but I'm afraid I can't.*

Don't use *wouldn't like* when refusing invitations.

▷   See also 225 B.

221   Advice

A   *must, ought to* and *should*

> *You **must** read this book. It's marvellous.*
> *You **ought to** go with a group. You **shouldn't** go alone.*
> ***Ought** I **to** insure the house?*

must is the most emphatic.

B   *had better* + bare infinitive (see also 107 C)

> *You'd **better** go now. You'd **better not** wait any longer.*

We can use it with other persons:
> *He'd **better** apply for a visa.*

C   *if I were you I should/would*

> *If I were you I'd go on foot; I wouldn't take the car.*

We can omit *if I were you* but must then stress the *I*:
> *'I should/would go on foot* OR *'I'd go on foot.*

D   *may as well*

We use this in the affirmative only for unemphatic advice:
  *You **may as well** read the letter.* (It would do no harm.)
We can use it for other persons:
  *As there's nothing for me to do here I **may as well** go home.*

E   *why don't you* or *why not* + bare infinitive

  ***Why don't you** apply?*   ***Why not** walk to work?*

F   *it is time you* + past tense (see also 217 C)

  ***It's time you** began looking for work.*

Exercise 221

▶ George has health problems. Give him some good advice.
  □ Advise him to stop putting on weight.
    It's time *you stopped putting on weight*.
  1 Advise him to go on a diet.   You ought _____.
  2 Advise him to walk to the station every morning.   Why
    don't _____?
  3 Advise him to take up squash.   If I _____.
  4 Advise him to give up smoking.   You had _____.
  5 Advise him to go to bed earlier.   You must _____.

222 Suggestions

A   *let's* or *shall I/we*

1   *let's* + bare infinitive:
    Let's go by car.

  We sometimes add *shall we?*
    Let's go by car, shall we?

  We make the negative with *let's not* or *don't let's*:
    *Let's not start too early/**Don't let's** start too early.*

2   *shall I/we* + bare infinitive:
    Shall we hire a car?
  We use this in the affirmative only.

3   We can answer with *Yes, let's* or *No, let's not*:
    Let's take a picnic lunch. ~ *Yes, **let's** (take a picnic lunch).*
    Shall we ask Bill to drive? ~ *No, **let's not** (ask Bill to drive).*

B *why don't you/we* or *why not* + bare infinitive

Why don't you take a taxi?/Why not take a taxi?

C *what/how about* + gerund or noun

I haven't made any soup. ~
Then *what about opening a tin?* OR *How about a tin?*

D *I/we suggest* + gerund or *that*-clause

I suggest sending the goods by air.
I suggest that we send them by air.

A *that*-clause with *should* is possible but more formal:
I suggest that we should send them by air.

Exercise 222

▶ Put in the words from the list. Use each word once.
why not, why don't we, what about, let's, let's not, shall we

□ Let's go to a theatre on Saturday, *shall we?*

1   No, ____ go to a theatre. Paul doesn't know much English.
2   Then ____ an opera? There's 'Otello' at the Coliseum. Shall we go to that?
3   Yes, ____. We can go by car.
4   ____ go by taxi? Parking there would be difficult.
5   All right, and ____ have supper out afterwards?

32   Verbs of liking and preference

223   *care for, like, dislike, love, hate, prefer*

A *care for* and *like*, used of feelings, are similar, but we use *care for* mainly in the negative and interrogative:

Do you care for ghost stories?/Do you like ghost stories?
No, I don't care for them/No, I don't like them. BUT
Yes, I like them. (*care for* would be very unusual here.)

B With *care for* (negative and interrogative), *like*, *dislike*, *love*, *hate* and *prefer* in the present and past we can use nouns, pronouns or gerunds:

> *Ann **loves** town life. Tom **prefers** the country.*
> *Bill **hated** school. Why **did** he **hate** it?*
> *Do you **dislike** writing letters?*

But infinitives are also possible after *like*, *love*, *hate*, *prefer* and are common in American English:

> *He **loved to watch** the trains go by.*

Infinitives are not used after *dislike* or *care for*.

Exercise 223

▶ Tom is telling Bill about the adventure centre they are going to. Complete Bill's replies.

□ We'll swim ~ Good; *I like swimming.*
□ . . . and fish. ~ But *I don't care for fishing.*
1 We'll ride ~ Good; ____.
2 and walk ~ But ____.
3 and explore underground caves ~ But ____.
4 and climb mountains. ~ Good; ____.

224 *would care for/would care* (negative and interrogative), *would like/love/hate/prefer*

A After *would care for*, *would like/love/hate/prefer* we can use nouns or pronouns:

> *Would you **like** coffee or would you **prefer** tea?*

B Verbs after *would care/like/love/hate/prefer* are usually infinitives:

> *Would you **care to live** here? ~ No, I **wouldn't care to live** in such a lonely place* OR *Yes, I'**d like to live** here.*

The perfect infinitive is also possible, but note the meaning:

> *I'**d like to have seen** it.* (I wanted to see it but I didn't get my wish.)

225 *would like* and *want*

A Examples of use in requests and answers to requests:

Customer: *I'd like six brown rolls, please.*
Baker: *I'm afraid I haven't any.* **Would you like** *white rolls?*
Customer: *No,* **I don't want** *white rolls, thanks.*

In requests we normally use *I would like*, which is more
polite than *I want*, but we use *I want* if we need
something urgently:

I want an ambulance.

would you like? is more polite and helpful than *do you want?*
so people dealing with clients and customers normally use
it. But there is a difference between the negative forms.
don't want means 'have no wish for', but *wouldn't like* means
'dislike'; so the customer above uses *don't want*.

B In invitations we use *would you like?*, not *do you want?*

Would you like *a lift to the station?* ~
Yes, please OR *Yes, I would (like a lift)* BUT
No, thanks OR *No, I don't want a lift, thanks.* (Not *I
wouldn't like a lift.* See A above.)

Would you like *to come to the match with me?* ~
Yes, I'd like to (come with you) very much OR
I'd like to, but I'm afraid I'm not free on Saturday.

C When we are not making requests or giving invitations,
we can normally use either *want* or *would like* in the
negative as well as affirmative or interrogative.

D Past forms of *want* and *would like*

In reported speech *want* becomes *wanted*, but *would like*
remains unchanged:

He said, 'I want to go/I'd like to go.'
He said he wanted to go/He said he'd like to go.

But *would like* as a main verb becomes *wanted* in the past:

Tom would like a lift today/Tom wants a lift today.
Tom wanted a lift yesterday.

We use *would like* + perfect infinitive (see also 224):

I'd like to have written to him. (But this was not possible.)

We can also use *would have liked* + noun/pronoun or present infinitive:
> *I'd have liked a day off.* (But I didn't get it.)

Exercise 225

▶ Complete these replies:
- □ We thought of going by car ~ Yes, *I'd like to go by car.*
- □ and starting at 2 a.m. ~ But *I don't want to start at 2 a.m.*
- 1 We thought of spending the first week picking grapes. ~ But ____.
- 2 And then we thought of camping by the Loire ~ Yes ____.
- 3 and swimming before breakfast ~ But ____.
- 4 and visiting the castles ~ Yes ____.
- 5 and going to museums ~ Yes ____.
- 6 and living very cheaply. ~ But ____.

226 *would rather/sooner* and *prefer*

would rather and *would sooner* have the same meaning and are used in the same way. But *would rather* is the more usual form. For convenience, we mention *would rather* only. *would* in both cases is usually contracted to *'d*.

A *would rather* + bare infinitive (+ *than*) and *prefer*

1 *would rather* can have a present meaning, so that:
> *He'd rather read than talk* can mean
> *He prefers reading to talking.*
Note the difference in construction here:
> *would rather* + infinitive + *than* + infinitive BUT
> *prefer* + gerund + *to* + gerund

2 *would rather* can also refer to a future action, and have the same meaning as *would prefer*:
> *Shall we go by train? ~ I'd rather fly (than go by train)* OR
> *I'd prefer to fly.*
Note that with *prefer* we mention the preferred action only, but that with *would rather* we can mention both actions.

3 We can put a noun/pronoun directly after *prefer*, but with *would rather* we need an infinitive. *have* is often used:
> *He'd prefer a house in the country but she would rather have a house in the town.*

B We can use *prefer* + object + infinitive or *would rather* + subject + unreal past. These have the same meaning. They refer to the present or future.

> *He wants to cycle to school; **I'd prefer him to go** by bus* OR
> ***I'd rather he went** by bus.* (*went* is an unreal past.)

C Past forms of *would rather* and **prefer**

1 *would rather* in reported speech remains unchanged:

> *He said, 'I'd rather fly than go by train.'*
> *He said he'd rather fly than go by train.*

But we cannot use *would rather* + present infinitive as a main verb in the past, so we normally express past preference by *preferred*: *Tom **preferred** to fly.*

2 Note the meaning of *would rather* + perfect infinitive:

> *We went by air, although I'd **rather have gone** by sea.*
> (I wanted to go by sea but we went by air instead.)

Exercise 226

▶ Complete these sentences.

    □ Ann prefers skating to skiing, but *I'd rather ski than skate.*
    1 Ann prefers talking to reading, but I'd ____.
    2 Ann prefers watching tennis to playing, but ____.
    3 Ann prefers cycling to walking, but ____.

▶ You and Tom are going on holiday. Your uncle, Bill, is paying for it. Give Bill's answers to your questions. Bill always prefers the first option in CAPITALS.

    □ Shall I HIRE a car or take your car? ~
       Bill: *I'd rather you hired a car.*
    4 Shall I DRIVE or shall I let Tom drive? ~ Bill: ____.
    5 Shall I CHOOSE the route or shall I let Tom choose it? ~
       Bill: ____.
    6 Shall we START ON MONDAY or Tuesday? ~ Bill: ____.

227 *wish* + subject + *would*

A We can use *wish* + subject + *would* to express regret that some other person (the subject of *would*) isn't willing to do what we want him to do. The action must obviously be one which the subject of *would* can control.

> ***I wish you would** come and see me more often.*

B We can use this form for present, usually habitual, or future actions:

> *I **wish** he **would** come home earlier in the evenings.* (I'm sorry he isn't willing to do this.)
> *I **wish** the children **would** eat vegetables.* (I'm sorry they refuse to eat vegetables.)
> *I **wish** Tom **would** stay at school for another year.* (I'm sorry that he intends to leave school this year.)

C We can also use *wish* + subject + *would* for future actions when the subject of *would* is a thing:

> *I **wish** it **would** stop raining.*   *I **wish** the sun **would** come out.*

Here *wish* + *would* expresses a not very optimistic wish about the future. If we were more optimistic we would use *hope* + subject + *will*:

> *I **hope** it **will** stop raining.*   *I **hope** the sun **will** come out.*

Exercise 227

▶ Complete these replies. Use the words in brackets.
   □ He gets up late in the mornings. (earlier) ~
      Yes, I wish he'd get up earlier.
   1 He doesn't eat a proper breakfast. ~ Yes, ____.
   2 He plays his transistor far too loudly. (more quietly) ~
      Yes, ____.
   3 He comes in very late at night. (earlier) ~ Yes, ____.
   4 And he makes a lot of noise. (less noise) ~ Yes, ____.
   5 He won't tell us where he goes. ~ Yes, ____.
   6 He won't answer our questions. ~ Yes, ____.

228 *wish* + infinitive, *wish* + noun, *wish* + past tense

A *wish* + infinitive

wish + infinitive has the same meaning as *want/would like* + infinitive, but is more formal:
but is more formal:

> *I **wish** to see the manager.*   *I **wish** to make a complaint.*

B *wish* + noun

This form has a restricted use. In sentences such as *He wants/wanted a house* and *She would like a flat*, we cannot replace *want* or *would like* by *wish*. But we can wish someone luck/a happy Christmas etc.:

> *He wished me luck.* (He said, 'Good luck!')

We can also *wish for* something, usually something we have no hope of getting. This phrase is used chiefly in exclamations:

> *How he wished for a good map!*

C Subject + *wish (that)* + subject + past tense (subjunctive)

The two subjects may be the same or may be different.

1 *wish (that)* + subject + past tense expresses regret about a present situation:

> *I wish I had more time.* (I'm sorry I haven't more time.)
> *I wish you could drive.* (I'm sorry you can't drive.)

We can put *wish* into the past without changing the other verb:

> *I wished I had more time.* (I was sorry I hadn't more time.)

2 *wish (that)* + subject + past perfect (subjunctive) expresses regret about a past situation or action:

> *I wish I had asked him.* (I'm sorry I didn't ask him.)
> *I wish you hadn't posted it.* (I'm sorry you posted it.)

We can use *wished* without changing the subjunctive:

> *I wished I hadn't posted it.* (I was sorry I had posted it.)

3 We can use *if only* instead of *wish (that)* in 1 and 2 above. *if only* has the same meaning but is more dramatic:

> *If only I knew his address!   If only you'd told me earlier!*

Exercise 228

▶ Complete these sentences:

☐ I *wish I could* park near my office. (But I can't park.)
1 I ____ nearer the centre. (But I don't live near the centre.)
2 I ____ afford a flat here. (But I can't afford a flat here.)
3 I ____ a well-paid job. (But I haven't (got) a well-paid job.)
4 I ____ French. (But I don't know French.)
5 I ____ to university after leaving school. (But I didn't go.)

33   Reported speech

229   Direct and reported speech

There are two ways of reporting what someone has said: direct speech and indirect, or reported, speech.

A When we use direct speech we repeat the speaker's exact words:

> Mary: *I've bought the tickets.*
> *She said, 'I've bought the tickets.'*

Note the comma after *said* and the quotation marks.

B In reported speech we give the exact meaning of what was said, without necessarily using the speaker's exact words:

> *She said (that) she'd bought the tickets.*

There is no comma after *say* etc. in reported speech. We often omit *that* after *say* and *tell* + object, but keep it after other introductory verbs like *complain* or *explain*.

When reporting a conversation verbally, we normally use reported speech, though we occasionally use direct speech for dramatic effect.

230   Pronouns, adjectives and adverbs

A First person pronouns and possessive adjectives change to third person:

> *He said, 'I've missed **my** train.'* →
> *He said he'd missed **his** train.*

except when the speaker is reporting his own words:

> *I said, 'I've lost my job.'* →   *I said I'd lost my job.*

you/your usually change:

> *He said, '**You're** late.'* →   *He said I was late.*
> *He said, '**You've** left **your** umbrella behind, Ann.'* →
> *He told Ann **she** had left **her** umbrella behind.*

But if we are talking to Ann, we leave the *you/your* unchanged:

> *He told you (that) you'd left your umbrella behind.*

B *this* (adjective) in time expressions often becomes *that*:
> *I said, 'I'll go later **this** week/month/year.'* →
> *I said I'd go later **that** week/month/year.*

this, used otherwise, and *these, that, those* (adjectives) usually change to *the*:
> *He said, 'I'll give you **this** book/**these** books.'* →
> *He said he'd give me **the** book/**the** books.*

this, that/these, those (pronouns) usually change to *it/them*:
> *'I made **this**,' she said.* → *She said she'd made **it**.*
But *that*, representing a clause, can remain unchanged:
> *'That's true,' he said.* → *He said that was true.*

C1 The following expressions change unless the speech is reported on the same day:

> *'today'* → *that day*   *'yesterday'* → *the day before*
> *'the day before yesterday'* → *two days before*
> *'tomorrow'* → *the next day/the following day*
> *'the day after tomorrow'* → *in two days' time*.

2 The following change unless the speech is reported in the same week/month/year:

> *'the next week/month/year'* → *the following week/month* etc.
> *'last week/month/year'* → *the previous week/month* etc.
> *'a week/month/year ago'* → *a week* etc. *before*

D *here* becomes *there* only when it is clear what place is meant:
> *The man in the bar said, 'I'll be **here** tomorrow.'* →
> *He said he'd be **there** the next day.*

In other cases *here* is usually reported by a phrase:
> *I said, 'Sit **here**.'* → *I told him to sit **beside me** etc.*
But *'Come here!'* is usually reported *He called* + object:
> *He said, '**Come here**, boys.'* → *He called the boys.*

Exercise 230

▶ Read this conversation and fill the spaces in the reported speech below:
> Mary: You'd enjoy yourself more, Paul, if you had your own flat.
> Paul: But my mother likes me living at home.

Mary: Your mother is quite different from mine. My mother doesn't want me at home. We get on quite well but we couldn't live together. Our ideas are too different.

Mary told Paul that (□) *he* would enjoy life more if (1) _____ had a flat of (2) _____ own. Paul said that (3) _____ mother liked (4) _____ living at home. Mary said that (5) _____ mother was quite different from (6) _____. (7) _____ mother didn't want (8) _____ to live at home. (9) _____ got on well but (10) _____ couldn't live together. (11) _____ ideas were too different.

▶ Read this conversation and complete the reported speech below:

Ann: I rang Bill yesterday to ask him to our party next week. But there was no answer.

Tom: Oh, Bill left his flat the day before yesterday and he won't be able to go to your party, Ann, because he's leaving London the day after tomorrow.

Ann said that (12) _____'d rung Bill (13) _____ to ask him to (14) _____ party (15) _____. Tom said that Bill had left (16) _____ flat (17) _____ and that he wouldn't be able to go to (18) _____ party because he was leaving London (19) _____.

231 Statements: tenses

A When the verb introducing the reported statement (*say*, *tell* etc.) is in the present, present perfect or future, we can report the direct statement without any tense changes:
    Tom (on phone to Ann): *I'll get a taxi.*
    Ann (to Mary, who is beside her): *He says he'll get a taxi.*

B The introductory verb is in the present tense when we are
    1 Reporting a conversation which is still going on, as above.
    2 Reading a letter and reporting what it says.
    3 Reading instructions and reporting them.
    4 Reporting what someone says quite often:
        He always says he can't come.
      We could also use a present perfect here:
        He has always said he can't come.

C But the introductory verb is more often in a past tense (*said, told* etc.). Verbs in direct speech then usually change to a corresponding past tense. (*that* has been omitted in the examples below.)

DIRECT SPEECH	REPORTED SPEECH
'*I never hurry*,' he said.	He said he never **hurried**.
'*I'm waiting* for Ann,' he said.	He said he **was waiting** for Ann.
'*I've found* a job,' she said.	She said she'**d found** a job.
'*We've been working*,' they said.	They said they'**d been working**.
'*We shall be here*,' they said.	They said they **would be there**.
'*Tom will help you*,' they said.	They said Tom **would help me**.
'*I shall/I will be working* in Spain,' I said.	I said I **would be working** in Spain.

Note that *He said, 'I shall . . .'* becomes *He said he would . . .* and *I said, 'I shall . . .'* normally becomes *I said I would . . . I said I should . . .* is possible but less usual.

D In modern conversation, however, statements about habitual actions are sometimes reported without a change of tense. So '*I never hurry*,' *he said* could be reported *He said he never hurries*.

Sometimes present continuous and present perfect tenses can also be reported unchanged.

E The past simple tense can become the past perfect:
    She said, 'I loved him.' → *She said she had loved him.*

This change is necessary in the above example as otherwise there would be confusion between past and present feelings. But when there is no risk of confusion we often leave the past simple unchanged:
    She said, 'I saw him on Monday' could be reported
    She said she saw him on Monday OR
    She said she'd seen him on Monday.

F When the past continuous tense (*was working*) is a main verb and there is no time expression, we usually change it to the past perfect continuous:
    He said, 'We were working there.' →
    He said they had been working there.

In other cases this tense is usually reported unchanged:
I said, 'When I saw them they were playing cards. →
I said that when I saw them they were playing cards.

Exercise 231

▶ Paul phones you and you report what he says at once to Ann:
- □ Paul: 'I've just arrived.'
  You: He says he *has* (or he *'s) just arrived.*
1 'I'm at the station.'   He says he ____.
2 'I'll be with you in about an hour.'   He says ____.
3 'I'll get a bus.'   He says ____.
4 'I know where to get one and I remember the number.'
5 'I think I know where to get off.'
6 'I've got presents for you.'

▶ Tom phoned you yesterday. Now report what he said.
- □ Tom: 'I'm leaving Jones and Co.'
  He said *he was leaving Jones and Co.*
7 'I've been offered a better job.'   He said ____.
8 'The salary is twice what I'm getting from Jones and Co.'
9 'There will be a chance of promotion.'
10 'Jones and Co. have refused to promote me.'

232 Subjunctives, modals and conditionals

A Subjunctives (unreal past tense)

Subjunctives are reported unchanged:
'I wish I knew his address,' she said. →
She said she wished she knew his address.

Note that subject + *had better* + bare infinitive usually
remains unchanged. But *you had better* . . . can also be
reported by *advise* + object:
'You'd better go to bed early,' he said. →
*He said I'd better go/He **advised me to go** to bed early.*

B Modals (*could, might, must, ought to, should, would, used to,
need*)

When these are used in the affirmative or negative we
can report them unchanged:
'The plane might be late,' I said. →
I said the plane might be late.

'The car wouldn't start,' he said. →
He said the car wouldn't start.

One exception: *you might* for requests is usually
reported by *ask* + object:
'You might give me your telephone number,' she said. →
She *asked me* to give her my telephone number.

Note also that *must, ought to* and *should* used for advice
can also be reported by *advise* + object:
'You ought to wear a coat,' she said to him. →
She *advised him* to wear a coat.
*The steward said, 'Passengers should keep their luggage
with them at all times.'* →
The steward *advised passengers* to keep their luggage . . .

C   Conditional sentences

Type 1 sentences change in the normal way (231 C):
'If I see him I'll tell him,' I said. →
I said if I *saw* him I'*d tell* him.

Type 2 sentences do not change:
'If she worked faster she'd earn more,' he said. →
He said if she *worked* harder she'*d earn* more.
(For requests with *would you?*, see 219.)

Type 3 sentences do not change:
He said, *'If I'd seen her I'd have asked her.'* →
He said if he'*d seen* her he'*d have asked* her.

Exercise 232

▶ Tom and Ann are expecting Bill but don't know when he's
coming. Report the conversation with *Tom said* or *Ann said*.
□ Tom: I wish Bill had told me when he was coming.
    Tom said he wished Bill had told him when he was coming.
1 Ann: He probably doesn't know about train times.
2 Tom: (Then) I wish he would ring up from the station.
3 Tom: Bill behaves as if we were a hotel.
4 Ann: (Well) it's time I started cooking supper.
5 Tom: You had better make something that you can keep
        hot.
6 Ann: If it's uneatable by the time he arrives, I'll tell him
        that's his own fault.

▶ Bob is going to the opera with Ann and you. But he rings up from the station to say that he'll be late. Report the conversation to Ann later. Begin *Bob said.*

□ I've missed my train, so I might be late.'
Bob said he'd missed his train, so he might be late.

7 'But you needn't wait for me.'
8 'You mustn't miss the first act.'
9 'You could leave my ticket at the box office.'
10 'It was all my own fault. I should have started earlier.'

▶ Now report this conversation. Begin *Ann said* or *Tom said.*

11 Ann: If I see any strawberries in the shops I'll get some.
12 Tom: If they are on sale already, they'll be expensive.
13 Ann: If we had a bigger garden we could grow our own fruit. (use *they, their*)

233 Infinitive and gerund constructions

Instead of *say (that)* + clause we can sometimes use the following.

A *agree/refuse/offer/promise/threaten* + infinitive:

'All right, I'll wait,' he said. → *He agreed to wait.*
'No, I won't sell it,' he said. → *He refused to sell it.*
'I'll help if you like,' he said. → *He offered to help.*
'I'll write, really I will,' I said. → *I promised to write.*

B *accuse . . . of/admit/apologize for/deny/insist on* + gerund:

'You lied!' he said. → *He accused me of lying.*
'I'm sorry I'm late,' I said. → *I apologized for being late.*
'I didn't steal it!' I said. → *I denied stealing it.*

Exercise 233

▶ Report this conversation between Mr Jones and Ann in the office. Use the verbs in brackets.

Mr Jones: Can you finish this letter before you go home?
□ Ann: Yes, I'll finish it.   (agreed)   *She agreed to finish it.*
1 Mr Jones: I'm sorry for keeping you so late, Ann. (apologized)
2 Mr Jones: I promise not to do it again this month. (promised)
3 Mr Jones: Can I give you a lift home?   (offered)

234 *say, tell* and other introductory verbs

A *say* with direct or reported speech

say (that) can introduce a reported statement:
  *Tom **said that** he was ready to start work.*

say can introduce or follow a direct statement:
  *Tom **said**, 'I've read the instructions'* OR
  *'I've read the instructions,' Tom **said**.*

When *say* is in end position we can invert *say* and noun
subject:
  *'I've read the instructions,' **said Tom**.*

say + *to* + the person addressed can follow a statement
in direct speech:
  *'I'm ready to start work,' he **said to me**.*

B *tell* + object (+ *that*) can introduce a reported statement:
  *He **told me (that)** it would be easy.*

tell + object can follow a direct statement:
  *'It'll be easy,' he **told me**.*

tell needs the person addressed except with *tell* + *lies/
stories/the truth*, when the person addressed is optional.

Note *tell* + object + *about/how*:
  *He **told us about** the plane crash.*
  *They **told us how** they had escaped.*

C Other common introductory verbs are:

add	object	remind + object
answer	point out	reply
complain	protest	warn (+ object)
explain	remark	

Exercise 234

▶ Report these sentences, using the verbs in brackets:
  □ 'The service is very slow,' he said.   (complain)
    He complained that the service was very slow.
  1 'Your bicycle has no brakes,' he said to me.   (warn)
  2 'I can manage without brakes,' I said.   (answer)
  3 'You've already had two accidents,' he said.   (remind)
  4 'The first accident wasn't my fault,' I said.   (point out)

235 Questions

A Tenses, pronouns, adjectives, adverbs change as in statements.

B The interrogative word order changes to the affirmative word order:

    'Who is she?' he said. → *He asked who she was.*

With affirmative questions we keep the affirmative form:

    'Who lives here?' he said. → *He asked who lived there.*

C If the introductory verb is *say*, we must replace it by *ask* (+ object) or by *inquire, wonder, want to know* etc.

After *ask* we can put the person addressed:

    *'What do you want?' he **asked me**.* →
    ***He asked (me)** what I wanted.*

But we cannot do this with *inquire, wonder* or *want to know*.

D If the direct question begins with a question word (*how* or *wh-*), we repeat this in the reported question (see above).

If there is no question word we normally use *if* or *whether*:

    'Do you know Tom?' he said. → *He asked if I knew Tom.*

whether can emphasize that a choice has to be made:

    'Do you want to go by air or by sea?' he asked. →
    *He asked **whether** I wanted to go by air or by sea.*

Exercise 235

▶ Mrs Jones is on holiday. She asked Bob, the holiday courier, some questions. Report her questions, using the verbs in brackets.

    □ 'Will breakfast be early?'   (asked)
      She asked if breakfast would be early.
    1 'What time does the coach leave?'   (wanted to know)
    2 'Can we stop to take photographs?'   (asked)
    3 'Where are we having lunch?'   (wanted to know)
    4 'Will there be time to do some shopping?'   (wondered)
    5 'Is this your first season as a courier?'   (asked)

236 Questions with *shall I/we?*

shall I/we? questions can be

A Requests for information or speculations:
'*When shall I hear the result of the test?*' *I asked.*
'*Where shall we be in the year 2000?*' *he said/wondered.*

We report these by *ask/wonder* + *would*:
I asked when I **would** *hear the result of the test.*
He wondered where they **would** *be in the year 2000.*

B Requests for advice or for instructions:
'*What shall I wear, Mother?*' *she said.*
'*Where shall I send your letters?*' *he asked.*

We report requests for advice by *ask* + *should*:
She **asked** *her mother what she* **should** *wear.*
and requests for instructions by *should* or *be* + infinitive
(104 B):
He asked (me) where he **should send** *my letters* OR
He asked me where he **was to send** *my letters.*

C Offers:
'*Shall I wait for you?*' → *He* **offered** *to wait for me.*

Note that '*Would you like me to wait?*' and '*I'll wait if you like*' could also be reported by *offer* as above.

D Suggestions:

These are usually in the form *shall we?*
'*Shall we meet tonight?*' → *He* **suggested** *meeting . . .*

(For suggestions, see 222.)

Exercise 236

▶ Report these offers and suggestions:
  □ '*Shall I bring a bottle of wine?*' *he said.* (offer)
    He offered to bring a bottle of wine.
  1 Tom (on phone): I've got tomorrow off. Shall we go for a drive? (suggest)
  2 Ann: That would be lovely. Shall I bring a picnic lunch? (offer)

3   Tom: That's a good idea. And shall we start early, before
    the rush?   (suggest)
4   Ann: Yes, let's.   (agree)
5   Tom: Shall I call for you at 7?   (offer)

237 Requests for permission with *can/could I?*
may/might I?

A   *can/could I? may/might I?* + *have* + noun

We can report these by *ask* (+ object) + *for*:
'Can I have a sweet?' said the little boy. →
The little boy **asked (me) for** a sweet.
'Could I have the weekend off?' asked Ann. →
Ann **asked (him) for** the weekend off.

B   *can/could I? may/might I?* + *see* . . . or + *speak to*

We can report these by *ask for* or *ask to see/to speak to*:
Could I speak to the manager, please?' I said. →
I **asked for** the manager OR I **asked to see** the manager OR
I **asked to speak** to the manager.

Do not put a noun/pronoun after *ask* here as this would
change the meaning.

C   *can/could I? may/might I?* with other verbs

We usually report these requests by *ask* (+ object) +
if/whether + *could*:
'May I use your phone?' →   He **asked if** he could use my
phone.
'May I/Could I keep the book for another week?' he said. →
He **asked (the librarian) whether** he could keep the book . . .

might is possible here but rather formal.

238 Offers and invitations

A   *will you have? would you like?* + noun

We report these by *offer* + noun:
'Will you have/Would you like some tea?' she said. →
She **offered** me some tea.

B *would you like? could you?* + infinitive

We report these by *ask/invite* + object + infinitive:
> *'Would you like to come too?'* she said. →
> *She **asked/invited** me to come too.*

Exercise 237–238

▶ Put the underlined sentences into reported speech:
- □ Bob: <u>Can I park here?</u>   *Bob asked if he could park there.*
- 1 Attendant: <u>Could I see your permit, please?</u>
    Bob: I've only just joined the staff. I haven't got a permit.
    Attendant: You'll have to ask Mr Jones for one, sir.
- 2 Bob (on the phone): <u>May I speak to Mr Jones, please?</u>
    Secretary: I'm afraid he's away today. Would you like to
    leave a message?
- 3 Bob: Yes. <u>Would you please say that Bob Smith rang about</u>
    <u>a parking permit?</u>
- 4 Secretary: Oh, we have one for you. <u>Could you come to the</u>
    <u>office and pick it up?</u>
- 5 Secretary: <u>Would you like a ticket for our concert?</u>
    Bob: Thanks very much.

239 Commands, requests and advice

A1 We usually report these by *tell/ask/advise* + object +
infinitive:
> *'Shut the door, Tom,'* he said. →
> *He **told Tom to shut** the door.*
> *'Could you pass the sugar, please,'* she said. →
> *She **asked me to pass** the sugar.*
> *'If I were you I'd wait,'* he said. →
> *He **advised me to wait**.* (For advice forms, see 221.)

2 For negative commands etc. we put *not* before the
infinitive:
> *'Don't tell anyone,'* he said. →
> *He **told me not to tell** anyone.*

3 Other verbs which we can use here include:

beg	forbid	order	request
command	implore	recommend	urge
encourage	invite	remind	warn

These verbs, like *tell* and *advise,* must be followed by the person addressed without *to.* If this person is not mentioned in the direct speech we must add a suitable noun or pronoun:

> *'Don't forget to lock the door,' she said.* →
> *She **reminded me to lock** the door.*
> *'Don't drive too fast,' she said.* →
> *She **warned him not to drive** too fast.*

ask follows the above rule except when used as shown in 238 B.

B We can also report commands by *say (that)* + subject + *be* + infinitive.

This is the usual form when the introductory verb is in the present tense:

> *He says, 'Wait till six.'* →
> *He says that **we are to wait** till six* OR
> *He says **to wait** till six.* (colloquial)
> *He says, 'Don't wait after that.'* →
> *He says that **we aren't to wait** after that* OR
> *He says **not to wait** after that.* (colloquial)

It is also useful when reporting a clause + command:

> *He said, 'If you see Ann, tell her to ring me.'* →
> *He said that if I saw Ann **I was to tell** her to ring him.*

Exercise 239

▶ Report this conversation, using the words in brackets:

☐ Solicitor: Could you please sign the document, Mr Smith?   (asked)
The solicitor asked Mr Smith to sign the document.

1 Mrs Smith: Don't sign till you've read it again.   (told)
2 Solicitor: Read the small print very carefully.   (warned)
3 Mr Smith: I haven't got my reading glasses with me. Would you mind reading it aloud?   (asked)
4 Solicitor: If I were you I'd take the document home and study it carefully.   (advised)

▶ A child has been kidnapped. The kidnapper rings the child's father. Complete what the father says to his wife.

☐ Kidnapper: Have £5,000 ready in used notes.
He says that we are to have £5,000 ready.

5 Kidnapper: If you haven't enough cash, go to the bank tomorrow morning.   He says _____.

6   Kidnapper: Wait by the telephone for instructions.
    He says ____.
7   Kidnapper: Don't tell anyone.   He says ____.

240 Suggestions

Suggestions (222) are usually reported by *suggest* +
gerund/noun/pronoun or *that*-clause:
> *'What about walking?/Let's walk,' said Tom.* → *Tom*
> *suggested walking*.
> *'What about a taxi?' I said.* → *I suggested a taxi*.
> *'Why don't you go, Bob?' I said.* →
> *I suggested that Bob went/should go*.

Exercise 240

▶ Report these suggestions. Use *suggested* in the way shown.
   □ *'Shall we have a 'bring and buy' sale?' said Mary.*
      She suggested having a 'bring and buy' sale.
   1   'What about a sponsored walk?' said George.
   2   'Let's do a house-to-house collection,' said Tom.
   3   'You need a permit for that,' Ann pointed out. 'Why don't
       you apply for one, Tom?' (*suggested that Tom . . .*)

241 *let's* in reported speech

A   *let's* + bare infinitive usually expresses a suggestion
    and is reported by *suggest* + gerund. *'Yes, let's'* in answer
    to a suggestion is usually reported by *agree*:
    > *'Let's invite Bill,' said Tom. 'Yes, let's, said Ann.* →
    > *Tom suggested inviting Bill and Ann agreed*.

B   *'Let us/Let's . . .'* is sometimes a call to action. We usually
    report this by *urge* + object + infinitive:
    > *'Let's do everything we can to help!' he said/urged.* →
    > *He urged us to do everything we could to help*.

242 Exclamations and *yes* and *no*

A   Exclamations become statements in reported speech, so
    the '!' disappears.

Exclamations beginning *What a . . .* or *How . . .* are usually reported by *say*, though *exclaim* is sometimes used:

'What a silly idea!' he exclaimed. →
He **said** that it was a silly idea.
'How unjust!' exclaimed Mary. →
Mary **exclaimed** that it was unjust.

Note also:

He said, 'Thank you.' →   He **thanked** me.
He said, 'Good luck!' →   He **wished** me luck.
He said, 'Congratulations!' →   He **congratulated** me.
He said, 'Idiot!' →   He **called** me an idiot.

B   *yes* and *no* are reported by subject + auxiliary verb:

'Can you swim?' ~ 'No.' →
He asked (me) if I could swim and I said (that) **I couldn't**.
'Do you play, Ann?' ~ 'Yes, I do.' →
He asked (Ann) if she played and she said (that) **she did**.

Exercise 242

▶ Report what Ann and Tom said:

□   'Something's burning!' exclaimed Tom. 'Can you smell it, Ann?'
    Tom said something was burning and asked Ann if she could smell it.

1   'No,' said Ann. 'You're just imagining it.'
2   'Are you cooking anything, Ann?' ~ 'No,' said Ann.
3   'Have you been burning rubbish in the garden, Tom?' ~ 'Yes, I have.'
4   'Did you leave the fire burning, Tom?' ~ 'No, I didn't.'

243   Reported speech: mixed types

Direct speech may consist of statement + question, statement + command, suggestion + statement etc.

A   Normally each requires its own introductory verb:

'I don't know the way. Do you?' he said. →
He **said** he didn't know the way and **asked** if I knew it.
'This place is dangerous. Go away!' he said. →
He **said** that the place was dangerous and **told** me to go away.

B   But sometimes we can use *as* instead of a second
introductory verb:
  'Could you open the window? It's very warm,' I said. →
  I asked him to open the window as it was very warm.

C   Sometimes the second introductory verb can be a participle:
  *'Don't drink too much. Remember that you'll have to drive
  home.'* →
  *She warned him not to drink too much, reminding him
  that he would have to drive home.*

Exercise 243

▶ Report this conversation, using *said, advised, asked, suggested*:
  1   Ann: I can't find my keys. Have you seen them, Peter?
  2   Peter: No. Can you remember when you last had them?
  3   Ann: No. Would you mind looking in your car?
  4   Peter (returning):   They're not in the car. Can you get into
      the house without them?
  5   Ann: Yes; my sister's at home. But what shall I do about
      the keys?
  6   Peter: Let's go back to the restaurant and ask there.

34   Linking words

244   *and, but, or, neither . . . nor, either . . . or, both . . . and*

A   *and, but, or* join pairs of nouns/adjectives/adverbs/
verbs/phrases/clauses:
  They eat fish and eggs.   *He is tall and strong.*
  It was sunny but cold.   *Shall we camp here or over there?*
  Can he sing or dance? ~ *He sings but he doesn't dance.*

B   *neither . . . nor, either . . . or, both . . . and* add emphasis.

1   Affirmative verb + *neither . . . nor* is more emphatic
than negative verb + *or*:
  *The forecast was 'cold and foggy', but it was neither cold
  nor foggy.* (It wasn't either cold or foggy.)
  He neither wrote nor phoned. (He didn't either write or
  phone.)

2 We can also use *either* with affirmative and interrogative verbs:

> We must (**either**) leave the room now **or** pay for another day.
> Could you ring me (**either**) today **or** tomorrow?

(For *neither*, *either* in additions to remarks, see 102 D.)

3 *both . . . and* is more emphatic than *and* alone:

> **Both** boys **and** girls should learn to cook.

Exercise 244

▶ Finish these sentences, using *neither . . . nor*:

☐ He said there were trees and flowers round the building. But *there are neither trees nor flowers*.

1 He said there was a playground and a roof garden. But ____.

2 He said that the rooms were large and bright. But these rooms ____.

3 He said that the furniture was modern and elegant. But this ____.

▶ Reply to these remarks, using *neither . . . nor*:
He says he used to:

☐ sing and dance. ~ Nonsense! *He neither sang nor danced*.

4 sing solos and train the choir. ~ Nonsense! ____.

5 play the piano and conduct the orchestra. ~ ____.

6 write and direct plays. ~ ____.

▶ Put in *both . . . and* or *either . . . or*:

☐ Maria: I'd like to be a full-time student. Can I come to *both* morning *and* afternoon classes?

7 Secretary: No, we don't take full-time students. You must come ____ in the morning ____ in the afternoon.

8 Maria: I want to study more than one language. Can I take ____ French ____ German classes?

9 Secretary: I'm afraid the French and German classes are at the same time. So you will have to take ____ French ____ German.

10 Maria: Do I have to pay now? ~ Secretary: No, you can ____ pay now ____ pay when the classes start.

245 *besides, however, otherwise, so, therefore, still, yet*

These can join sentences or clauses, but all except *therefore* can also be used in other ways. Their position will vary according to how they are used.

A *besides* (preposition) means 'in addition to/as well as':
*He works full-time and **besides** that he helps his wife.*

besides (adverb) means 'moreover/also':
*I'm not ready to go out now; **besides**, it's raining.*

We can also use *anyway* or *in any case* instead of *besides*:
***Anyway**, it's raining.*

B *however* (adverb of degree) precedes its adjective/adverb:
*You won't earn much there, **however** hard you work.* (no matter how hard)

however (conjunction) usually means 'but'. It often follows the first word or phrase, but can also precede or follow the clause:
*He agreed to support us. Later, **however**, he changed his mind/He changed his mind later, **however**.* (He agreed to support us but later (he) changed his mind.)

C *otherwise* (adverb) can mean 'in other ways/apart from this':
*Your spelling is poor. **Otherwise** your work is good.*

otherwise (conjunction) means 'if not/or else':
*We must take a taxi. **Otherwise** we'll be late.*

D *so* (adverb of degree) precedes its adjective/adverb:
*Her heels were **so** high that she couldn't walk fast.*

so (conjunction) precedes its clause:
*My case was heavy **so** I took a taxi.*

E *therefore* can replace *so* (conjunction) in formal English. It can precede its clause or precede the main verb or follow the first word or phrase:
*There was fog at Heathrow. **Therefore** the plane was diverted* OR *The plane **therefore** was diverted* OR
*The plane was **therefore** diverted.*

F *still* and *yet* can be adverbs of time (43 C):
*Prices are **still** high. They haven't come down **yet**.*

still (conjunction) joins two clauses or sentences and
means 'I admit that, but in spite of that':
*I'm not rich. ~ **Still**, you could give something.* (I admit
that you aren't rich, but . . .)

yet (conjunction) also joins two clauses. It means 'in
spite of that':
*They're ugly and expensive; **yet** people buy them.*

Exercise 245

▶ Put in *besides, however* or *otherwise*:
  □ Bill: Go by air; *otherwise* you'll spend hours in a train.
  1 John: But I have to go by train; ____ my boss won't pay.
  2 John: If there's a train strike ____, he'll pay my air fare
    home.
  3 Bill: Do you mind travelling by train? ~ John: No, I like
    it. ____, when I travel by train my wife can come too.
  4 Bill: You'd better be at the station in good time, ____ you
    won't get seats.

▶ Now put in *still* or *yet*:
  5 Alex: Are you ____ thinking of leaving your present job?
    Jim: Yes, I am.
  6 Alex: Have you found anything else ____?
  7 Jim: No. Actually I'm ____ thinking of starting my own
    business, but I haven't discussed it with my wife ____.
  8 Alex: I ____ think you should look for another job.

246 *though/although* and *in spite of/despite*

A *though/although* usually introduces a clause of concession:
__Although__ it was foggy he drove fast OR
He drove fast __although__ it was foggy.
*He has a full-time job __though/although__ he hasn't got a
work permit.*

We can use either *though* or *although* except as in B below.

B We can also use *though* (but not *although*) to link two main
clauses. *though* here means 'but' and follows its clause:
He says he'll pay; I don't think he will, __though__.

C *in spite of* + noun/pronoun/gerund can sometimes
replace *though/although* + clause:
> *In spite of the fog he drove fast* OR
> *He drove fast in spite of the fog.*
> *He has a full-time job in spite of having no work permit* OR
> *In spite of having no work permit he has a full-time job.*

D *despite* can replace *in spite of*. It is often used in newspapers:
> *Despite the bad weather, the cyclists completed the course.*

Exercise 246

▶ Put in *in spite of* or *although/though*:

☐ Tom's wife drives better than he does, *although* he won't
   admit it.

1 Tom is proud of his driving ____ he isn't a good driver.

2 He's had several accidents and has been fined for
   speeding; ____ that he still drives too fast.

3 Last night ____ there was a lot of fog on the road, he didn't
   slow down at all.

4 Of course, lots of people drive fast ____ bad weather
   conditions and warnings from the police.

5 ____ the weather was bad, we arrived on time.

247 *while, when* and *as* used for time

A *while* can mean 'during the time that'.

We use it with simple tenses when we have parallel
actions:
> *One of us slept while the other drove.*
> *While she painted he cooked and cleaned.*

But *while* with a continuous tense is more usual in
sentences like:
> *While we were swimming someone stole our clothes.*

B *when*

1 *when* with simple or continuous tenses can mean 'in
   this period':
> *When I lived/was living in Bath I used to cycle to work.*
> *I met him when I was living in Bath.* (The continuous
> tense is usual here. *while* would also be possible.)

2 *when* with simple tenses can mean 'at this point in time':
> *When I arrived they were watching television.*

or 'immediately after/soon after':
> *When the lift stops the doors open.*

or 'whenever' (= every time):
> *When the bell rings the dogs bark.*

C We use *as* with simple tenses

1 when the second action happens before the first is finished:
> *As I stepped off the pavement I was knocked down by a cyclist.*
> (Perhaps I had one foot still on the pavement.)

We could also use *as* or *when* with a continuous tense in this sentence. But note that *when* + past simple tense would mean 'after I stepped off'.

3 for parallel development:
> *As the wind rose the noise increased.* (the more wind, the more noise)
> *As he grew older he became more confident.*

If we use *when* here we lose the idea of parallel development.

4 for parallel actions (*while* is also possible here):
> *He sang as he worked.   PAYE = Pay as you earn.*

But note that *as = when/while* can be used only with certain verbs (248 A).

Exercise 247

▶ Put in *when* or *whenever* or *while*:

(□) *When* he left college he rented an attic studio. It was uncomfortable and (1) ____ it rained the roof leaked. He was very poor and (2) ____ the landlady came round for the rent he used to climb on to the roof. (3) ____ she sat in the studio waiting for him to come in, he sat on the roof waiting for her to go away. But (4) ____ (= during the time that) he was there he did his best work. Later (5) ____ he had begun to sell his pictures, he got married. She was a writer and (6) ____ he painted she wrote short stories. (7) ____ she sold a story she gave a party. He didn't like some of her friends and, one day, (8) ____ he told her not to invite them she became very angry. Next day, (9) ____ he returned from his studio he found the house empty.

▶ Put in *as* or *when*:
(10) _____ I went shopping yesterday I was wearing a pair of rather loose shoes. (11) _____ I got onto the bus, one of them fell off. I jumped out but (12) _____ I bent down to pick it up a dog seized it and ran away with it. (13) _____ I turned round I found that the bus had gone.

248 *as* = *when/while* and/or *as* = *because*

A We use *as* = *when/while* mainly with verbs of action or development. So we don't use it with the types of verbs listed in 142, *belong, feel, love, see* etc., or with verbs such as *live, remain,* and *stay*.

B *as* with the verbs mentioned in A above normally means 'because':
   As he has a car he can get here easily. (Because he has a car . . .)
   I'll go first as I know the way. (. . . because I know)

C We can also use *as* = *because* with verbs of action. With these verbs, therefore, *as* can mean either *because* or *when/while*:
   As I cycle a lot I keep fairly fit. (Because I cycle . . .)
   As I cycle past the bus queues I feel sorry for them. (When I cycle . . .)

D *as* + noun can mean either *when/while* or *because*:
   As a student he'd been very poor. (When he was a student . . .)
   As a student he gets cheap fares. (Because he's a student . . .)

Exercise 248

▶ In the following passage AS means either 'because' or 'when/while'. Say which meaning each AS has.

(1) AS you're a student you'll get in free. (2) AS you go round the gallery look out for paintings by Turner (3) AS there's going to be a lecture on him tomorrow. (4) AS you go down the steps outside the gallery, look at the new statues on your left. They're ugly but the gallery had to accept them (5) AS the sculptor has also given them some very fine pictures.

35 | Purpose

249 Infinitives of purpose

A We often express purpose by the infinitive:
>   *He went to Paris to study art.*

If the main verb has a person as its object the infinitive
may refer to this person and not to the subject:
>   *She sent Tom to the shop to buy some milk.* (Tom was to
>   buy the milk.)

B We also use either *in order* or *so as* + infinitive

1 with a negative infinitive to express a negative purpose:
>   *We talked quietly in order/so as not to wake the children.*

2 with *to be* and *to have*:
>   *He started early in order/so as to be there in good time.*
>   *She gave up her job in order/so as to have more time at home.*

We can usually put *in order/so as* before the affirmative
infinitive of other verbs also, but this is not necessary
and it is safer to use these phrases only as shown above.

C We can also use

1 noun + infinitive:
>   *I have an essay to write.*   *I have things to do.*

2 noun + infinitive + preposition:
>   *He needs a table to work at and a chair to sit on.*

3 noun + infinitive + noun + preposition:
>   *Have you got a safe to put this money in?*

In 3 we are talking about a particular purpose. For a
general purpose we use *for* + gerund:
>   *A corkscrew is a tool for opening bottles (with).*

D We don't normally put an infinitive of purpose
immediately after the imperative or infinitive of *go* and
come.

Instead of *go/come* (imperative) + infinitive of purpo...
we use *go/come* + *and* + another imperative:

Go and wash your hands.   *Come and have* lunch, boys.

And instead of *(to) go/come* + infinitive of purpose we
use *(to) go/come* + *and* + bare infinitive:

I'll have to go and help my mother.
You must come and taste our wine.

But with other forms of *go* and *come* we can use
infinitives of purpose:

I went to help my mother.   *I'm coming to taste* your wine.

Exercise 249

▶ Complete these sentences:
   □ Peter's father studied music in Paris.
      And now *Peter has gone to Paris to study music.*
   1 Mary's mother read history at Oxford. And now Mary has
      gone ____.
   2 Bill's father studied art in Florence. And now Bill ____.
   3 Tom's mother painted (pictures) in Holland. And
      now Tom ____.

▶ Join the two parts of the sentences by *in order* or *in order not* +
   infinitive. (*so* or *so as not* are also possible.)
   Use *be*, *disturb*, *have* or *reach*.
   □ We decided to catch the first ferry *in order to be* in Calais by
      ten.
   4 We had to get to Dover by six ____ late for the first ferry.
   5 We left home very early on Monday morning ____ Dover
      by six.
   6 We did all our packing on Sunday night ____ more time
      on Monday morning.
   7 We left the house very quietly on Monday ____ anyone.

▶ Read this:
   Would you please cut the bread and ham into slices and make
   sandwiches, and put the sandwiches on a large plate. Oh, and
   could you put the fruit into a bowl, and open the bottles.

   Now complete these replies:
   □ All right, but I'll need a carving knife *to carve the ham with.*
   8 I'll need a breadknife ____.
   9 A large plate ____.
   10 A corkscrew ____.
   11 A bowl ____.

250 Clauses of purpose and alternative forms

A We can also express purpose by a clause. We form
purpose clauses with *so that + will/would +* infinitive or
so that +can/could + infinitive.

Future Present Present perfect	+ *so that + will/can +* infinitive
Conditional Past Past perfect	+ *so that + would/could +* infinitive

B We use a clause of purpose when we have to mention
the subject of the action we wish to happen:
> *The notices are in several languages **so that** foreign tourists
> **will/can understand** them.*
> *He bought the field behind his house **so that** nobody **would/
> could build** on it.*

C Instead of purpose clauses we sometimes use the
following constructions:

to enable + object *+* infinitive
> *They make coins in various sizes **to enable blind people to
> tell** the difference between them.* (so that blind people can
> tell . . .)

to avoid + gerund
> *Raiders wear masks **to avoid being** recognized.* (so that the
> victims won't recognize them)

to prevent + object *+* gerund
> *He wrote his diary in code **to prevent his wife reading** it.*
> (so that his wife wouldn't be able to read it)

D An *in case* clause is sometimes similar to *to prevent +*
gerund:
> *Don't wash it in very hot water **in case** it shrinks.* (to
> prevent it shrinking)
> *I kept the medicine cupboard locked **in case** the children tried
> to open it.* (to prevent the children opening it)

But an *in case* clause can have a different (conditional) meaning:

> *I keep candles in the house **in case** there is a power cut.* (to use if there is a power cut)

Here the subject is merely taking precautions against a possible future action, not trying to prevent it.

(For *in case* and *if*, see 189.)

E Tenses with *in case*

Future Present Present perfect	+ *in case* +	present tense or *should* + perfect infinitive
Conditional Past Past perfect	+ *in case* +	past tense or *should* + perfect infinitive

Exercise 250

▶ (a) Combine these pairs of sentences, using *so that*:
  □ There are burglar alarms on all the windows. He doesn't want anyone to get in secretly.
     There are burglar alarms on all the windows so that no one can get in secretly.
  1 The outer gates are locked when it gets dark. He doesn't want anyone to drive up to the house during the night.
  2 He has guard dogs running round at night. He doesn't want anyone to approach the house on foot.
  3 He has dark glass in his car windows. He doesn't want anyone to see who is in the car.

▶ (b) Now combine them using *to prevent* + gerund:
  □ *There are burglar alarms on all the windows to prevent anyone getting in secretly.*

▶ Use *in case* or *so that* to link the following pairs of clauses:
  □ Write his name in the book *in case* you forget who lent it to you.
  4 Write his name in the book ____ you won't forget who lent it to you.
  5 I cashed a cheque ____ I needed more money.
  6 He took a tent with him ____ he wouldn't have to depend on youth hostels.

36   Subordinate clauses

251   What is a subordinate clause?

A sentence can consist of a main clause only:

He lived with his parents.

or of a main clause and one or more subordinate clauses:

He lived with his parents till he got married.

A subordinate clause is a group of words containing a subject and verb and forming part of a sentence. It does the work of a noun, adjective or adverb.

For examples of subordinate clauses, see:

1   noun clauses 256–258
2   adjective clauses (relative clauses) 67–75
3   adverb clauses of comparison 39; condition (*if*-clauses) 183–189; purpose 250; reason 253; result 254; time 255.

252   The sequence of tenses in subordinate clauses

When the main verb of a sentence is in a past tense, the verb in the subordinate clause normally has to be in a past tense also.

In the following examples the main verbs are in heavy type and the subordinate clauses are underlined:

*I'll **turn on** the heating <u>when I get back</u>.*
*I **turned on** the heating <u>when I got back</u>.*

*I'll **go** <u>as far as I can</u>.*
*I **went** <u>as far as I could</u>.*

*She **rides** better <u>than he does</u>.*
*She **rode** better <u>than he did</u>.*

*I **believe** <u>what he says</u>.*
*I **believed** <u>what he said</u>.*

37 | Clauses of reason, result and time

253 Clauses of reason introduced by *because* or *as*

A We use *because*, not *as*, when we are answering a question:
   *Why did you go?   I went **because** Tom told me to go.*

B We can use *because* with *not*, *but* and *only*. We cannot use *as* in this way:
   *He was angry **not because** we were late **but because** we made a noise.*
   *She **only** smokes **because** he does* OR *She smokes only because he does.*

C But with most clauses of reason we can use either *because* or *as*:
   *He couldn't read the letter **because/as** it was in Japanese.*
   ***As/Because** it was in Japanese he couldn't read it.*
   as is a little more usual than *because* when the clause of reason comes first.

D When the reason is obvious or is already known we normally use *as*:
   ***As** you are here you can give me some help.*

E We can use *since* instead of *because* or *as* in the sentences in C and D above:
   ***Since** it was in Japanese he couldn't read it.*

F We can also use two main clauses joined by *so*:
   *You're here **so** you may as well help me.*

Exercise 253

▶ Put in *as* or *because*. In some of the sentences both forms are equally suitable.
   □ Why are you going to the lake? ~ *Because* Bill wants to see it.
   1 It's his last chance to see it ____ he leaves tomorrow.
   2 Why is he taking his camera? ~ ____ he wants to take photos of the birds.

3 ____ I know the way I'll go first.
4 We'll take a picnic lunch ____ there isn't a restaurant there.
5 ____ we aren't going to a restaurant we can take the dogs.
6 We arrived late not ____ of the traffic but ____ we left late.

254 Clauses of result introduced by *such/so . . . that*

A We use *such* before an adjective + noun (except as shown in C below):

> *He has **such** big feet that he can't buy shoes to fit him.*
> *He's **such** a slow worker that he never finishes in time.*
> *It's **such** an easy exam that everyone passes it.*

Note the position of *a/an*.

B We use *so* before adverbs or adjectives without nouns:

> *He works **so** slowly that he never finishes in time.*
> *His feet are **so** big that he can't buy shoes to fit him.*
> *The exam is **so** easy that everyone passes it.*

C We also use *so* with *much* and *many*, even when they are followed by nouns:

> *I make **so** many mistakes that I always get low marks.*
> *He drank **so** much milk that he got quite fat.*

Exercise 254

▶ Put in *so* or *such* before these phrases. Note their use.
  □ *so* many cars
  1 ____ heavy traffic   4 ____ many tourists
  2 ____ much dust   5 ____ long delays
  3 ____ a crowd of people

▶ Now join these sentences, using *so . . . that* or *such . . . that*:
  □ I had a good time in New York. I'd like to go again.
    I had such a good time in New York that I'd like to go again.
  6 I was invited out (very) often. I hardly ever had a meal alone.
  7 I met a lot of people. I can't remember all their names.
  8 Some of them spoke (very) fast. I couldn't understand what they said.
  9 But everything was very expensive. I couldn't buy many presents.
  10 It was a short holiday. I didn't see all I wanted to see.

255   Time clauses

A   These are introduced by conjunctions of time such as:

after	*hardly . . . when*	*till/until*
as	*immediately*	*when*
as soon as	*since*	*whenever*
before	*the sooner*	*while*

He got home **before** I did.

We can also use *the minute, the moment*:
I recognized him **the moment** I saw him.

(For *as/when/while*, see 247; for *since*, see 81 B.)

B   We don't use a future form in time clauses, i.e. in time clauses we do not use *after/when* etc. + *will* or *would*. (But see note below.)

1   Future forms usually become present simple tenses in time clauses, as shown below. Time clauses are underlined.

She'**ll be back** soon. I'll stay till <u>she **gets back**</u>.
He'**s going to apply** for the job. <u>The sooner he **applies**</u> the better.
He'**s leaving** at two. We'll have lunch <u>before he **leaves**</u>.

But we can have a continuous tense in a time clause when we are using the tense for a continuous, not a future action:

He'**s giving** a lecture tomorrow. <u>While he'**s giving** it</u> (during this time) we'll go for a walk.

2   Future perfect tenses change to present perfect:

I'**ll have finished** this book by the end of the week. <u>As soon as I'**ve finished** it</u> I'll lend it to you. (See also 3 below.)

3   *would* + infinitive changes to a past tense:

He said he **would come**. He told us to wait here <u>till he **came**</u>.

NOTE
We can use *when* with the future or *would* + infinitive when *when* introduces a main clause: *When will you be back?* or a noun clause: *He asked when we would be back.*

C   Perfect tenses in time clauses

1   We can use a perfect or a past tense with *after* and with *hardly . . . when*:

> *After you **have checked** the figures, write the total here.*
> *We had hardly left the house when it **began** to rain.*

2   We can also use perfect tenses after *when, as soon as* and *till/until* to emphasize that the action in the time clause will be complete before the other action begins:

> *When he **has done** his homework he usually watches TV.*

or was complete before the other action began:

> *When he **had done** it he was allowed to watch TV.*

If we use simple tenses in time clauses, as in *When he does his homework* etc., we give the impression that he does his homework and watches TV at the same time. If we say *When he did his homework* etc., we give the impression that he did his homework and watched TV at the same time.

3   *before* + perfect tense emphasizes that the action in the time clause is not complete before the other action begins:

> *He writes reviews before he **has read** the whole book.*
> *He wrote the review before he **had read** the whole book.*

Exercise 255

▶ Put the verb in brackets into the correct tense:

   □   It will stop raining soon. As soon as it *stops* (stop) raining we'll go out for a walk.

   1   The shop will open soon. When it _____ (open) I'll buy some milk.

   2   Immediately the kettle _____ (boil) I'll make the tea.

   3   Your father will be home in half an hour. When he _____ (get) home we'll tell him our news.

   4   Dinner will be ready soon. The moment it _____ (be) ready I'll call you.

▶ Now put these verbs in brackets into the correct tense:

   □   When the lecture *has ended* (end) the students will ask questions.

   5   As soon as the lecturer _____ (answer) the questions everyone will leave.

   6   When you _____ (read) this book, I want you to answer some questions on it.

   7   (at a level crossing) The train will go by in a few minutes. When it _____ (go) by, the gates will open.

38 Noun clauses

Noun clauses can be introduced by *that* and so are often called '*that*-clauses'. But we frequently omit the *that* in speech.

256 Noun clauses after adjectives/participles and nouns

We can use noun clauses after the following.

A *it* + *be* + adjective/present participle

Common adjectives here are: *certain, likely, possible, probable, lucky, disappointing, interesting, surprising* and *odd, sad, strange*.
> It's **disappointing** that you can't come.
> It's **strange** (that) he hasn't answered your letter.

B *it* + *be* + *a* + noun or phrase

We can use *a nuisance/pity/shame/relief/wonder* and *a good thing* here.
> It's **a pity** (that) he can't speak French.
> It's **a good thing** you had a map with you.

C Subject + *be* + adjective/past participle

Common adjectives are *certain, sure* (29 C); *glad, sorry;* and *afraid* (29 A).
Common participles: *delighted, disappointed, pleased, relieved, surprised*.
> I'm **glad** (that) you were able to come.   I'm **sorry** it's so wet.
> I'm **surprised** he didn't pass the test.

D Certain abstract nouns

Common nouns: *belief, fact, fear, hope, knowledge, news, report, rumour, suspicion*. We need *that* with nouns.
> **The hope** that they would be freed gave the hostages courage.

257 Noun clauses after verbs

A We can use noun clauses after a large number of verbs. These include verbs of communication, mental activity and discovery. After the starred verbs (*) in the list below the *that* is usually kept; after the others it is often omitted in speech.

add*	find out	reply
admit	forget	reveal
agree	hear	say
answer*	hope	see
it appears	imagine	it seems
assure + object	know	suggest*
believe	learn	suppose
complain	point out*	suspect
decide	promise	tell + object
deny	pretend	think
discover	realize	it turns out
expect	remark*	understand
explain	remember	warn + object
feel	remind + object	wish

*He **admitted** (that) he'd told a lie.*
*He **pointed out** that I'd made a mistake.*
*I **saw** (that) she was worried.*

B Noun clauses beginning with *how, what, when, where, who* or *why* can follow the following verbs:

ask	forget	realize	think
decide	hear	remember	understand
discover	imagine	say	want to know
explain	know	see	wonder
find out	learn	tell	

*She **asked why** I wanted to go.   I **saw what** you did.*
*He **explained what** had happened.*
*I **know where** it is.   He **told me who** he was.*
*I **wonder where** he lives.*

Most of the above verbs can also take other constructions.

Exercise 257

► Complete these replies. Use affirmative verbs.
  □ Where does he live? ~ I've forgotten *where he lives*.
  1 What did he say? ~ I didn't hear ____.
  2 Where did they go? ~ I didn't see ____.
  3 When are they coming back? ~ I don't know ____.
  4 Who was he? ~ I never found out ____.
  5 Why did she leave him? ~ I can't remember ____.

258 *so* and *not* instead of noun clauses

A *so* after *believe, expect, suppose, think*:
     Will Tom be at the party? ~ I **expect so**. (*so* = that he will.)
     Will Ann be there too? ~ I don't **suppose so**. (*so* = that
     she will.)

B *so* after *say* and after *tell* + object:
     Prices are going up. The paper **says so**. (*so* = that they are.)
     How do you know he loved her? ~ Did he **tell you so**? (*so* =
     that he did.)

C *so* and *not* after *hope* and *be afraid*:
     Is Tom coming? ~ I **hope so**. (*so* = that he is.)
     Will there be queues? ~ I'm **afraid so**. (*so* = that there will.)

   For the negative we put *not* after an affirmative verb:
     Is it going to rain? ~ I **hope not**. (*not* = that it isn't.)
     Have you any change? ~ I'm **afraid not**. (*not* = that I
     haven't.)

Exercise 258

► Add *not* or *so*:
  □ Have we missed the bus? ~ I hope *not*.
  1 But there's no one at the bus stop. We must have missed
     it! ~ I'm afraid ____.
  2 Will there be another one soon? ~ I don't suppose ____.
     It's a very irregular service.
  3 Doesn't any other bus come this way? ~ I don't
     think ____.
  4 Could we get a taxi? ~ I suppose ____.
  5 Have you got enough money for a taxi? ~ I'm afraid ____.

39   Phrasal verbs

259   Form

A   After certain verbs we can put adverbs or prepositions, like *away, back, down, in, off, on, out, over, round, through, up* and *after, at, for, into, with, without.* In this way we give the verbs a variety of meanings.

B   Verb + *away, back, down, in, off, on, out, over, round, through, up*

1   Some of these combinations are transitive (need an object):
put on (clothes)   *take off* (clothes)   *try on* (clothes)
*She **tried on** the coat to see if it was the right size.* (The object is *coat*.)

Some are intransitive (cannot have an object):
go away, come back   stand up, sit down
turn up (= arrive/appear)
*He didn't **turn up** till after dark.* (no object)

Some have several meanings and are transitive in some and intransitive in others. *take off*, used of clothes, is transitive:
*He **took off** his wet shoes.*
take off, used of aeroplanes, means 'leave the ground' and is intransitive:
*The plane **took off** half an hour late.*

2   Noun objects here can come either after the combination:
*He **took off** his shoes.   He **put on** his slippers.*
or immediately after the verb:
*He **took** his shoes **off**.   He **put** his slippers **on**.*

Pronoun objects (*me, you, him, her, it, us, them*) usually follow the verb:
*He **took** them **off**.   He **put** them **on**.*

C Verb + *after, at, for, into, to, with, without*

These combinations are transitive:
   look after (= take care of)
   run after (= pursue/try to catch)
   look for (= search for/seek)
   see to (= deal with/attend to/put right)
The object comes at the end:
   They **ran after** the ball OR They **ran after** it.

D Combinations with three words are also possible.
These are always transitive.
   look forward to (= expect with pleasure)
   put up with (= bear patiently)
The object comes at the end:
   We're **looking forward to** your party OR
   We're **looking forward** to it.

E A gerund object is sometimes possible:
   We're **looking forward to** seeing you.
   He **gave up** smoking. (He stopped smoking.)

Exercise 259

▶ Put in *put on, take off, try on* or *put out*:

In some of the sentences a phrasal verb (*put on*) + pronoun object (*it*) is necessary. Put the pronoun object immediately after the verb (*put it on*).

  □   I wonder if this coat would fit me. ~ Why don't you *try it on* and see?

  1   You can take off your shoes and ＿＿ the slippers. They're more comfortable on a long flight. ~

  2   But my shoes are quite comfortable. Why should I ＿＿? Besides, I think these slippers are too small. ~

  3   ＿＿ and see. If they're too small you can ask for a bigger pair.

  4   By the way, you'd better ＿＿ your cigarette. There's a no smoking sign. ~

  5   OK. I'll ＿＿. But I thought you could smoke on planes. ~

  6   We can smoke after the plane has ＿＿ (left the ground).

260 Examples of common phrasal verbs

In this section these are marked 'tr' (= transitive) or 'intr' (= intransitive). When the object can come only at the end of the expression, this will be shown.

Some of the following expressions have other meanings besides those given. For these and for other phrasal verbs, see a good dictionary.

get back (intr) = return to one's starting point:
If we start early we'll get back before dark.

get back (tr) = regain possession of:
People whose bicycles are stolen don't usually get them back.

get on (intr) = make progress, meet with success/ failure:
How are you getting on with your painting? ~ Very well. I've nearly finished.

get on (intr) (used with plural subjects) = live/play/ work amicably together:
The two boys didn't get on; they were always fighting.

look for (tr; object at end) = try to find, search for:
I'm looking for a parking place.

look up (tr) = look for (information) in a dictionary/ directory/timetable etc.:
I'll look up his telephone number/look it up.

put off (tr) = postpone:
Go to the dentist today. Don't put it off any longer.

put up with (tr; object at end) = bear patiently:
Camping is fun if you can put up with the discomfort.

turn down (tr) = refuse (an offer), reject (an application/applicant):
She turned down an offer of £500,000 for her house.
He wanted to join the navy but they turned him down.

turn up (intr) = arrive, appear:
I arranged to meet him at the station, but he didn't turn up.

40   Numbers, dates and measurements

261   Cardinal numbers

A   Examples of forms

1 *one*	21 *twenty-one*
2 *two*	22 *twenty-two*
3 *three*	23 *twenty-three*
4 *four*	24 *twenty-four*
5 *five*	25 *twenty-five*
6 *six*	26 *twenty-six*
7 *seven*	27 *twenty-seven*
8 *eight*	28 *twenty-eight*
9 *nine*	29 *twenty-nine*
10 *ten*	30 *thirty*
11 *eleven*	31 *thirty-one* etc.
12 *twelve*	40 *forty*
13 *thirteen*	50 *fifty*
14 *fourteen*	60 *sixty*
15 *fifteen*	70 *seventy*
16 *sixteen*	80 *eighty*
17 *seventeen*	90 *ninety*
18 *eighteen*	100 *a/one hundred*
19 *nineteen*	1,000 *a/one thousand*
20 *twenty*	1,000,000 *a/one million*

Also   0 *nought/zero*

B   When writing in words, or saying, a number made up
of three or more figures we put *and* before the last two
figures, unless they are noughts:

713 *seven hundred **and** thirteen*
5,102 *five thousand, one hundred **and** two* BUT
6,100 *six thousand, one hundred*

We also use *and* with hundreds of thousands:

320,410 *three hundred **and** twenty thousand, four
hundred **and** ten*

and hundreds of millions:

303,000,000 *three hundred **and** three million*

C *a* is more usual than *one* before a single *hundred, thousand, million* etc.:

    100 *a hundred*   1,000 *a thousand*
    100,000 *a hundred thousand*

We can also use *a hundred and one, a hundred and two* etc. up to *a hundred and ninety-one* and *a thousand and one* etc. up to *a thousand and ninety-nine*. Otherwise we use *one*, not *a*:

    1,040 *a/one thousand and forty* BUT
    1,140 *one thousand,* **one** *hundred and forty*

D *hundred, thousand, million* and *dozen* are singular when we are talking about a definite number:

    six **hundred** *men   ten* **thousand** *pounds   two* **dozen** *eggs*

but plural when used loosely, to suggest a large number:

    hundreds *of people   thousands of birds   dozens of times*

In this case *of* is placed after *hundreds, thousands* etc.

E We use '·' (decimal point) to show decimals. In speech we say 'point':

    10·9 *'ten* **point** *nine'*

After a decimal point we speak each figure separately and usually call a zero 'nought':

    8·04 *'eight point* **nought** *four'*

But 'o'/əʊ/ and 'zero' are also possible.

262 Ordinal numbers

A Examples of forms

first	*eleventh*	*twenty-first*	*thirty-first* etc.
second	*twelfth*	*twenty-second*	*fortieth*
third	*thirteenth*	*twenty-third*	*fiftieth*
fourth	*fourteenth*	*twenty-fourth*	*sixtieth*
fifth	*fifteenth*	*twenty-fifth*	*seventieth*
sixth	*sixteenth*	*twenty-sixth*	*eightieth*
seventh	*seventeenth*	*twenty-seventh*	*ninetieth*
eighth	*eighteenth*	*twenty-eighth*	*hundredth*
ninth	*nineteenth*	*twenty-ninth*	*thousandth*
tenth	*twentieth*	*thirtieth*	*millionth*

Notice the spelling of *fifth, eighth, ninth* and *twelfth*.

B   When ordinal numbers are written in figures the last two letters of the word must be added, except in dates (263 B):
> *first = 1st   second = 2nd   eightieth = 80th*

C   We normally put *the* before ordinal numbers:
> ***the** sixtieth day*   ***the** fortieth visitor*

D   In ordinal numbers made up of three or more figures the rule about *and* is the same as for cardinal numbers:
> *101st = the hundred **and** first*

E   Titles of kings etc. are written in Roman figures:
> *Charles V   James III   Elizabeth II*

    But in spoken English we use the ordinal with *the*:
> *'Charles **the** Fifth'   'James **the** Third'   'Elizabeth **the** Second'*

F   When writing in words or speaking fractions like ½, ⅓ and ¼ we use *a* or *one*. *a* is more usual.
> *½   **a/one** half   ⅕   **a/one** fifth   ¹⁄₂₀   **a/one** twentieth*

    With other fractions we use a mixture of cardinal and ordinal numbers:
> *⅗   three fifths   ⁷⁄₁₀   seven tenths*

    A whole number + a fraction can be followed directly by a plural noun:
> *2¼   miles = two and a quarter miles*

    ½ (*half*) can be followed directly by a noun but other fractions require *of* before a noun:
> *half a second* BUT *a quarter of a second*

263   Dates

A   Days of the week   Months of the year

Days of the week	Months of the year	
Sunday (Sun.)	*January (Jan.)*	*July*
Monday (Mon.)	*February (Feb.)*	*August (Aug.)*
Tuesday (Tues.)	*March (Mar.)*	*September (Sept.)*
Wednesday (Wed.)	*April (Apr.)*	*October (Oct.)*
Thursday (Thurs.)	*May*	*November (Nov.)*
Friday (Fri.)	*June*	*December (Dec.)*
Saturday (Sat.)		

Days and months are always written with capital initial letters.

B We use ordinal numbers for dates, so in speech we say:
March the tenth, July the fourteenth etc. OR
the tenth of March etc.

They can, however, be written in a variety of ways.
March the tenth could be written:

10 March	March 10	10th of March
10th March	March 10th	March the 10th

C We can abbreviate dates using points or strokes:
10.3.90, 10/3/90. In American English the day and the month are reversed.

D When speaking the year we use *hundred* but not *thousand.* The year 1990 is spoken as *nineteen ninety* OR *nineteen hundred and ninety.*

264 Measurements

A We add *s* to form the plural of *ounce, pound, ton, kilo* etc. when they are used as nouns:
*six **pounds** of sugar   two **kilos** of apples*

B When there is more than one inch/mile/centimetre etc. we normally use the plural form of these words:
*one inch, ten **inches**   one mile, four **miles**
one centimetre, five **centimetres***

But when there is more than one foot we can use either *foot* or *feet*. *foot* is more usual in heights. We can say:
six foot tall OR *six feet tall   two foot long* OR *two feet long*

C When used in compound adjectives units of measure never take the plural form:
*a two-**mile** walk, a six-**inch** ruler
a five-**litre** can of petrol, a 24-**hour** delay*

41 | Spelling rules

For noun plurals, see 10–12.
For verb forms, see 140 B, 143 B, 147 B.

Vowels: *a e i o u*
Consonants: *b c d f g h j k l m n p q r s t v w x y z*

265 Doubling the consonant before a suffix

A In words of one syllable which have one vowel and
which end in a single consonant (other than *w, x* and *y*)
we double the consonant before a suffix beginning
with a vowel:

hit + ing = hitting   BUT   *keep, keeping* (two vowels)
knit + ed = knitted   *help, helped* (two consonants)
run + er = runner   *love, lover* (ending in a vowel)

u is not counted as a vowel after *q*: *quit, quitting.*

B When two- or three-syllable words end in a single
consonant after a single vowel we double the final
consonant when the stress falls on the last syllable.

ac'quit + ed = acquitted   BUT   *'murmur + ed = murmured*

C We usually double the *l* of words ending in *l* when it
follows a single vowel or two vowels pronounced
separately:

cruel, cruelly   *model, modelling*   *quarrel, quarrelling*

266 Omission of a final *e* before a suffix

A We leave out the final *e* before a suffix beginning with a
vowel when it follows a consonant:
love + ing = loving   *move + able = movable*

Words ending in *ce* or *ge* sometimes retain the *e* (267 A).

age keeps its *e* before *ing* except in American English:
   age, ageing

likable can also be spelt *likeable*.

B We keep the final *e* before a suffix beginning with a consonant:
   engage, engagement   fortunate, fortunately

But the final e in adjectives ending in a consonant + le is dropped in the adverb form:
   comfortable, comfortably   simple, simply

The final *e* is also dropped in the following words:
   argue, argument   due, duly   true, truly
   whole, wholly (notice the double *l* here)

C When a word ends in *ee* we do not drop the final *e* before a suffix:
   agree, agreed, agreeing, agreement

267 Words ending in *ce* and *ge*

A When a word ends in *ce* or *ge* we keep the *e* before a suffix beginning with *a* or *o*:
   replace, replaceable   courage, courageous
This is done to avoid changes in pronunciation, because *c* and *g* are generally pronounced soft before *e* and *i*, but hard before *a* or *o* (or *u*).

B Words ending in *ce* change the *e* to *i* before *ous*:
   grace, gracious   space, spacious

268 The suffix *ful*

When *full* is added to a word the second *l* is dropped:
   beauty + full = beautiful (but note adverb *beautifully*)
   use + full = useful (but note adverb *usefully*)

If the word to which the suffix is added ends in *ll* the second *l* is dropped here also: *skill + full = skilful*.

Note *full + fill* = fulfil.

269 Words ending in *y*

When a word ends in a consonant + *y* we change the *y* to *i* before any suffix except *ing*:
   carry + ed = carried   BUT *carry + ing = carrying*

y following a vowel does not change:
   obey + ed = obeyed   play + er = player

270 *ie* and *ei*

The normal rule is that *i* comes before *e* except after *c*:
   believe, sieve   BUT   *deceive, receipt*

There are however exceptions. Some of these are:

eight	*height*	*reign*	*vein*
either	*neighbour*	*seize*	*weigh*
foreign	*neither*	*their*	*weight*

271 Hyphens

We use hyphens as follows.

A In adjective phrases before nouns:
   a badly-built house   *well-trained dogs*
   a six-foot wall   *a coal-mining area* (18 D)
(Note that the number, *six* etc., is followed by a singular noun.)

B In some noun + adverb combinations:
   hold-up   look-out   make-up   take-off

C In some numbers: *twenty-one, forty-six* etc. (261 A, 262 A)

D After most prefixes:
   anti-social   ex-soldier   mid-June   self-employed

With *co* and *re*, however, we can omit the hyphen; so we can write *coeducation* or *co-education* and *redevelop* or *re-develop*. But it is more useful to keep the hyphen in words such as *co-operate* and *re-employ* in order to avoid the double vowel.

E To divide a word when it comes at the end of a line and there isn't room for all of it. Only words of two or more syllables should be divided and the break should come between syllables.

▷ For possible uses of hyphens in compound nouns, see 18 D.

272 Capital letters

Capital letters are necessary at the beginning of certain words:

A Names and titles of people and names of places:
Captain Wilson   Tom Smith   Piccadilly Circus

But a title without a name is often spelt with a small letter: *The captain smiled*.

B Days, months and the names of festivals:
Wednesday   April   Easter   Christmas   New Year's Day

C Nouns and adjectives connected with nationality, regions or religion:
She's an Austrian   French cooking   a Catholic church

D The first and other important words in the titles of books, magazines, newspapers, films, plays, etc.
War and Peace   The Merchant of Venice

273 Abbreviations

A A full stop is used after shortened forms of words:
adj. (adjective) *Apr.* (April) *Co.* (Company)
and sometimes after a single letter which stands for a word, name or title:
a.m.   e.g.   G. B. Shaw

B But full stops are often omitted if the abbreviation is frequently used:
NATO   USSR   VIP   Mr Smith   Mrs Wilson

Key to exercises

Exercise 1

1 an	5 a	9 –	13 a;–
2 an	6 an	10 a	14 an
3 a	7 an	11 –	15 –
4 an	8 a	12 an	16 a

Exercise 2

1 one	3 One	5 one	7 a
2 a	4 a	6 a	8 one

Exercise 3

1 the	4 a	7 the
2 the	5 The	8 the
3 the	6 a	

Exercise 4

1 the	7 the	13 the
2 –	8 the	14 –
3 the	9 –	
4 the	10 the	
5 –	11 the	
6 the	12 the	

Exercise 5

1 –	9 the
2 the	10 your
3 –	11 the
4 –	12 the
5 The	13 your
6 –	14 the
7 –	15 Your
8 –	16 his

Exercise 6

1 –	4 –	7 The	10 –
2 –	5 –	8 the	11 the
3 –	6 the	9 –	

Exercise 7

1 these	3 That	5 those
2 those	4 this	

Exercise 9

4 daughter	13 lioness
5 cow	14 spinster
6 niece	15 widow
8 bitch	17 hostess
9 waitress	20 sister-in-
11 manageress	-law
12 aunt	21 bride

Exercise 10

1 boxes	7 days
2 buses	8 matches
3 bushes	9 potatoes
4 cases	10 taxes
5 cliffs	11 tomatoes
6 clocks	12 kisses

Exercise 11

1 babies	11 men
2 children	12 photos
3 countries	13 pianos
4 aircraft	14 sheep
5 feet	15 shelves
6 keys	16 storeys
7 kilos	17 stories
8 women	18 thieves
9 leaves	19 teeth
10 loaves	20 wives

Exercise 12

1 brothers-in-law
2 house agents
3 juke-boxes
4 lady doctors
5 MPs
6 runners-up
7 time bombs
8 women drivers

Exercise 13

1 are 2 is 3 was 4 lead

Exercise 14

1 a	4 a	7 −; a
2 −; −	5 −; −	8 a
3 −	6 −; a	9 a; −

Exercise 15

1 the child's room
2 the children's clothes
3 Mr Smith's car
4 the VIP's luggage
5 her son-in-law's flat
6 the workers' canteen

Exercise 16

1 week's holiday
2 Today's newspaper
3 ten minutes' wait
4 Last year's fashions
5 month's wages
6 Yesterday's news

Exercise 18

1 the corner shop
2 the waiting room
3 the car keys
4 a coffee ice-cream
5 a reading lamp
6 a silk dress
7 a gold mine

Exercise 20

1 a yellow and green flag
2 a big, red car
3 He was tall and thin.
4 He was a tall, thin man.
5 a cold, wet day
6 interested; interesting
7 annoying; annoyed
8 amusing; amused
9 tired; tiring

Exercise 21

1 upset
2 little
3 dark
4 sure
5 sorry
6 late

7 ready
8 good
9 sour
10 ill
11 horrible
12 interesting

Exercise 22

1 a heavy old leather case
2 her new blue dress
3 expensive handmade shoes
4 a nice sharp carving knife
5 a noisy little English car
6 a lovely sunny day

Exercise 23

1 braver, bravest
2 busier, busiest
3 cleverer, cleverest
4 drier, driest
5 fatter, fattest
6 more, most
7 worse, worst
8 more beautiful, most beautiful
9 more difficult, most difficult
10 more exciting, most exciting
11 farther, farthest/further, furthest
12 better, best

Exercise 24

1 more crowded than
2 more expensive
3 cheaper
4 quickest
5 more difficult than
6 than
7 than
8 as; as
9 the; the
10 the

Exercise 25

1 I did/me
2 he has/him
3 he does/him
4 we do/us
5 we are/us
6 we had/us/we did
7 we can/us

Exercise 26

1 small ones
2 the eldest (one)
3 an early one; the best (one)
4 than a soft one

Exercise 27

1 The unemployed
2 the disabled
3 the deaf
4 The Welsh

Exercise 28

1 It was stupid of him to forget the key.
2 It was foolish of her to arrive late.
3 It was kind of you to offer to help.
4 It is dangerous to hitch-hike alone.
5 It is difficult to park in the high street.
6 It is not safe to leave cars unlocked.
7 It was terrible to feel the house shaking.
8 It was dreadful to see the cars burning.
9 It was exciting to canoe down a fast river.
10 I was glad to hear that he had got the job.
11 He was disappointed to see nobody he knew at the party.
12 She was delighted to see him again.

Exercise 30

1 far
2 a long way
3 far
4 far; far
5 nearest
6 nearer
7 quite near
8 nearer

Exercise 31

1 a few
2 a little
3 a few
4 a few
5 a little
6 very few
7 very little
8 very little

Exercise 32

1 a lot of
2 much
3 more
4 a lot of/a great many
5 most/a lot of
6 a lot of/more
7 much
8 more

Exercise 34

1 once
2 home
3 rather
4 late
5 quietly
6 then
7 so
8 away
9 that morning
10 suddenly
11 about
12 upstairs
13 quite
14 still
15 very
16 fast

Exercise 35

1 manner
2 frequency
3 place
4 degree
5 manner
6 place
7 manner
8 degree
9 time
10 there
11 before
12 then
13 in a hotel
14 much less
15 On our second day
16 halfway up a mountain
17 immediately
18 slowly
19 Soon
20 completely

Exercise 36

1 gently
2 angrily
3 sincerely
4 beautifully
5 legibly
9 legibly
10 simply
11 easily
12 carefully

Exercise 37

1 quietly	12 enough
2 straight	13 truthfully
3 really	14 slowly
4 early	15 well
5 fast	16 warmly
6 back	17 loudly
7 slowly	18 late
8 well	19 low
9 still	20 long
10 carefully	21 direct
11 long	22 straight

Exercise 39

1 more cheaply
2 earlier
3 more quietly
4 badly; worse
5 soon
6 harder
7 sooner; sooner
8 further/farther

Exercise 41

1 He pays his staff badly.
2 He spoke to me politely./He spoke politely to me.
3 He speaks politely to all his regular customers./He speaks to all his regular customers politely.
4 He doesn't get on well with some of his staff.

Exercise 42

1 We came home without a penny.
2 She buys her clothes abroad.
3 He went there with his wife.
4 She sent the children upstairs.
5 They ran away from me.

6 He has gone back to Rome.
7 somewhere
8 anywhere
9 anywhere
10 somewhere 13 anywhere
11 everywhere 14 Nowhere;
12 Anywhere anywhere

Exercise 43

1 WRONG — Bill arrived late.
2 RIGHT (other positions also possible)
3 RIGHT (end position also possible)
4 WRONG — We stop work early on Saturday./On Saturday we stop work early.
5 RIGHT (other positions also possible)
6 WRONG — Stay in bed today.
7 RIGHT (but front position also possible)
8 We're not taking on any more staff just now./Just now we are not taking on any more staff.
9 We have just finished lunch.
10 Just then there was a knock on the door./There was a knock on the door just then.
11 yet; still 13 yet 15 still
12 still 14 yet; still

Exercise 44

1 Some tennis players play best on hard courts.
2 The children go to school by bus.
3 He waited impatiently outside the telephone box./He waited outside the telephone box impatiently.

4 She sang beautifully at the Festival Hall.
5 He often spends the weeked quietly at home./Often he spends the weekend quietly at home.
6 In foggy weather I don't drive fast on motorways./I don't drive fast on motorways in foggy weather.
7 He says he always sleeps well on a hard bed./He always says he sleeps well on a hard bed.

Exercise 45

1 Ann always goes by bus.
2 Usually the buses are very crowded./The buses are usually very crowded./The buses are very crowded usually.
3 Often she has to stand all the way./She often has to stand all the way.
4 But she is never late for work.
5 You've been late three times this week.
6 Once he fell asleep at the controls./He fell asleep at the controls once.
7 Take these pills twice a day for the first week.
8 He woke us up again last night.
9 never; ever
10 ever; never
11 never; hardly ever

Exercise 46

1 wasn't big enough
2 was rather expensive
3 are extremely high
4 The house we nearly bought
5 got it fairly cheaply
6 a very bad state of repair
7 were much stronger
8 was badly injured
9 nearly lost his temper
10 We almost won.
11 we don't train enough
12 If we trained more
13 Were the children well fed?
14 The church was badly damaged by fire.
15 The workcrs were badly paid.
16 full of well-paid officials
17 It will only take a minute./It will take only a minute.
18 I had just enough money
19 He only lent it to me.
20 We will just have time
21 He didn't even say 'Goodbye'.

Exercise 47

| 1 rather | 3 rather | 5 fairly |
| 2 fairly | 4 rather | |

Exercise 49

1 have hardly any (money)
2 I'll have hardly any (spare time)
3 have hardly any (records)
4 hardly ever watches (TV)
5 hardly ever reads a paper
6 hardly ever eats fruit
7 can hardly lift it
8 can hardly read it
9 could hardly hear it

Exercise 50

1 far	12 longer
2 farthest	13 long
3 farther	14 long
4 a long way	15 a long time
5 too far	16 too long
6 near	17 very much
7 quite near	18 much
8 near	19 a lot; much
9 nearer	20 much
10 nearest	21 more
11 too near	22 a lot

Exercise 52

1 Neither of us can swim.
2 Neither of them would wait.
3 Neither of us knew the area.
4 Neither of them saw the programme.
5 either of them
6 either of us
7 either of you
8 either of them
9 either of you

Exercise 53

1 He goes everywhere on his bicycle.
2 He has seen everything.
3 Everyone admires him.
4 You see tourists everywhere.

Exercise 54

1 you both/both of you
2 us both/both of us
3 them both/both of them
4 them both/both of them
5 us both/both of us
6 They both help.
7 We both went.
8 You both pay.
9 We were both there.
10 We've both seen it.

Exercise 55

1 Some; any	3 some	5 no
2 None	4 any	6 any

Exercise 56

1 someone
2 anything
3 somewhere
4 No one
5 something
6 anyone else
7 no one else
8 somewhere else
9 anywhere else

Exercise 57

1 Others	4 some/others
2 another/one	5 One
3 Some	6 the other

Exercise 58

1 Who drove them to the station?
2 What delayed them?
3 Who rang Tom?
4 Which of them left an umbrella in the car?
5 Which train did they miss?
6 Which train did they catch?
7 What did she leave in the car?
8 Who did she ring?
9 Who was Ann travelling with?
10 Who did she speak to on the phone?
11 What did she ask about?

Exercise 59

1 What was the (TV) programme like?
2 What does she look like?/ What is she like?
3 What's he like?
4 What's it for?

5 What's the restaurant like?
6 How tall is he?
7 How deep is the river?
8 How long is the swimming pool?

Exercise 60

1 When 4 Why
2 Where 5 Where
3 How

Exercise 62

1 Mary is his sister.
2 Mary is her daughter.
3 Mary is their daughter.
4 Bill is their son.
5 Tom is her husband.
6 Yes, I'm sure they're hers.
7 Yes, I'm sure it's yours.
8 Yes, I'm sure it's ours.
9 Yes, I'm sure it's mine.
10 Yes, I'm sure it's theirs.

Exercise 63

1 Joan bought it for her father/ for him.
2 I showed them to my mother/to her.
3 She read it to her children/to them.
4 We got it for Ann/for her.
5 I made it for you.
6 Tom sent them to me.

Exercise 64

1 It's raining.
2 It's six miles.
3 It'll take two hours.
4 It's a pity (that) you couldn't find a less expensive hotel.
5 It's a good thing (that) you have plenty of money.
6 It's a shame (that) Ann can't come with you after all.
7 It was foolish of her to book

8 It was good of you to offer
9 It was kind of him to invite her to stay.

Exercise 66

1 yourselves 5 itself
2 themselves 6 himself
3 herself 7 ourselves
4 himself 8 myself

Exercise 67

All answers begin: No, it was

1 John who sent out the invitation
2 Tom who bought the wine
3 Jill who prepared all the food
4 Tom who got drunk
5 Alan who sang for us
6 George who drove us home

Exercise 68

1 The family who have just bought the flat below me seem noisy too.
2 The man who sweeps the stairs doesn't sweep out the lift.
3 The men who wash the windows haven't been for six months.
4 The men who are repairing the roof want hot water for tea.
5 The girl we saw sitting at the desk is Tom's secretary.
6 The man we heard telephoning in the next room is Tom's partner.
7 The woman we passed in the corridor is Tom's accountant.

Exercise 69

1 my brother lent me
2 I brought from my old flat
3 I've just made

4 I bought on Monday
5 the last tenant left behind

Exercise 70

1 to read
2 to eat
3 to talk to
4 waiting
5 arriving
6 leaving
7 announcing
8 selling
9 collecting

Exercise 72

Answers 1–6 begin: This is

1 Peter, who does the filing
2 Mary, who keeps the accounts
3 Joan, who manages the switchboard
4 John, who makes the tea
5 Mrs Jones, who is my assistant
6 Tom, who works the lift
7 Bill, who she didn't much like, asked her
8 She . . . was sorry to see Tom dancing with Mary, who had apparently come with him.
9 She knew that Mary's father, who was Tom's employer, wanted them
10 Bill, who worked in a jeweller's, said that Tom had recently bought

Exercise 73

1 which   3 which
2 whose   4 whose

Exercise 74

1 He told her what he knew, which didn't comfort her much.

2 He . . . knocked at the door, which opened at once.
3 In the safe he found only a small folder, which he took out.
4 . . . some papers, which didn't seem secret or important.
5 He rang Paul, who said, 'The briefcase must be somewhere; go on looking.'
6 what
7 which
8 what
9 which
10 which

Exercise 77

1 give a cheque to anyone else
2 offer a job to anyone else
3 show these photos to anyone else
4 didn't get me a ticket
5 didn't buy me a book
6 didn't find me a job
7 I gave him one last year.
8 I'm sending them to Ann.
9 I'd better send Mary some too.

Exercise 78

1 –   3 –   5 –
2 –   4 to

Exercise 79

1 in   4 on   7 in
2 in   5 on
3 on   6 at

Exercise 80

1 by   6 then
2 after   7 after
3 before   8 then
4 after   9 then
5 after   10 then; then

Exercise 81

1 till/to
2 for
3 at
4 till
5 till
6 don't finish till
7 didn't ring till
8 am not starting till
9 don't arrive till

10 since	16 during
11 for	17 for
12 for	18 during
13 since	19 during
14 since	20 for
15 for	21 for

Exercise 82

1 by	6 on	11 off
2 from	7 at	12 on
3 to	8 in	13 off
4 in	9 at	14 into
5 to	10 onto	15 out

Exercise 84

1 in	5 at
2 in	6 at
3 at	7 at
4 in	8 in

Exercise 85

1 before	7 at
2 behind	8 down
3 on	9 Before
4 up	10 down
5 about	11 behind
6 below	

Exercise 86

1 under the fence
2 over the river
3 under the bridge
4 under a tree
5 above the river
6 below the village

Exercise 87

1 Ann is sitting beside Tom, and opposite George.
2 Tom is sitting between Ann and Mary, and opposite Joan.
3 Mary is sitting beside Tom, and opposite Bill.
4 Mr Jones is behind Mr Smith. Mr Smith is in front of Mr Jones.

Exercise 88

1 with a beard
2 with a pipe
3 with ear-rings

Exercise 90

1 good at
2 proud of
3 keen on
4 interested in
5 good for
6 tired of
7 afraid of
8 waiting for
9 insists on
10 care for
11 object to
12 succeeded in

Exercise 92

1 Bill's	6 We'd
2 Paul's	7 I'll
3 We're	8 That'll
4 That's	9 you've; you'll
5 We've	

Exercise 93

1 doesn't	7 it'd
2 don't	8 didn't
3 can't; that's	9 doesn't; I do
4 didn't	10 he does
5 haven't	11 can't
6 won't	12 couldn't

13 isn't
14 you'll
15 Here's
16 it'd
17 He never goes out.
18 He eats no meat.
19 He hardly ever writes letters.
20 He talks to nobody.
21 He does nothing.

Exercise 94

1 What's	4 What'll
2 Why's	5 Where'd
3 Where've	6 Who's

Exercise 96

1 Why can't you start tonight?
2 Why haven't you got your ticket?
3 Why haven't they sent it?
4 Why didn't it reach them in time?
5 Why didn't you send it first class?

Exercise 99

1 Yes, I am.	6 No, you/we can't.
2 No, I haven't.	
3 Yes, it is.	7 No, they won't.
4 Yes, she does.	
5 Yes, we did.	

Exercise 100

1 Yes, we must.
2 Yes, it does.
3 Yes, it is.
4 No, we couldn't!
5 No, we wouldn't!
6 Yes, we will.
7 Yes, there are.
8 No, they haven't!
9 No, it hasn't.
10 Yes, I have!
11 No, it isn't.
12 Yes, we must!
13 Yes, he will!

Exercise 101

1 aren't they?	7 hasn't it?
2 shouldn't he?	8 don't they?
3 wouldn't it?	9 has he?
4 won't they?	10 did he?
5 couldn't he?	11 does he?
6 isn't there?	12 is it?

Exercise 102

1 is Bill
2 does his brother
3 we haven't
4 we can't
5 Ann was
6 had the second
7 could the cyclists
8 the second one has

Exercise 104

1 (a) She wasn't cooking.
    (b) Was she cooking?
2 (a) They aren't waiting.
    (b) Are they waiting?
3 (a) He isn't employed by the bank.
    (b) Is he employed by the bank?
4 (a) The house isn't being watched.
    (b) Is the house being watched?
5 (a) He hasn't been arrested.
    (b) Has he been arrested?
6 are to have
7 is to be
8 was to have landed
9 was to have started/was to start

Exercise 105

1 were hungry
2 is/'s afraid

3 was thirsty
4 am/'m cold
5 is/'s hot
6 is/'s
7 were
8 isn't
9 won't be/isn't
10 is/'s; has there been
11 there was
12 is it; It is/It's
13 is there/Will there be
14 there is/there's
15 There is/There's
16 it is/it's
17 There is/There's; it isn't;
   there are

Exercise 107

1 No, I have them developed.
2 No, I'm having it typed.
3 No, I had it built.
4 No, she is having them
   made.
5 No, I have them cleaned.
6 You'd better get some
   traveller's cheques.
7 You'd better book a seat in a
   non-smoker.
8 You'd better insure your
   luggage.
9 You'd better be early.
10 You'd better not travel on a
   Bank Holiday.

Exercise 108

1 you have/you've got; do
   you often have
2 I don't have; I have
3 Have you got/Do you have
4 I've got/I have; it hasn't
   got/it doesn't have
5 Does he often have
6 we had; they are having
7 Did you have
8 Everyone always has

9 I haven't (got)/I don't have;
   We are having/We have
10 do you have; We have

Exercise 110

1 But he didn't answer my
   letter!
2 But I don't make mistakes!
3 But you didn't write to me!
4 But she doesn't do her
   homework!
5 did   7 did   9 do
6 do   8 do   10 do

Exercise 111

1 do they usually do
2 are you doing
3 Do you still do; I do; I don't
   do
4 didn't do
5 does he do; He doesn't do
6 Do demonstrations do; do

Exercise 113

1 But you can't carry them in
   the streets.
2 So I can't carry a knife, can
   I?
3 No, you can't.
4 Can my sister carry her
   umbrella?
5 Oh yes, she can carry her
   umbrella.
6 If someone tries to mug her,
   can she hit him with her
   umbrella?
7 She can't hit him first, but if
   he hits her, she can hit back.
8 Candidates who finish
   early may leave the hall.
9 But candidates who leave
   may not return.
10 If we finish early we can
   leave the hall.
11 But we can't return.

Exercise 114

1 Can/Could I borrow your timetable?
2 May I/Might I use your phone?
3 Can I go out and play?
4 May I/Might I/Could I look at your paper?
5 May I/Could I photocopy a page of this book?

Exercise 115

1 couldn't/weren't allowed to
2 couldn't/weren't allowed to
3 was allowed to
4 couldn't/weren't allowed to
5 were allowed to

Exercise 116

1 It may/might be windy.
2 And if it was windy people mightn't want to eat out of doors.
3 Your brother may/might bring his dogs.
4 Yes, he said that he might bring them.
5 If other people bring their dogs there may/might be a dog fight.

Exercise 117

1 he may/might have lent
2 he might have sent
3 he may/might have given
4 may/might have forgotten
5 might have hidden

Exercise 118

1 couldn't have got
2 may/might/could have got
3 couldn't have reached
4 may/might/could have used

Exercise 120

1 can't; Can
2 have been able to
3 has been able to
4 can; will be able to
5 will be able to

Exercise 121

1 couldn't   5 was able to
2 was able to   6 could
3 could
4 was able to

Exercise 122

1 could have saved
2 could have written
3 could have rung

Exercise 124

1 Yes, he should cut his hair more often.
2 Yes, he should get up earlier.
3 Yes, he shouldn't borrow your shirts.
4 Yes, he shouldn't use your razor.
5 Yes, he should try/should be trying to find a job.

Exercise 125

All the answers begin: That was bad.
1 They should've carried your luggage up.
2 The central heating should've been on.
3 It should've been served at 7.30.
4 They should've called you at 7.

Exercise 129

1 will/'ll have to
2 have to
3 must

4 will/'ll have to
5 will have to
6 must
7 will/'ll have to

Exercise 131

1	need not	4	need not
2	must not	5	must not
3	need not		

Exercise 132

1 don't have to
2 needn't
3 don't have to
4 needn't
5 don't have to
6 don't have to

Exercise 134

1 needn't have ironed
2 needn't have put
3 needn't have ordered
4 needn't have boiled
5 needn't have bought
6 needn't have brought

Exercise 135

1 must spend
2 must have
3 must drive
4 must have let
5 must have switched
6 must have had
7 must have known
8 can't get
9 can't know
10 can't have

Exercise 136

1 He won't be at home now.
2 He'll still be in his office.
3 No, he should have finished by now.
4 He should be on the train home.

5 His wife will be waiting at the station with the car.

Exercise 137

All the answers begin: Oh no, he

1 didn't dare (to) ask for a rise
2 didn't dare (to) complain
3 didn't dare (to) refuse to do overtime
4 doesn't dare (to) go home early
5 doesn't dare (to) take a weekend off

Exercise 138

1 Yes, he did. I used to drink champagne every night too.
2 Yes, he did. I used to drive a Rolls Royce too.
3 Yes, he did. I used to go to the Bahamas every year too.
4 bus would meet
5 they'd swim
6 staff would organize
7 we'd play
8 we'd sunbathe

Exercise 140

1	carrying	12	seeing
2	crying	13	shopping
3	eating	14	sitting
4	forgetting	15	standing
5	having	16	staring
6	liking	17	stealing
7	marrying	18	stopping
8	permitting	19	swimming
9	playing	20	taking
10	preferring	21	travelling
11	quarrelling	22	winning

Exercise 141

1 Ann's working
2 are you working
3 I'm not doing; I'm looking

4 are waiting
5 they're helping
6 he's not paying/he isn't paying
7 What he doing?
8 He's talking; He's making
9 They're going
10 he's not paying; She's paying

Exercise 142

1 It smells
2 Ann's just tasting; it needs
3 she thinks; She's looking
4 I don't like
5 It looks; It tastes
6 It doesn't need

Exercise 143

1 catches   5 relaxes
2 hurries   6 watches
3 has   7 says
4 gets

Exercise 144

1 work   6 likes
2 works   7 is enjoying
3 goes   8 feels
4 he's travelling
5 he's meeting

Exercise 146

1 (a) He wasn't practising when I saw him yesterday.
   (b) Was he practising when you saw him?
2 (a) They weren't playing when I saw them yesterday.
   (b) Were they playing when you saw them?
3 (a) She wasn't doing her shopping when I saw her yesterday.
   (b) Was she doing her shopping when you saw her?

4 (a) He wasn't going home when I saw him yesterday.
   (b) Was he going home when you saw him?
5 (a) They weren't watching TV when I saw them yesterday.
   (b) Were they watching TV when you saw them?
6 (a) She wasn't writing letters when I saw her yesterday.
   (b) Was she writing letters when you saw her?

Exercise 147

1 applied   21 broke
2 buried   22 brought
3 cried   23 bought
4 died   24 came
5 dropped   25 chose
6 entered   26 cut
7 fitted   27 drank
8 grabbed   28 felt
9 hurried   29 got
10 knitted   30 went
11 obeyed   31 heard
12 occurred   32 kept
13 played   33 left
14 quarrelled   34 lay
15 referred   35 paid
16 signalled   36 put
17 stayed   37 saw
18 stopped   38 shut
19 travelled   39 woke
20 tried

Exercise 148

1 had; came
2 took
3 put
4 didn't you hang
5 rang; wanted
6 met
7 was working
8 (was) sharing

9 got
10 moved out
11 rang
12 told
13 said
14 was looking
15 (was) trying
16 advised

Exercise 150

1 No, they've only just gone.
2 No, it's only just left.
3 No, he's only just bought it.
4 No, I've only just sent it.

Exercise 151

1 I've been
2 Have you tried/Did you try
3 I tried; I didn't hear
4 happened; got; has left

Exercise 152

1 didn't go
2 hasn't opened
3 hasn't written
4 didn't hand in
5 hasn't paid

Exercise 153

1 Have you ever seen
2 I have; I saw
3 I've never been; I've seen
4 played; got; hasn't played
5 Have you ever seen
6 I did

Exercise 154

1 So you've been a vegetarian for two years.
2 So you've worn glasses for three months.
3 So you haven't taken sleeping pills for three weeks.
4 So you haven't smoked for five years.

Exercise 155

1 for   3 since   5 for
2 for   4 since

Exercise 158

1 have told you
2 has he picked
3 has she been doing
4 has she grilled
5 I've written
6 I've been writing
7 He's been painting
8 We've cut up

Exercise 160

1 His wife had left him.
2 He'd quarrelled
3 He'd lost
4 He'd crashed
5 He'd broken
6 His landlord had put up

Exercise 162

1 No, she'd been painting portraits for quite a long time.
2 No, she'd been selling her paintings for quite a long time.
3 No, she'd been dieting for quite a long time.
4 No, she'd been looking for a house for quite a long time.

Exercise 165

1 arrives   5 docks
2 returns   6 disembark;
3 embark   board
4 sails

Exercise 166

1 At 11 I'm playing golf with Bill.
2 At 11.30 Ann's having a driving lesson.

3 At 7.30 we're going to a concert.
4 On Sunday morning we're driving to Sevenoaks.
5 We're having lunch with Ann's parents.
6 Bill and Mary are coming to supper.

Exercise 169

1 it's going to break down
2 it's going to explode
3 it's going to collapse
4 we're going to have
5 is going to erupt

Exercise 170

1 it'll		4 shall	7 won't
2 We won't		5 We'll	
3 We'll		6 We'll	

Exercise 171

1 he'll like   4 he'll be
2 won't suit   5 he'll have
3 he'll take

Exercise 172

1 I'll buy the wine.
2 I'll hire the glasses.
3 I'll open the bottles.
4 I'll make the coffee.
5 Bill's buying the wine.
6 Tom's hiring the glasses.
7 George's opening the bottles.
8 Mary's making the coffee.

Exercise 173

1 Are you going to climb
2 I'm going to climb
3 I'll come
4 are you going to fish
5 I'm going to fish
6 I'll row
7 are you going to do
8 I'm going to sit
9 I'll do

Exercise 174

1 I don't want to; I'll
2 wants to
3 I'll
4 I don't want to
5 I'll

Exercise 175

1 won't be coming
2 I'll ask
3 won't drive
4 won't be going; we'll be going
5 won't go

Exercise 176

All the answers begin: So by the end of the year

1 you'll have written 365,000 words
2 you'll have run 1,825 miles
3 you'll have lost 6 kilos
4 you'll have learnt 600 new words

Exercise 179

1 he would (come)/he'd come
2 he would (get it)/he'd get it
3 he would (like them)/he'd like them
4 she would (object)/she'd object
5 she would (want to move)/she'd want to (move)

Exercise 184

1 If I get a house in the suburbs, I'll have a garden.
2 If I rent a flat in the centre, I'll be able to walk to work.
3 If I'm able to walk/If I can walk to work I'll save money.
4 you had better   6 you can
5 why don't you   7 could you

Exercise 185

1 if they weren't/if it wasn't so expensive
2 if I could park near the office
3 if I had a bicycle
4 if it wasn't rather dangerous
5 liked   7 played
6 belonged   8 offered

Exercise 186

1 If I'd known her number I'd have rung her.
2 If he'd given me his address I'd have written.
3 If they'd sent me a bill I'd have paid it.
4 If she'd asked for help I'd have helped her.
5 he'd have caught his train
6 he'd have been in time for work
7 wouldn't have been annoyed
8 he'd have gone out to lunch
9 he wouldn't have felt so hungry in the afternoon

Exercise 188

1 Unless he puts money in the meter
2 Unless he pays his telephone bill
3 Unless you speak French
4 Unless you book at once
5 Unless you need help, don't ask for it.
6 you are   9 you can
7 you would   10 you don't
8 you haven't

Exercise 189

1 Take some sandwiches in case there isn't a café at the station.
2 Take a coat for Bob in case it turns cold.
3 Take a spare pair of gloves for him in case he loses one of his.
4 Take the pushchair in case he gets tired on the walk.

Exercise 191

1 No, it would be a pity to dig up the rose bushes.
2 No, it would be a mistake to plant rhododendrons.
3 Yes, it would be a good idea to cut the grass.
4 No, it would be a waste of time to sweep up the leaves.

Exercise 192

1 he offered to help us
2 he forgot to buy any
3 he threatened to shoot him
4 he tried to ring her

Exercise 193

1 how to open it
2 who to ask
3 what to do
4 which to choose
5 which to take
6 how to get there
7 what to say
8 who to ask

Exercise 194

1 I'd like you to read it.
2 I'd like you to listen to it.
3 I'd like you to watch it.
4 I'd like you to do it.
5 I'd like you to learn how to use it.

Exercise 195

1 Yes, they invited us to go with them.

2 Yes, they reminded us to book in advance.
3 Yes, they persuaded us to insure ourselves.
4 No, they advised us not to drink the water.
5 No, they warned us not to go out alone at night.

Exercise 197

1 to play tennis
2 to take photos
3 to sit in the garden
4 is too high to reach
5 is too heavy to move
6 is too thick to use
7 is she strong enough to cycle 100 miles a day?
8 is he young enough to get another job?
9 are they tall enough to join the police?
10 It isn't strong enough to use as a tow rope.
11 It isn't light enough to carry far.
12 It isn't ripe enough to pick yet.

Exercise 198

1 he may be coming by train
2 he may be bringing his girlfriend
3 they may be waiting at the station
4 he may have lost it
5 he may have got lost on the way here
6 his car may have broken down on the way here
7 must have left them
8 must have made it
9 must have bought it
10 seems to be asking him to move

11 he seems to be arguing with the traffic warden
12 she seems to be giving him a parking ticket

Exercise 200

1 finding a guest house is
2 booking in advance is
3 climbing alone is
4 going with a group is
5 starting early is

Exercise 201

1 shocking her
2 making the same mistake
3 marrying him
4 paying for it

Exercise 202

The participle phrase can also come first as shown in 1.

1 He went off by himself instead of waiting for us./ Instead of waiting for us, he went . . .
2 I lived in York before coming here.
3 She lost her way after driving a few miles.
4 He set off for York without wasting any time.
5 He arrived in time in spite of starting late.
6 of waiting for George
7 ringing his home
8 getting away
9 giving him another ten minutes
10 wasting any more time

Exercise 205

All the answers begin: Yes, he advised us

1 to start with an easy climb too
2 to get up early too

3 to climb with a group too
4 to use ropes too

All the answers begin: They used to allow

5 parking
6 swimming
7 fishing
8 camping

All the answers begin: Yes, he's beginning

9 to talk
10 to eat solid food
11 to read

Exercise 206

1 to take
2 crossing
3 to camp
4 carrying
5 risking
6 remember kicking my sister/her
7 remember breaking her toys
8 stealing apples
9 remember running away
10 bringing me home
11 to read your letters
12 borrowing your clothes
13 using your phone
14 to invite his friends to your parties

Exercise 208

1 I saw him taking it out
2 I saw him reading it
3 I heard it ringing
4 I heard him answering it
5 I saw him throwing it into the fire
6 I smelt it burning

Exercise 209

1 him going up her big pear tree
2 him climbing along a thin branch
3 the branch break/breaking
4 him fall/falling
5 him lying at the foot of the tree
6 riding with Tom
7 the whole day riding
8 riding with us
9 too much time riding

Exercise 210

1 Expecting to find her at home, he brought
2 Hearing no sound, he knocked
3 Thinking she might be in the garden, he went
4 Finding nobody there, he went

Exercise 211

1 Seeing a policeman, I decided
2 Going up to the policeman, I told him
3 Taking out his notebook, he asked for
4 Walking past just then, the man nodded
5 Putting away his book, the policeman said
6 Thanking the policeman, I hurried, on feeling rather foolish.

Exercise 213

1 was left open
2 was stolen
3 will be caught
4 being questioned
5 the bank manager been told
6 should have been answered earlier
7 needn't be typed
8 must be photocopied

9 ought to be posted today
10 It may have been stolen.
11 He must have been drugged.
12 They could have been bribed.
13 He might have been murdered.

Exercise 214

1 he's supposed to be writing
2 he's said to be living
3 he's believed to be building
4 he's thought to have been responsible
5 he's believed to have smuggled explosives
6 he's supposed to have died

Exercise 217

1 knew   3 were
2 owned   4 had built
5 it's time we had a meeting
6 it's time we made some plans
7 it's time we wrote to Tom/ him

Exercise 218

1 That's not a good idea. Don't buy an old bicycle.
2 That's a good idea. Go on foot.
3 That's a good idea. Learn another language.
4 That's a good idea. Stay at home next summer.
5 That's not a good idea. Don't borrow money.
6 That's not a good idea. Don't get more credit cards.

Exercise 219

1 to ring for a taxi
2 waiting
3 would hurry

4 check that the windows are shut
5 Would you like a drink?
6 Will you have a cigarette?
7 Could you have coffee with me tomorrow?

Exercise 221

1 You ought to go on a diet.
2 Why don't you walk to the station every morning?
3 If I were you I'd take up squash.
4 You had better give up smoking.
5 You must go to bed earlier.

Exercise 222

1 let's not
2 what about
3 let's
4 Why not
5 why don't we

Exercise 223

1 I like riding
2 I don't care for walking
3 I don't care for exploring underground caves
4 I like climbing

Exercise 225

1 I don't want to spend the first week picking grapes
2 I'd like to camp by the Loire
3 I don't want to swim before breakfast
4 I'd like to visit the castles
5 I'd like to go to museums
6 I don't want to live very cheaply

Exercise 226

1 I'd rather read than talk
2 I'd rather play than watch
3 I'd rather walk than cycle

4 I'd rather you drove.
5 I'd rather you chose.
6 I'd rather you started on Monday.

Exercise 227

All the answers begin: I wish
1 he'd eat a proper breakfast
2 he'd play his transistor more quietly
3 he'd come in earlier
4 he'd make less noise
5 he'd tell us where he goes
6 he'd answer our questions

Exercise 228

1 I wish I lived
2 I wish I could afford
3 I wish I had
4 I wish I knew
5 I wish I had gone

Exercise 230

1 he	11	Their
2 his	12	she
3 his	13	the day before
4 him	14	their
5 his	15	the following week
6 hers	16	his
7 Her	17	two days before
8 her	18	her/their
9 They	19	in two days' time
10 they		

Exercise 231

1 He says he's at the station.
2 He says he'll be with us in about an hour.
3 He says he'll get a bus
4 He says he knows where to go to get one and he remembers the number.
5 He says he thinks he knows where to get off.
6 He says he's got presents for us.

7 He said he'd been offered a better job.
8 He said the salary was twice what he was getting from Jones and Co.
9 He said there would be a chance of promotion.
10 He said Jones and Co. had refused to promote him.

Exercise 232

1 Ann said (that) he (Bill) probably didn't know about the train times.
2 Tom said (that) he wished Bill would ring up from the station
3 and that he behaved as if they were a hotel.
4 Ann said (that) it was time she started cooking supper.
5 Tom said she'd better make/advised her to make something that she could keep hot.
6 Ann said (that) if it was uneatable by the time he arrived, she would tell him that it was his own fault.
7 Bob said (that) we needn't wait for him.
8 Bob said (that) we mustn't miss the first act.
9 Bob said (that) we could leave his ticket at the box office.
10 Bob said (that) it was his own fault. He should have started earlier.
11 Ann said (that) if she saw any strawberries in the shops she'd get some.
12 Tom said (that) if they were on sale already they'd be expensive.

13 Ann said (that) if they had a bigger garden they could grow their own fruit.

Exercise 233

1 He apologized for keeping her so late
2 and promised not to do it again that month.
3 He offered her a lift home.

Exercise 234

1 He warned me that my bicycle had no brakes.
2 I answered that I could manage without brakes.
3 He reminded me that I'd already had two accidents.
4 I pointed out that the first accident hadn't been my fault.

Exercise 235

1 She wanted to know what time the coach left.
2 She asked if they could stop to take photographs.
3 She wanted to know where they were having lunch.
4 She wondered if there would be time to do some shopping.
5 She asked if it was his first season as a courier.

Exercise 236

1 Tom told Ann (that) he'd got the next day off and suggested going for a drive.
2 Ann said it would be lovely and offered to bring a picnic lunch.
3 Tom said that was a good idea and suggested starting early.
4 Ann agreed.

5 Tom offered to call for her at 7.

Exercise 237–238

1 The attendant asked to see/if he could see Bob's permit.
2 Bob asked to speak to Mr Jones/asked if he could speak to Mr Jones.
3 Bob asked the secretary to say that Bob Smith had rung about a parking permit.
4 She asked him to come/if he could come to the office and pick it up.
5 She offered him a ticket for their concert.

Exercise 239

1 Mrs Smith told her husband not to sign till he had read it again.
2 The solicitor warned him to read the small print very carefully.
3 Mr Smith asked him to read it aloud.
4 The solicitor advised him to take the document home and study it carefully.
5 if we haven't enough cash we're to go to the bank tomorrow morning
6 we are to wait by the telephone for instructions
7 we're not to tell anyone

Exercise 240

1 George suggested a sponsored walk.
2 Tom said their were too many sponsored walks and suggested doing a house-to-house collection.
3 Ann pointed out that they needed a permit for that and

suggested that Tom should apply for one.

Exercise 242

1 Ann said (that) she couldn't and that Tom was just imagining it.
2 He asked Ann if she was cooking and/but she said (that) she wasn't.
3 She asked if he had been burning rubbish in the garden and he said (that) he had.
4 She asked if he had left the fire burning but he said (that) he hadn't.

Exercise 243

1 Ann said she couldn't find her keys and asked Peter if he had seen them.
2 He said he hadn't and asked (her) if she could remember when she had last had them.
3 She said she couldn't and asked him to look/if he'd mind looking in his car.
4 He said they weren't in his car and asked if she could get into the house without them.
5 She said she could, as her sister was at home. But she wondered what she should do about the keys.
6 Peter suggested going back to the restaurant and asking there.

Exercise 244

1 there is neither a playground nor a roof garden
2 are neither large nor bright
3 is neither modern nor elegant

4 He neither sang solos nor trained the choir.
5 He neither played the piano nor conducted the orchestra.
6 He neither wrote nor directed plays.
7 either; or
8 both; and
9 either; or
10 either; or

Exercise 245

1	otherwise	5	still
2	however	6	yet
3	Besides	7	still; yet
4	otherwise	8	still

Exercise 246

Though can replace *although* here.
1 although   4 in spite of
2 in spite of 5 Although
3 although

Exercise 247

1	when/ whenever	8	when
2	when/ whenever	9	when
		10	When
3	While	11	As
4	while	12	as/when
5	when	13	When
6	while		
7	When/ Whenever		

Exercise 248

1 because   4 when/while
2 when/while   5 because
3 because

Exercise 249

1 to Oxford to read history
2 has gone to Florence to study art

3 has gone to Holland to
   paint
4 in order not to be
5 in order to reach
6 in order to have
7 in order not to disturb
8 to cut the bread with
9 to put the sandwiches on
10 to open the bottles with
11 to put the fruit into

Exercise 250

1 The outer gates are locked
   when it gets dark (a) so that
   no one can drive . . . (b) to
   prevent anyone driving . . .
2 He has guard dogs running
   round at night (a) so that no
   one can approach . . . (b) to
   prevent anyone
   approaching . . .
3 He has dark glass in his car
   windows (a) so that no one
   can see . . . (b) to prevent
   anyone seeing . . .
4 so that   6 so that
5 in case

Exercise 253

1 as/because
2 Because
3 As
4 as/because
5 As
6 because; because

Exercise 254

1 such
2 so
3 such
4 so
5 such
6 I was invited out so often
   that I hardly ever had
7 I met such a lot of people
   that I can't remember

8 Some of them spoke so fast
   that I couldn't understand
9 Everything was so
   expensive that I couldn't b
10 It was such a short holiday
   that I didn't see

Exercise 255

1 opens   5 has answered
2 boils   6 have read
3 gets   7 has gone
4 is

Exercise 257

1 what he said
2 where they went
3 when they're coming back
4 who he was
5 why she left him

Exercise 258

1 so   4 so
2 so   5 not
3 so

Exercise 259

1 put on   4 put out
2 take them off   5 put it out
3 Try them on   6 taken off

Index

References are to sections.